G. Richard Dimler

Friedrich Spee's *Trutznachtigall*

German Studies in America

Edited by Heinrich Meyer

No. 13

G. Richard Dimler

Friedrich Spee's *Trutznachtigall*

Herbert Lang & Co. Ltd.
Bern and Frankfurt/M.
1973

Friedrich Spee's *Trutznachtigall*

by

G. Richard Dimler

Herbert Lang & Co. Ltd.
Bern and Frankfurt/M.
1973

ISBN 3 261 00848 2
© Herbert Lang & Co. Ltd., Bern (Switzerland)
Peter Lang Ltd., Frankfurt/M. (West-Germany)
1973. All rights reserved.

Printed by Lang Druck Ltd., Liebefeld/Berne (Switzerland)

PREFACE

To say that Friedrich Spee von Langenfeld is unknown in the English-speaking world is hardly an understatement. Aside from some scattered articles in scholarly journals, nothing has appeared in English which analyzes Spee either as a writer or as a historical figure. An extended treatment would seem to be called for because of his not inconsiderable accomplishments as poet and social-crusader in early seventeenth-century Germany. While the major emphasis in the present work is on a literary analysis of Spee's *Trutznachtigall* and *Güldenes Tugend-buch,* attention is also given to significant biographical details, especially his personal heroism in condemning the injustice of the witchcraft trials in his book, *Cautio Criminalis.* For Spee was unique in that he was one of the very few who cried out for justice. The modern plea for justice, equality and concern for one's neighbour has long since been anticipated in the singular cry of this courageous Jesuit priest.

Through this work the author hopes to introduce Spee more fully to the English-speaking world. Though the final word on Spee's position within baroque literature is still forthcoming, the present work hopefully will provide materials for such a judgment.

I wish to thank Professor Eli Sobel of U.C.L.A. and Professor Heinrich Meyer of Vanderbilt University for their encouragement and many helpful suggestions.

TABLE OF CONTENTS

I. SPEE: THE HISTORICAL BACKGROUND 9

II. SPEE AND THE BAROQUE LITERARY CONTEXT:
    PROBLEMATIC AND ORIENTATION 15

III. ANALYSIS OF IMAGERY 24

    A. Elemental Images (Inorganic) 24
        1. Light 24
        2. Night-Darkness 27
        3. Color 29
        4. Water-Images 31
        5. Fire, Heat, Flame, Burning 34
        6. Stars 37
        7. Firmament 44
        8. Air, Wind and Clouds 47
    B. Organic Nature 51
        1. Flowers 51
        2. Trees 56
        3. Seasons of the Year, Hours of the Day 61
        4. Animals 64
    C. Human Existence 68
        1. Love 68
        2. Heart 76
        3. Pain and Sorrow 81
        4. Wounds 85
        5. Joy 88
        6. Sighs 91
        7. Tears 97
        8. Taste and Smell 101
        9. The Human Anatomy 103
     10. Death 106
    D. Realia 111
        1. Arrows 111
        2. Precious Objects 116

IV. CONCLUSION 119

V. TABLE OF IMAGE-CATEGORIES 122

VI. REFERENCE TABLES 127

A SELECTED BIBLIOGRAPHY 151

INDEX 155

CHAPTER I
SPEE: THE HISTORICAL BACKGROUND

The early seventeenth-century in Europe and above all in Germany was a time of turbulence and transition. Seven years after Friedrich Spee von Langenfeld decided to enter the Jesuit novitiate in Trier, the Thirty Years War (1618—1648) was about to commence. What began as a Habsburg war against Bohemian religious separatism, through the election of the Protestant Frederick of the Palatinate to the throne of Bohemia, took a decided political form. The Habsburgs sought to strengthen their political power and centralize their hold in hereditary dominions, and the Counter-Reformation, of which the Jesuits formed an important part, was a vital instrument. This was a war in which mixed political and religious motives dominated. These events were to be the immediate political background to Spee's life in the early part of the seventeenth-century.

By the time of the Treaty of Westfalia (1648) much of Germany lay in ruins and was utterly devastated. It is estimated that the density of population of Germany as a whole decreased by nearly two-thirds. The population of the duchy of Wurtemberg, for example, was reduced from 400,000 to 48,000 people.[1] The plagues, the destruction and ruin resultant from the devastation of war contribute also to the prevalent barock themes of *memento mori,* the vanity of existence and the deep pessimistic strain which runs through the literature of seventeenth-century Germany. Superstitious beliefs generated a pathological craving for the miraculous, the mysterious and the occult. In the later sixteenth- and throughout the seventeenth-century witchcraft trials extended all over Germany. It is estimated that during this period 100,000 victims were executed, among them were men, women, and children, princesses, ladies of noble birth, councilors and princes, priests, monks and pastors.[2]

It was also during the late sixteenth-century and even into the early part of the seventeenth-century that the Society of Jesus, of which Spee was to become a member, became such an instrumental force in the Counter-Reformation. Founded by Ignatius Loyola in 1534, the Jesuits became a leading exponent of intellectual and church reform. Their grammar schools were the best of the time, and the Jesuit drama became a dominant aspect of seventeenth-century Catholic culture. Much of the inner dynamism and thrust behind the Jesuit movement is derived from the principles which Ignatius had set down in his book, the *Spiritual Exercises.* Service of the Church and the Pope, self-sacrifice for Christ

---

1 Cf. Kurt F. Reinhardt, *Germany: 2000 Years,* 2nd ed., Vol. I (New York: Ungar, 1961), p. 292.
2 Cf. Reinhardt, *Germany,* I, pp. 292ff.

and His Kingdom, self-mastery and a profound awareness of God working in the world and through men in the establishment of His Kingdom are some of the main themes in Ignatian Spirituality. Peter Canisius (1521–1597), the first prominent Jesuit in Germany, was a key figure in implementing these Ignatian principles throughout Germany and among the Catholic youth. Through his efforts and his fellow Jesuits, the schools of the Society of Jesus in Germany became model institutions and their influence extended even to the leading Catholic universities of the empire.

Some six years before Canisius' death in 1597, at a time when Shakespeare was beginning his career as a playwright with the *Comedy of Errors,* the most famous German Jesuit poet and author was born. Friedrich Spee von Langenfeld, author of the famous moral treatise on witchcraft, the *Cautio Criminalis,*[3] is little known in the English-speaking world except among students of German literature and specialists in seventeenth-century literature. Even among his brother North-American Jesuits of the 1970's, Spee is practically unheard of and his biography has not yet appeared in English. That he was a distinguished poet of the early seventeenth-century is generally agreed upon by literary critics. Although Spee's poetry is not conceded the poetic stature of such baroque poets as Gryphius and Grimmelshausen, nonetheless the *Trutz-nachtigall* and the *Güldenes Tugend-buch* truly merit the solid position they have attained in the early German baroque tradition.

Although a primary aim of the present work is a study of his poetic imagery, the heroic stature of his life and the impact of his courageous work, the *Cautio Criminalis,* which condemns the unjust treatment of women denounced for witchcraft, should not be overlooked in an overall assessment of Spee as a poet, as a Jesuit and as a human being. Thus a brief summary of his life as background to his poetic achievement is not out-of-place at this point in our inquiry.

Friedrich Spee von Langenfeld was born on February 25, 1591, the oldest of five children, at Kaiserswerth near Cologne in Germany. He was the son of the castellan of the Archbishop-Elector of Cologne, Peter Spee von Langenfeld. The family had a noble origin. (Charles the Sixth raised the family of Spee to the level of Count on May 9, 1739.) Spee was raised as a son of royalty and attended the Jesuit gymnasium (comparable to the American junior-college), Tricoronatum, in Cologne beginning in 1602. He became a member of the Jesuit sodality, youths dedicated to the Virgin Mary, in 1604. In 1608 he was accepted in the humanities division of the University of Cologne and received his baccalaureate on March 9, 1609. The following year, on November 22, 1610, Spee entered the Society of Jesus at the age of nineteen and became a novice in Trier. (The Jesuit college in Trier had already in the 1580's and 1590's become involved in

---

[3] German translation by Joachim-Friedrich Ritter, 2nd ed. (Darmstadt: Wissenschaftliche Buchgesellschaft, 1967).

witchcraft scandals.) Because of the plague in Trier at that time, he continued his training as a Jesuit novice in Fulda where he pronounced his first religious vows of poverty, chastity and obedience. From 1612–1615 he pursued philosophical studies in Wurzburg, received his masters degree, and in 1617 he taught poetry and rhetoric at the Jesuit college in Worms.

At this time he suffered his first great disappointment. He volunteered for the Foreign Missions in the Far East in direct imitation of his Jesuit hero and saint, Francis Xavier. (Spee dedicated a poem of the *Trutznachtigall* (18) to Xavier.) However, Spee was refused permission to go to the Foreign Missions by the Jesuit General P. Vitelleschi. In the fall of 1618, four months after the famous defenestration in Prague, which led to the Thirty Years War, Spee began his theological studies in Mainz and completed them in 1622. It is also possible that during his years of theological study, Spee first began writing serious poetry in the form of hymns in German and made a considerable contribution to the Jesuit hymnals of the time.[4] In these early hymns he makes use of *Contrafaktur,* the incorporation of a worldly melody, and adopts it to a sacred theme in a hymn. This was a typical Jesuit trait. Just as such Jesuit missionaries to the East as Matteo Rici and Adam Schall adopted Chinese customs and habits of dress in order to bring Christianity to China, so Spee uses secular melodies to popularize his hymns. This trait will reappear later in his mature poetry. Spee does not hesitate to use classical and Petrarchan motifs in the Eclogues and love poetry of the *Trutznachtigall.* He was ordained a priest the same year at the age of thirty-one. From 1623–1626 Spee was Professor of Logic, Physics and Philosophy at the Jesuit College in Paderborn. He became an outstanding father-confessor during this time, but due to the outbreak of the plague in Paderborn in 1626, he was sent to Speyer to begin the third year of spiritual novitiate. Perhaps at this time he first became aware of the injustice of the witch-trials which were then taking place with regularity there as well as in Wurzburg. It was later because of his avowed opposition to the injustice of these trials, that he was to become a highly controversial figure in the Society. A patron of the Jesuits, Dietrich von Fürstenberg (1585–1618), had already become one of the leading persecutors of those accused of witchcraft. Ferdinand of Bayern, the Archbishop of Cologne, under whose authority the bishopric of Paderborn fell, was well-known for his support of these trials. In 1628 Spee most probably began work on the first draft of the *Cautio Criminalis* in Cologne where witch-trials were also in progress. The celebrated case of a patrician, Katharina von Henot is discussed in the *Cautio, Dubium XXXIX.* She was finally burned to death after forced confessions under heavy torture.

---

4 Cf. Emmy Rosenfeld, *Friedrich Spee von Langenfeld. Eine Stimme in der Wüste* (Berlin: de Gruyter, 1957), pp. 25ff.

It is generally conceded that Spee's *Cautio* is one of the noblest and most enlightened writings of the century, in which he advocates a thorough reform of court procedure and prisons. Although Spee does not deny outright the existence of witchcraft, he clearly asserts that the victims he examined were not guilty, and that the cruel methods of examination would have brought about the same confessions had there been no substance at all in the charges. Spee himself had first-hand experience with the condemned as father-confessor and he even accompanied them to the places of execution (*Cautio, Dubium* XIX). Leibniz reports the story that Philip of Schönborn, the Archbishop Elector of Mainz, met Spee at this time and inquired why his hair was so grey at such a young age. Spee is reported to have answered that he was prematurely grey as a result of having to accompany innocent women accused of witchcraft to their deaths.

It was during these initial investigations into the nature and justification for these trials, that Spee became more and more a bone of contention to the Jesuit authorities. His difficulties with Hermann Bavingh, now the Jesuit Provincial, increased. Consequently, Bavingh seized an opportunity to remove Spee from Cologne and in 1628 Spee was sent to Peine near Hildesheim to do missionary work in a predominantly Lutheran area. He worked with great success, even winning the respect of the Lutherans, until he was nearly assassinated on April 29, 1629, suffering severe head and shoulder wounds from an assailant's bullets. Spee recovered from his injuries late in 1629 and was sent back to teach moral theology at Paderborn. In 1630 and 1631 he experienced even greater difficulties with his superiors because of his controversial views regarding the witch-trials, and his apparently liberal interpretation of certain customs in the Society of Jesus. In fact, his rector, Hermann Bavingh, took away his professorship in the middle of the school year in 1631 after the anonymous publication of the *Cautio* that same year.

Spee returned to the *Tricoronatum* in Cologne and while he was there, the whole question of sorcery and diabolic possession increased in fury. Spee was openly condemned by his fellow Jesuits, secular priests and the civil judges. They were particularly incensed by his statements in the *Cautio* in *Dubia* 30, 39 and 52 where religious superiors and authorities are criticized for allowing unscrupulous, biased and openly prejudiced men and priests to become seriously involved in the trials.

Spee's situation in the order became even more critical when a second edition of the *Cautio* with further corrections in his own hand appeared without his knowledge. Here Spee openly criticized the Electors, among them Maximilian and Ferdinand of Bavaria who were Jesuit benefactors and friends. The Jesuit General sought his removal from the order but the provincial hesitated. After some two years Spee's position in the order gradually improved and he was sent to teach moral theology in Trier in the fall of 1633. During the siege of Trier by the French in 1635 another outbreak of the plague developed. In truly heroic fashion and fully aware of the dangers to his health and life Spee volunteered to do chaplain work in the hospitals among the soldiers stricken with the plague and he himself contracted the plague and died in Trier on August 7, 1635.

Testimony to the courage, single-mindedness, zeal and intellectual integrity of this great personality was not lacking among Spee's contemporaries. The future General of the Society, Nickel, was convinced of Spee's saintliness. Later even the great Leibniz was so impressed with Spee's life that he wrote a biography of him. (Leibniz' *Théodicée* is greatly influenced by Spee's *Tugendbuch.*) One can scarcely realize the courage and spirit Spee possessed to write such a controversial book as the *Cautio* in the face of such opposition from his own superiors and brother Jesuits, which almost led to his dismissal from the order. The truly astounding fact, however, is that one of the most attractive personalities and one of the most courageous men of the seventeenth-century found the time under such trying and perplexing conditions to write the peaceful, almost mystical love songs of the *Trutznachtigall.*

As will become clear from the central motifs, metaphors and themes of his work, his poetry seems on the surface to be a flight from the mean-ness and narrow-minded attitudes of human beings which he experienced all too frequently, and from his frustrations in trying to secure justice for innocent people accused of witchcraft to the Beauty of God, His Love, Providence and Presence. This poetic beauty sustained him in his love for God and his creatures and touches upon the very elemental forces of his personality. This beauty and love are the central themes of his poetry, capturing the basic Ignatian ethic in the *Spiritual Exercises,* that God is a loving God, caring for His creatures and showering them with His love, and therefore worthy of our praise and devotion. How Spee expresses this beauty and praise in the imagery and motifs of his poetry will be a central concern in the present analysis. These images and motifs should help to lead us to a greater realization of Spee's commitment to justice, his love for his fellow men and his artistry as a poet.

Spee's commitment to his fellow men in seeking justice for those unjustly accused of witchcraft, in risking assassination and death in preaching God's word to man, and finally in realizing that he would certainly contract the plague and die in his volunteering to work among the sick soldiers in Trier in 1635 is an established fact. These accomplishments bear testimony to his profound desire to expend himself in serving his fellow man. Moreover, in a very real sense his poetic writings document his commitment and enable us to see beyond externals and to contact the inner-man, so to speak, in his emotional relationship to God. It is this inner commitment to God and His love which gave Spee the courage and strength to undergo many trials and endure much anxiety for the sake of suffering mankind, whether it be a dying soldier or a terrified woman accused of consorting with Satan.

As Spee writes in his introduction to the *Trutznachtigall,* he intends a new spiritual Parnassus *(kunstberg)* to the greater glory of God, where God will be praised and His name heard. Thus, in a true sense, his poetry records his emotional and spiritual commitment to God, a counterpart to his logical and reasoned declamations in the *Cautio.* His poetry spells out his inner fervor and dedication. In his imagery we find the expression of his love for God and desire to praise Him, which are basically the principles of his Ignatian and Jesuit commitment. But since Spee lived at a certain time and place, early seventeenth-century Germany, his poetic imagery will of necessity embody the motifs, themes and ideas of his age. Thus in assessing the imagery of the *Trutznachtigall* several problem areas emerge: how does Spee fuse secular and spiritual motifs and images in his poetry, and to what extent does he employ the typical baroque imagery of his time as a vehicle for his poetic ideas? Such an analysis of his poetic style can help to reveal Spee both as Jesuit priest and as baroque poet.

CHAPTER II
SPEE AND THE BAROQUE LITERARY CONTEXT:
PROBLEMATIC AND ORIENTATION

Before beginning a direct analysis of Spee's imagery, it would be well to situate him within the literary context of his age and indicate the basic reactions of twentieth-century criticism to Spee and baroque imagery as it applies to him. Within the past decade European and American scholars have shown extensive and lively interest in German baroque imagery. Several studies have appeared since 1965; the first, by Manfred Windfuhr, is a general analysis of the image in German baroque lyric poetry based on his six categories of style: (1) affective-pathetic, (2) mystical, (3) decorative, (4) bombastic, (5) grotesque, and (6) conceited.[1] A second important study is an analysis of Gryphius' imagery; Dieter Jöns, *Das 'Sinnen-bild' bei Gryphius* (Stuttgart: Metzler, 1966). Gryphius' imagery is analyzed from the standpoint of medieval-Christian symbolism according to a schema of fourteen image-topics.[2] Whereas Gerhard Fricke's earlier study, *Die Bildlichkeit in der Dichtung des Andreas Gryphius* (Berlin: Dümmler, 1933), compares Gryphius' baroque imagery with the classical imagery of the age of Goethe, Jöns' analysis extends into previous literary and cultural history to seek the background for these image-topics.

Windfuhr's study, however stimulating and necessary for an overall assessment of seventeenth-century imagery, cannot be a substitute for a detailed and thorough study of the images of the individual poet, such as the Gryphius monographs presented by Jöns and Fricke.[3] Windfuhr's analysis is further limited because it is confined to three major image-fields. Most seventeenth-century poets employ imagery based on far more categories than these three utilized by Windfuhr. Fricke's study of Gryphius was based on more than thirty image-categories.

---

[1] *Die Barocke Bildlichkeit und Ihre Kritiker* (Stuttgart: Metzler, 1966). His analysis is confined, for the most part, to three major image-areas or *Bildfelder:* (1) the world, man and God; (2) descriptions of feminine beauty; (3) cosmic and terrestrial nature.

[2] In his study of Gryphius' imagery Jöns employs the following fourteen *Bildfelder:* (1) Nacht und Licht, (2) Sterne, (3) Sonne und Sonnenlauf; (a) Morgen, (b) Mittag, (c) Abend, (d) Nacht und Morgen, (e) Jahreslauf der Sonne; (4) Schatten, (5) Meer und Seefahrt, (6) Brunnen und Quelle, (7) Regen, Tau und Wind, (8) Bäume, (9) Pflanzen und Blumen, (10) Tiere, (11) Stein, (12) Gold und Eisen, (13) Künstliche Gegenstände and (14) Hominis fragilitas et mundi vanitas. These *Bildfelder* are listed in his outline on page V. Cf. also articles on baroque style in *Colloquia Germanica,* I (1967), 2—110.

[3] Windfuhr, *Barocke Bildlichkeit,* p. 180. Windfuhr admits as much, since seventeenth-century poets invariably exhibit more than one stylistic trait and the isolated presentation of various categories of style such as Windfuhr has done cannot be expected to grasp the total esthetic of any one poet.

Friedrich Spee's position within the context of German baroque lyric poetry is still being assessed. Scholars have shown continued interest in the *Trutznachtigall*. Since 1950 several studies have appeared concerned with Spee's mysticism (Bankl, Zeller, Zoepfl),[4] on the relationship between his theology and esthetic (Margarete Gentner, "Das Verhältnis von Theologie and Asthetik in Spees 'Trutznachtigall'," [diss. Tübingen, 1965]), an analysis of Spee's love-imagery and emblematic from the standpoint of medieval and Petrarchan motifs (Eric Jacobsen, *Die Metamorphosen der Liebe und Spees "Trutznachtigall"* [Copenhagen, 1954]), an analysis of his pastoral motifs (Elfriede Eikel, "Die Entstehung der religiosen Schäfer-Lyrik von Petrarca bis Spee" [diss. Heidelberg, 1956]; Wolfgang Nowak, "Versuch einer motivischen Analyse des Schäferhabits bei Friedrich von Spee" [diss. Berlin, 1954]), and a general study of literary parallels and sources of the *Trutznachtigall* in Emmy Rosenfeld, *Friedrich Spee von Langenfeld. Eine Stimme in der Wüste* (Berlin: de Gruyter, 1958), and Emmy Rosenfeld, *Neue Studien zur Lyrik von Friedrich von Spee* (Milan: Univ. Boccocini, 1963). A systematic analysis of Spee's imagery in the *Trutznachtigall* was still lacking and, in particular, an analysis by types and methods employed in the approaches of Jöns and Fricke toward the imagery of the individual German poet of the seventeenth-century.

Pre-World War II studies on Spee have also been deficient with regard to an exhaustive, complete treatment of Spee's poetic imagery. Scholars either confined themselves to particular aspects of Spee's imagery, such as nature and cosmology in the *Trutznachtigall*, or they have avoided an overall analysis which would necessarily have incorporated images based on areas of human existence as love, death, joy and sorrow. Other researchers have superficially analyzed certain image-fields without adequate investigation into their poetic function, semantic structure, or style, particularly in the relationship of each image-field to the total context of the *Trutznachtigall*.

Alphons Jungbluth in his study, "Beiträge zu einer Beschreibung der Dichtersprache Friedrichs von Spee" (diss. Bonn, 1906), devoted scarcely one-third of his analysis to Spee's imagery. Heinrich Schachner, "Naturbilder und Naturbetrachtung in den Dichtungen Friedrichs von Spee," *Programm des Obergymnasiums Kremsmünster* (1906), 1–62, and Ilse Märtens, "Die Darstellung der Natur in den Dichtungen Friedrichs von Spee," *Euphorion*, 29 (1925), 564–592, limit their studies to either "Naturbilder," "Naturbetrachtung," or "Naturdarstellung" in the *Trutznachtigall*. An example of an attempt to assess Spee's esthetic contribution through a selective analysis of his poetic

---

[4] Susanne Bankl, "Friedrich von Spee von Langenfeld und die europäische Mystik" (diss. Wien, 1959); Paul Zeller, "Friedrich von Spee und seine Weltschau" (diss. Fribourg, 1956); Friedrich Zoepfl, "Die Frömmigkeit Friedrichs von Spee," *Geist und Leben. Zeitschrift für Aszese und Mystik*, 20 (1947), 36–53.

production is the study by Margarete Gentner. Her aim, as stated in her introduction, is "Mit der Betrachtung eines einzelnen Gedichts der 'Trutz-nachtigall,' dessen Vorlage eindeutig nachweisbar ist, soll das Ganze der Speeschen Dichtkunst in den Blick kommen."[5]

However, a study based on a selective analysis of Spee's *Bilder* cannot be sufficiently productive of fundamental conclusions with respect to his overall esthetic contribution in the baroque period of German literature. A sufficient diversity and complex of image-fields must be chosen and analyzed if the *Trutznachtigall*, as a total work of art, is to emerge through these image-aspects. However, such a study has not previously been undertaken. Through such a careful and detailed study of these images Spee's poetic personality and position within the seventeenth-century and his relationships to medieval mystics, Petrarchan motifs, and Jesuit spiritual themes emerge. This requires a comprehensive analysis of his predominant image-fields. When Spee's use of traditional and contemporary images is seen against the background of his other images, such as joy, sorrow, love, fire, and tears, and their function within the general thematic of the *Trutznachtigall*, then the unity of his poetic expression becomes clearer.

A study of Spee's images presents a further problem that has often been neglected or overlooked in previous studies of the *Trutznachtigall*. Twenty-four of the poems which Spee later incorporated into the *Trutznachtigall* were taken from his earlier devotional work (written in the summer of 1632, for the benefit of his spiritual children),[6] the *Güldenes Tugendbuch, das ist, Werck und Übung der dreyen Göttlichen Tugenden, des Glaubens, der Hoffnung, und der Liebe. Allen Gott-liebenden, andächtigen, frommen Seelen, und sonderlich den Kloster- und Welt-Geistlichen Personen sehr nutzlich zu gebrauchen.* In the fall of 1633 Spee incorporated these twenty-four *GTB* poems into the *Trutznachtigall*. The *editio princeps* contains fifty-two poems, although the manuscripts have fifty-one.[7] These songs play an important role in the methodology and structure of the *GTB*, and this aspect of Spee's creativity will be investigated at appropriate points in this study. The songs incorporated into the *Trutznachtigall* were frequently partial or total summaries of Spee's theological and spiritual aims as expressed in the exercises of the *GTB*. In the main they are lyrical

5 *Das Verhältnis von Theologie und Ästhetik*, p. 3.

6 Cf. E. Rosenfeld, *Neue Studien*, p. 18. Spee collected the various exercises or chapters of the *Güldenes Tugendbuch* — hereafter referred to under the abbreviated form as *GTB* — and originally addressed to different spiritual charges, into the devotional book as it now exists, at the behest of one of his spiritual daughters mentioned in the introduction to the *GTB*. Cf. also Theo Van Oorschot, "Friedrich Spees Güldenes Tugend-Buch II Literarische Abhandlung" (diss. Nijmegen, 1968), pp. 19—20.

7 Cf. Robert M. Browning, "On the Numerical Composition of Spee's *Trutznachtigall*" in *Festschrift für Detlev W. Schumann*, hrsg. A. R. Schmitt (München: Delp, 1970), pp. 28ff.

responses written for the soul's use in her intimate colloquies with God or Christ. The structure and function of the imagery in these *GTB* poems is frequently determined by their position and function in the *GTB*. Their later position within the *Trutznachtigall*, their poetic thrust and schema, require that their original context within the *GTB* be taken into account.

Scholarship on Spee has made known the crucial role that the *GTB* has for an understanding and assessment of the *Trutznachtigall*. Paul Zeller, "Friedrich von Spee und seine Weltschau" (diss: Fribourg, 1956), p. 52, maintains that these two works of Spee are, in reality, two different versions of the same "Gedanken- und Gefühlsinhaltes." He also maintains that the *Trutznachtigall* can only be understood after an analysis of the *GTB* has been made (p. 52). Frederick W.C. Lieder, "Friedrich Spee and the Théodicée of Leibniz," *JEGP*, II (1912), 160, says that the relationship between them is such that: "The poems of the *Trutznachtigall*, as can be seen from a hasty perusal of their titles, are merely poetic versions of the principles laid down by the *Güldenes Tugendbuch*." Jean-B. Neveux, "Friedrich von Spee SJ (1591–1635) et la société de son temp. La grâce et le droit," *Études germaniques*, 19 (1964), 413, calls the *GTB* the prose complement of the *Trutznachtigall*. Theo Van Oorschot first intended a stylistic analysis of the *GTB* as a preparation for an evaluation of the literary, spiritual and intellectual aspects of the *Trutznachtigall*. He had to abandon this project until a reliable, edited text of the *GTB*, as well as a historical and source analysis of the *GTB*, were available. With the recent appearance of a reliable critical edition of the *GTB*, through Van Oorschot's own efforts (Friedrich Spee, *Güldenes Tugend-Buch*, ed. Theo Van Oorschot [Munich: Kösel, 1968] — Friedrich Spee, *Sämtliche Schriften*, Historische-kritische Ausgabe in drei Bänden, ed. Emmy Rosenfeld, Vol. II) an analysis of the mutual relationship between the *Trutznachtigall* and the *GTB* can now be made with reliability. Van Oorschot's critical edition of the *GTB* is an indispensable aid in an analysis of Spee's poetic imagery.

With the exception of Jacobsen's study limited to problematic aspects of Spee's love-imagery, no work on Spee has yet appeared which has thoroughly analyzed the mutual interaction and relationship between the *Trutznachtigall* and the *GTB*. As Van Oorschot states, "Eine Abhandlung über das GTB als *Grundlage* der TrN steht also noch aus" ("GTB II," p. 166). Jacobsen uses the *GTB* more for purposes of clarification of the *Trutznachtigall* than to show the influence of the *GTB* on the *Trutznachtigall*: "Dass die TN in vollem Umfang nur unter Ausnutzung des GTB verstanden und beurteilt werden kann, wird hoffentlich aus dem Folgenden hervorgehen. Eine wissenschaftliche Neuausgabe des GTB ist deshalb für die weitere Speeforschung eine unbedingte Voraus- setzung."[8] In the most recent study of Spee's esthetic, the work by M. Gentner,

---

[8] Eric Jacobsen, *Die Metamorphosen der Liebe und Friedrich Spees 'Trutznachtigall'. Studien zum Fortleben der Antike*, I (Copenhagen: Filolog. Medd., 1954), p. 10.

the unity between the two works is stressed but not their mutual effect on one another. An accurate analysis of the *Trutznachtigall* in the light of the *GTB's* philosophy and spirituality is not present in Gentner's study. A primary goal of the following analysis is also the investigation of the mutual effect and influence of the *GTB* on the *Trutznachtigall*. Only in this manner can an accurate assessment of Spee's imagery be given, together with a clarification of the total function of imagery in his two works.

The present analytic approach to the imagery in the *Trutznachtigall* is similar to the schema in Fricke's work on Gryphius. His excellent and exhaustive analysis of Gryphius' imagery according to *Stoffgruppen* and *Bedeutungs-gruppen* has equal validity when applied as an external schema to the *Trutznachtigall*. Just as Fricke was able to catalogue Gryphius' imagery into some thirty-five elemental and thematic image-categories, a similar analysis of Spee's *Trutznachtigall* has produced some twenty-four categories. For a study of Spee's works certain specific image-groups such as: "sighs," "joy," and "sorrow" have been treated since Spee emphasizes themes and motifs whose purport lies elsewhere than does that of Gryphius.[9] Spee writes predominantly about religious themes, but includes motifs from contemporary baroque pastoral poetry and Petrarchan images that either do not occur in Gryphius or rarely appear.

The ability to catalogue baroque imagery, where themes and image-groups permeate poets from Opitz to Neukirch and Weise without undergoing any significant change in motif, is peculiar to the seventeenth-century.[10] The similar type of analysis, presented in the following chapters, could not be as easily applied to the classical and romantic poets; e.g., Goethe, Hölderlin and Kleist, since their poetic expression is much more subjective and introspective when compared to the more objective types of the baroque creative process.[11] The enormous proliferation of baroque handbooks and collections of symbols, metaphors, emblems and similes which run their courses unchanged throughout the baroque period give adequate testimony to this more objective type of image.[12] Fricke's approach rests mainly on the objective imagery of a secular

---

[9] This can be seen by comparing the image-index in Fricke, pp. v and vi, with the index to this study.

[10] Cf. Fricke, *Bildlichkeit,* p. 33; Windfuhr, *Bildlichkeit,* p. 180; Marian Szyrocki, *Die deutsche Literatur des Barock. Eine Einführung* (Hamburg: Rowohlt, 1968), p. 29; and Elisabeth Frenzel, *Stoff-Motiv- und Symbolforschung,* 2nd ed. (Stuttgart: Metzler, 1966), p. 48.

[11] Ferdinand Van Ingen, *Vanitas und Memento Mori in der Deutschen Barocklyrik* (Gröningen: Wolters, 1966), pp. 32ff., and Paul Böckmann, *Formengeschichte der deutschen Dichtung. Von der Sinnbildsprache zur Ausdruckssprache* (Darmstadt: Wissen-schaftliche Buchgesellschaft, 1967), 327.

[12] For the abundance of "Schatzkammer" in existence at this time cf. Windfuhr, *Bildlichkeit,* pp. 72ff., and August Langen, "Deutsche Sprachgeschichte vom Barock bis zur Gegenwart," *Deutsche Philologie im Aufriss,* 2nd ed., I (Munich: Schwartz, 1957), 1114.

poet such as Gryphius, but the following analysis and its results propose that baroque objectivity also existed in seventeenth-century religious poetry of the type written by Spee. Spee's imagery also lends itself to objective categorizations, as demonstrated by the application of the approximately twenty-four image-categories in the following analysis.

Analysis does not consist merely in the statistical isolation of images by frequency of occurrence, although this forms part of the study. The frequency of occurrence of a particular image can be enlightening for purposes of comparison with other German baroque poets, and for a determination of the predominance of a particular mode of stylistic expression such as the decorative, mystical, grotesque, and the affective-pathetic modes. It is also profitable, and necessary, to discover how German baroque poets apply a common image-field to different themes if more is to be learned about the nature and the function of seventeenth-century imagery. A complete catalogue of baroque imagery does not exist.[13] This is a desideratum if the baroque image is to be studied in terms of its depth and extension. Detailed analysis of Spee's poetry will contribute to this need. The individual *Bildbereich* in Spee has been analyzed according to: (a) its structure—tropes, paraphrases, figures of speech; (b) its function in the development of Spee's theme, i.e., the relation of the isolated light-image to its function in the expression of the soul's sorrow for sin or joy at Christ's presence; and (c) its style or mode of expression—grotesque, metaphysical, pietistic, affective or mystical. These three aspects of the image-field are present simultaneously and concomitantly in Spee's lyrical expression. Function, structure, and style are interrelated in Spee's imagery.

Image-function, image-structure, and image-style are not treated in isolation from one another. For example, the light-images in the *Trutznachtigall* will be seen to operate on a basic three-fold level of function: (a) as "compositions of place;" (b) as corroborative or contrastive to the soul's mood of joy or sorrow; and (c) in the development of theological themes regarding the Holy Spirit, Christ Himself, and the Holy Eucharist. The question then arises for a methodology that concerns the type of image (image-structure) or the style of image Spee uses in the development of these functions. Do his light-images which function as "compositions of place" appear in the decorative or affective mode? Does he use figures of paraphrase, simile, or personification to express these moods of sorrow in the soul? Do the light-images applied to Christ take the form of personification or paraphrase? What is the overall function of the light-image throughout the entirety of the *Trutznachtigall* and not just in any one isolated poem? How does the light-image in poem 6 of the *Trutznachtigall*

13 Windfuhr, *Bildlichkeit,* p. 180.

compare or differ with the light-image in poem 29? The methodological procedure here followed will demonstrate that the nature of Spee's imagery can be analyzed and assessed in its entirety and in its mutual interrelationships.

Through a correlation of Spee's image-aspects the inner gist and substance of the *Trutznachtigall* become apparent. Valid statements concerning Spee's spirituality, theology, mysticism, and the role of Christ in the *Trutznachtigall* toward the soul and Spee himself find better support from the text itself. The larger context of Spee's heroic commitment to his fellow man becomes clearer. A proper evaluation of the motifs from the Petrarchan school and the medieval mystics can be made only in conjunction with a total analysis of the poems of the *Trutznachtigall*. To deduce the esthetic qualities of Spee's imagery or his inner spirituality on the basis of one or few of his poems, as has been done by previous investigators, is to distort his poetry. Historical analogies and parallels to Spee and the seventeenth-century can be made by means of the following methodological approach which has produced a nearly total perspective for his poetry. This method views the *Trutznachtigall* as a totality in itself and in the light of its historical relationship to such problems as Jesuit spirituality, contemporary motifs and the Bible. To base a description or aspect of Spee's mysticism on an analysis of one section of a poem is unwarranted and unsupportable. To say that Spee writes in the mystical mode of style is an oversimplification. This analysis hopes to avoid such pitfalls. The work of art is a totality but a totality that is composed of varying and divergent heterogeneous strata. The image and its structure, function and style constitute one of the essential bases for this analysis of the totality of the *Trutznachtigall* as a work of literary art, and for giving greater insight into Spee's heroic figure in contemporary baroque society.

The elemental images which are catalogued in the first section of the analysis are divided into inorganic images: light, darkness, color, water, fire, heat, flame, stars, the firmament, air and wind. The second division is built around images of organic nature: flowers, trees, seasons, hours and animals. A third category has images derived from the human organism and from aspects of human existence: love, the heart, pain, wounds, joy, sighs, tears, taste, parts of the human anatomy, and death. The fourth, and final category is composed of *realia:* arrows, quivers, bows, jewels, and precious objects. For citations from the *Trutznachtigall*, the following rubric is employed: for example TN 24:14,2–5 refers to poem number 24 of the *Trutznachtigall*, fourteenth verse, lines two to five of the Arlt edition.[14] In poems from the *TN* which the Arlt edition has not divided into numbered stanzas, the first numbers after the poem number itself refer to the pages of the Arlt edition of the *TN,* as in the following rubric:

---

14 Friedrich Spee, *Trutznachtigall,* ed. Gustave Otto Arlt, *Neudrucke deutscher Literaturwerke des XVI. und XVII. Jahrhunderts,* 292–301 (Halle/Saale: Niemeyer, 1936).

TN 45:292,2—5 refers to poem number 45, page 292 of the Arlt edition, lines two to five. Those poems in the *TN* which originally were written in the chapters of the *GTB* will be enclosed in parentheses in the text as *TN* (6) which appears in *GTB* II, chap. 16. References to the *GTB* will be made as follows: *GTB* 203.2 refers to page 203 of the Van Oorschot edition of the *GTB*, line two. Following the analysis of the image-fields, an attempt will be made to synthesize the results of the present inquiry in the concluding section of this work.

Since an analysis of Spee's poetic imagery will be the major concern of the present work, several aspects of his imagery and poetic language in general will be detailed at this point. Terms such as simile, metaphor, personification and styles such as mystical and decorative will recur repeatedly in the text. Those baroque figures, tropes and stylistic levels and themes which occur most frequently and are most predominant in Spee are now listed (the reader is referred to the alphabetical listing on Spee's imagery in Chapter V):

(1) *affective:* Refers to a level of baroque style characterized by highly emotional content and a tendency to emotion-laden images. This style occurs for example in Spee's images of night in *TN* (7) and (47).

(2) *allegory:* A form of extended metaphor in which objects or persons are equated with meanings which lie outside the poem itself. The allegorical use by Spee in *TN* (13), where a flower is allegorized as human existence is an example.

(3) *antithesis:* A figure of speech characterized by strongly contrasting words, clauses or ideas as when Spee speaks of God's love as both cooling and burning at the same time in *TN* (3):6,5—8.

(4) *conceit:* An ingenious or fanciful notion or conception, usually expressed stylistically by means of an elaborate analogy and pointing to a striking parallel between two dissimilar things. The parallelism in *TN* (7):14,6 is a good example.

(5) *image-function:* Cf. discussion above.

(6) *decorative:* A stylistic mode characteristic of the baroque period in which picturesque metaphors predominate; e.g., pearly teeth, ivory forehead, alabaster neck or the dominant use of precious materials to describe the beloved as in *TN* 44 where Christ's hands and feet are called ivory.

(7) *metaphor:* An implied analogy which imaginatively identifies one object with another. In *TN* 29 Spee uses wind images to express the inner relationship within the Trinity.

(8) *mystical:* A style characterized by images applied exclusively to the soul's relationship to God. Spee's application of bitter-sweet love images and formulas to the Spouse's love for Christ in *TN* 9 is an example of this mystical style.

(9) *oxymoron:* A rhetorical antithesis bringing together two contradictory terms. An example occurs in *TN* (11):10,8 "von schatten klaren schein."

(10) *paraphrase:* The restatement of an idea in such a way as to retain the meaning while changing its diction and form. In *TN* 27:12,5 Spee calls brooks "reines wasser-glas."

(11) *personification:* A figure of speech which endows animals, ideas, and inanimate objects with human characteristics. In *TN* 26:1,1—2 Spee calls on stringed-instruments to speak with silver tongues.

(12) *simile:* A figure of speech in which a similarity between two objects is directly expressed as in *TN* (28):12,1 where snow falls from heaven like soft wool.

(13) *symbol:* An image which evokes an objective, concrete reality and has that reality suggest another level of meaning. For example, "schnee-Weisser tag" [TN (11):21,6] which symbolizes for Spee the day of final union of the spouse and Christ.

Chapter VI contains a complete catalogue of Spee's imagery and follows the scheme of images listed in the table of contents. (cf. pp. 127ff.)

CHAPTER III
ANALYSIS OF IMAGERY

A. Elemental Images (Inorganic)

Investigation into the *TN* begins with an analysis of Spee's treatment of images taken from inorganic nature.

1. Light

Light-images are a frequent occurrence in Spee. Approximately sixty-five instances are noted, compared to a lesser number of images of night and darkness. The light-images are frequently closely related to the sun, moon and stars (cf. Table 1.1, p. 127). These light-images fall into three functional categories. Spee uses them as introductions for coming themes somewhat as "compositions of place" in the *Spiritual Exercises of St. Ignatius*.[1] They help to set the mood for the action and theme of the poem and to focus attention on the coming poetic action. In this respect Spee seems to be influenced by the Ignatian schema of meditative prayer. Just as Ignatius in the *Spiritual Exercises* recommends, in the prelude to the coming meditation and consideration, that attention be focused by means of a "mental representation of the place," this same general method of approach is reflected in Spee.[2] This "composition of place," "seeing the spot," focussing the attention on the coming action was a practice of great importance for religious poetry, particularly in the seventeenth century.[3] Interestingly, Spee shows an affinity here with his English fellow Jesuit and poet, Robert Southwell.[4] In the *GTB* Spee employs a similar methodological approach in his exercises. Frequently he asks the spiritual daughter to picture in her imagination a scene for meditation and reflection introduced by the phrase "bilde dir für." The exercise in Book II, chap. 3, p. 126 is one example among many. Actually many of these light-images occur within the early stages of the poems in the *TN* and follow in this regard the fundamental structure of the Ignatian meditative-

---

[1] Forthcoming references to the *Spiritual Exercises* are based on the new translation by Louis J. Puhl. S.J. (Westminster, Md.: Newman, 1952).

[2] An example from Ignatius occurs in no. 112, p. 52 of Puhl's translation: "This is a mental representation of the place. It will consist here in seeing in imagination the way from Nazareth to Bethlehem. Consider its length, its breadth; whether level, or through valley and over hills."

[3] Cf. Louis Martz, *The Poetry of Meditation. A Study in English Religious Literature of the Seventeenth Century* (New Haven: Yale University Press, 1954), pp. 27ff.

[4] Cf. Martz, pp. 207—209, and Warren R. Maurer, "Spee, Southwell and the Poetry of Meditation," *CL,* XV (1963), 15—22, and Van Oorschot, "GTB II," pp. 106—107.

scheme. *TN* (3):3—4; (8):3,5—6; 9:1,6—7; (13):2,1—4; (21):2,1—2; and (22):1,6 offer us a few examples of this. In *TN* 26:3,3—4, the comparison of the stars to a proud peacock is another example of one such image functioning analogously as an Ignatian "composition of place:"

> Zu nacht er uns den himmel blau/
> Mit flämmlein schön bespritzet/
> Die glantzen wie der stoltze Pfau
> Wan er voll spieglen glitzet.

This image helps to focus attention on the main thrust of the poem (*TN* 26) which is an exhortation to creation to offer proper and fitting praise to its Creator.

A second group of light-images functions either to contrast or to corroborate the mood of the soul in its relationship with God.[5] For example, in *TN* (11), because the lover: "Mein einigs hertzen-liecht" has been taken away, Mary Magdalen cries out in anguish: "Ade liecht/lufft und leben // Ade schnee-weisser tag" [*TN* (11): 21,5—6]. She wishes to be enveloped in darkness if her beloved is absent. Her "Ade" to the brightness of creation corresponds to her mood of soul. In *TN* (7): 14,6 antithesis is used to show the pain of the love experienced between the spouse and her beloved: "Bey Sonnenschein ist schatten." In *TN* 39:18,7—8 and 19,1—5, the moon and the stars stop giving off light when they behold Christ suffering in Gethsemane. On the other hand, when the soul experiences joy at the presence of the beloved she cries out: "Wil fröligkeit nit sparen // Beim lieben Sonnen-schein" [*TN* (17):3,7—8].

Light is traditionally a symbol for things of the spirit and for spiritual strength.[6] Sacred Scripture employs the theme of conflict between the powers of light and the powers of darkness, above all in the Fourth Gospel of St. John.[7] This theme in Spee is found where light corresponds to joy, strength, love and harmony. Darkness, on the other hand, corresponds to sin and lack of grace. In *GTB* 124.7—8, "liecht und glantz" leave the soul when she is in a state of sin. A

---

[5] The soul is the most prominent figure in the *TN* aside from the Spouse, Christ Himself. Spee's inspiration for the figure came undoubtedly from the Canticle of Canticles and is another guise for Spee himself. Cf. Rosenfeld, *Neue Studien*, p. 72; and *Fr. Spee*, p. 222.

[6] J. E. Cirlot, *A Dictionary of Symbols*, tr. Jack Sage (London: Routledge, 1962), p. 179.

[7] Karl Rahner, *kleines theologisches Wörterbuch* (Freiburg im Breisgau: Herder, 1961), pp. 188—189; and Raymond Brown, "The Gospel of St. John and the Johannine Epistles," *New Testament Reading Guide*, XIII (Collegeville, 1960), 16ff.

similar use of symbolism occurs in Gryphius.[8] For the medieval mystics God appears as "lux aeterna."[9]

A third extension of the light-images is their function on the theological and religious level.[10] For example, the soul calls Christ "Das rein und liechtes liecht" [TN (6):13,2]; "mein einigs hertzen-liecht" [(11):21,1,2]; "Jesus wares Liecht" (49:320,3). God is addressed as "das schönes liecht" (GTB 211.28—32; 226.9—12). God is the source of light (TN 26:11,5; 50:13,1—8) and He suffuses us with the light of day (TN 26:3,2f.; 31—185,2—3). The Holy Spirit is called "gülden stral" (TN 29:31,3). In TN 27:2,5—8 the light of God far outshines the luminous stars. However, the light-image in Spee is applied in a theological sense to the Holy Eucharist. In TN 51:14,7 the Eucharist is called "Sonnen-glantz." In images clearly patterned after the Apostles Creed which is still in use in contemporary Catholic Liturgy at the Credo of the Mass,[11] Christ is called: "O Sohn / du deines Vatters glantz! // O Liecht / vom Liecht gezündet" (TN 29:7,5—6); and "Der Schein / von eben seinem schein" (TN 29:18,5—6) and also in TN (42):5,6.[12]

There is a structural and stylistic progression in these images of light. When light-images occur as "compositions of place" or as introductions to the main action of the poem, they appear mostly in the decorative mode and their structure is that of simple paraphrase or, less rarely, personification [TN (8):3,5—6]. However, in the second functional-category, where the light-image either reflects the mood of the soul or contrasts with it, the image-structure becomes more complex. Antithesis occurs: "Bey Sonnenschein ist schatten" [TN (7):14,6]; oxymoron: "von schatten klaren schein" [TN (11):10,8]; or the repetition of modifiers or substantives in close proximity [TN (11):21,5—6]. This tendency toward more complex rhetorical structures is continued and further intensified when the images are employed in a religious and theological sense. To describe Christ the word Licht is purposefully repeated as in: "liechtes liecht" [TN (6):13,2]; to describe God's luminous substance another repetition occurs: "Wie klar muss er den leuchten selb // Wie wunder/wunder glitzen? (TN 27:2,5—5); to describe the generation of the Son from the Father ("filiation" in

---

[8] Jöns, Sinnen-bild, pp. 132ff., expresses this symbolism as follows: "Die Nacht gilt — und das ist ihr häufigste Bedeutung — als Sinnbild der Sündhaftigkeit und in der äussersten Schärfe dieser Seinsverfassung als Sinnbild des Zustandes der Gnadenlosigkeit."

[9] Cf. Grete Lüers, Die Sprache der Deutschen Mystik des Mittelalters im Werke der Mechthild von Magdeburg (Darmstadt: Wiss. Buch, 1966), p. 214, for references to Mechthild, Tauler and Seuse.

[10] For examples from among other baroque poets, cf. Eva Lüders, "Die Auffassung des Menschen im 17. Jahrhundert. (Dargestellt an Hand der Poetischen Handbücher)" (Diss. Köln, 1934), pp. 38—39.

[11] Cf. F. X. Murphy, "The Creed," The New Catholic Encyclopedia, IV (New York: McGraw-Hill, 1967), 432—438, for the meaning of the Apostles Creed.

[12] Cf. GTB Book I, chap. 1 for Spee's version of the Tridentine Credo.

theological terminology),[13] light generates light (*TN* 29:7,5–6); beam flows from beam (*TN* 29:18,1); light merges with light.

From a stylistic point of view these images occur predominantly in the decorative mode in the first functional-category. In the second functional-category the style tends toward the metaphysical conceit,[14] with its emphasis on antithesis and oxymoron. On the theological level there is a mixture of both the mystical and conceptual modes — to describe the process of divine filiation, and the person of Christ as "liechtes licht."

2. Night-Darkness

As light stands for the divinity, its power and essence, and for joyfulness of spirit, so darkness in Spee is applied to the troubled soul, to its harassed state of introspection, its consciousness of sin and *contritio cordis*. Sorrow for sin and the necessity for penance are dominant themes in the *GTB*. Moreover the following chapters in the *GTB* are directly concerned with these themes that appear in the poems of the *GTB* and those transferred to the *TN*: Bk. II, chapters 5 and 6, and Bk. III, chapter 9. In this use of darkness to portray the troubled soul, Spee shows a marked affinity with Gryphius.[15] However, images of darkness are less frequent (25) than those of light (65). Occasionally, darkness is used antithetically with light in *TN* (7):14,6, as shown above: "Bey Sonnenschein ist schatten" to describe the soul's pain of absence from Christ. In comparison to God who is called "schönes Licht" (*GTB* 211.28), the light of the sun, moon and stars is dark: "Nur dunckel gantz: ist all ihr glantz" (*GTB* 211.34). Aside from these antitheses frequent use of paraphrase (cf. Table 2.1, p. 127), or personifications (cf. Table 2.2, p. 127) occurs.

Images of darkness in the *TN* function either: (a) in a context of religious contemplation as "contemplations- of place" [*TN* 45:291,24; *TN* (7):1,1–2; 21,1–2; (38):10,1–2; 44:1,5–6]; (b) to express a mood of penitence, "zerknirschung des herzens" [*TN* (15):1,1–2; 12,8; 13,3–4] plus the oxymoron in (15):14,4–6: "In dunkler nacht / ich bin bedacht // Mein tag / ohn tag verbringen;" or (c) within a context of praise of God as in [*TN* 30:183, 17–18; *TN* 26:3,1–2; (25):4,3–4 and *TN* (25):3,7–8]. On two occasions the image of darkness is used to contrast with joy. In *TN* 49:324,4–5 after the "braune

---

13 For the notion of generation or filiation in the context of the Trinitarian processions, cf. Pietro Parente, *Dictionary of Catholic Theology* (Milwaukee: Herder, 1957), pp. 230–231.

14 For a general discussion of this style in the seventeenth century, cf. Windfuhr, *Bildlichkeit*, pp. 261ff.

15 Cf. Fricke, *Bildlichkeit*, pp. 40–41.

Stunden sind entronnen," the soul gives way to joyfulness of spirit. In *TN* (18):2,2 the soul tells pain and sorrow: "Fliehet hin zur Finstren nacht" so that sorrow may give way to joy and that she may walk with Jesus in the sweetness of love.

Spee's use of the image of darkness to indicate sinfulness, sorrow, and separation from God stands in the tradition of medieval mystical terminology which in turn is based on Sacred Scripture. Meister Eckhart, Seuse, Mechthild von Magdeburg and Tauler use the image of darkness to convey the soul's separation from God.[16] Interestingly many images of darkness in Spee applied to penitence, sinfulness and sorrow for sin originate in *GTB* Bk. III, chapter 9 "Noch andere Werck der liebe, und ist Zerknirschung des Herzens" where Spee compares God's majesty and love for the soul with her ingratitude and sinfulness. The importance of the *GTB* for an understanding of this theme in Spee becomes clear. It is also of interest to note in the analysis above the number of poems in the *TN* originally written in the *GTB* which reflect this theme. In *GTB* Bk. III, chapter 9, Spee portrays the deep interpersonal relation existing between God and the soul, and the general conflict between darkness and light present in the Johannine Gospel, which was certainly well known to Spee and which was commented upon above. In this same chapter of the *GTB*, and with similar imagery, Spee has the soul cry out to God for forgiveness using an image of brightness and light (snow) as a symbol of grace: "Mach mich recht schnee- und schwanenweiss" [*GTB* 330.3 and *TN* (15):7,3]. In addition, Spee's use of antithesis in *GTB* 211.34, where God appears as all light and the luminous elements as darkness, is a further reflection of the cosmology expressed in the Prologue to St. John's Gospel: "A light that shines in the dark, a light that darkness could not understand" (I,5).[17]

The structure of these images of darkness does not vary with their three-fold function outlined above. Rather, personifications and paraphrases are found irrespective of function. Stylistically, the affective-pathetic mode of metaphor predominates although images involved in the praise-function tend more to the decorative style. Finally, Spee's paraphrases exhibit a remarkable uniformity in both modifiers and in verbal forms.[18]

---

[16] Lüers, *Sprache,* pp. 173–174; and August Langen, *Der Wortschatz des deutschen Pietismus,* 2nd ed. (Tübingen: Niemeyer, 1968), p. 127.

[17] All scriptural quotations are taken from the *Jerusalem Bible,* ed. Alexander Jones (London: Darton-Todd, 1966).

[18] Cf. the examples listed in Windfuhr, p. 198, and in Fricke, *Bildlichkeit,* pp. 141ff. There is definite similarity here with Gryphius. The image in *GTB* 211.28–34 bears some resemblance to the conceits that characterize the metaphysical mode as found in John Donne. Cf. Martz, *Meditation,* p. 105.

3. Color

Spee's use of color-images is more varied and extravagant than that of Gryphius, who uses predominantly black and white contrasts. Black and white image-contrasts have already been indicated in the categories of light and darkness specifically with regard to the soul's relationship to God and as expressive of her own introspective state. In Spee's poetic use of other colors of the spectrum he falls within the baroque decorative mode that uses great varieties of color. When Spee's color-images are compared with those of Harsdörffer, Lohenstein, Zesen and Fleming, his affinity with the decorative mode of style of these poets is evident. The emphasis on picture-images, on the Horatian *ut pictura poesis,* found among these decorative poets, manifests itself in the German baroque tendency toward the ornate style over the other stylistic categories of clarity and *puritas.*[19]

The words "color" and "paint" occur frequently in Spee in a metaphorical sense (cf. Table 3.1, p. 128). In describing the fading flower in *TN* (13):7,3–5, a symbol of the fragility of existence and beauty, Spee writes: "All dein gefarbten schein / Dich bald nur wirst entferben." *Entferben* is a verbal metaphor indicating not a sudden process but a slow deterioration. This is typical of the baroque decorative style that uses verbal forms of the types: *verschwinden, verbleichen, vergehen, verwehen, erblassen,* and *weichen.* The affective-pathetic style employs verbal forms that express more active and destructive forces such as: *zerbeissen, abfretzen, entreihen, verstreuen, zertreten.*

A favorite baroque image, "Braune nacht," is found in Spee in *TN* (16):1,5 and (15):1,1. "Braune stunden" occurs in *TN* 49:324,5. The image "braune Stunden" is considered to be characteristic of the decorative style.[20] But "braune Nacht" occurs in the *TN* only in a context of sorrow and penance, and does not function in a merely decorative sense.[21] Both poems *TN* (16) and (15) were used in the *GTB* within a context of sorrow for sin. The color "brown" in medieval mystical writing is used to describe the lower, sensual part of the soul

---

19 For a discussion of these styles in the seventeenth-century context, cf. Joachim Dych, *Ticht-Kunst. Deutsche Barock-poetik und rhetorische Tradition. Ars Poetica* I (Bad Homburg: Gehlen, 1966), p. 68. It is at this point in the analysis of Spee's color-images where Fritz Strich's statement on the nature of baroque imagery becomes significant when he states: "Die barocke Bildwelt entsteht, indem auch das geistigste Gefühl . . . als eine Farbe, ein Ton, eine Süssigkeit, ein Parfum empfunden wird." "Der Lyrische Stil des 17. Jahrhunderts," *Deutsche Barockforschung,* hrsg. R. Alewyn (Köln: Kiepenheuer Witsch, 1966), p. 251.

20 Gryphius uses "braune Nacht." Cf. Lüders, "Die Auffassung," p. 40.

21 For Spee's use of "night" as brown in the sense of "reproduktive Naturschilderung," cf. Märtens, "Darstellung der Natur," 585.

as in Mechthild's *Fliessendes Licht der Gottheit*.[22] There does seem to be a relationship between the sensual, the sinful, and the color brown in Spee.[23]

The adjective "falbe" modifies death [TN 46:302,1; (11):12,8; (43):2,5]. This is evidently a translation of Ovid's *pallida mors*.[24] Christ's forehead and the weeping moon are also described as "falb" (TN 9:9,1 and 45:292,5). The red-white color contrast is variously applied (cf. Table 3.2, p. 128). This color-antithetic is a Petrarchan trait often applied as a type of conceit.[25] It is also found in the Canticle of Canticles.[26]

Other color usages in the decorative mode are apparent in those that are applied to the beloved, Christ (cf. Table 3.3, p. 128). Many of these colors are variously applied to nature (cf. Table 3.4, p. 129). From these examples it is evident that Spee has a decided preference for image-composites of color and animal or color and precious jewel. In this respect he manifests traits of the baroque decorative style.[27]

A theological application of color-images occurs in the phrase "schnee-weisser tag" [TN (11):21,6], which is the symbol in Spee for the day of final union of the spouse and Christ. Moreover, the petition which the soul makes for purification from sin and her request to be made "schnee und schwanen weiss" [TN (15):7,3] shows the color "white" to be a symbol of grace and purity from sin, a traditional medieval mystical application.[28] A further extension of this image occurs in GTB 52.17—24:

> Wie scharlach, und wie rotes blut
> > Von sünden bin geferbet:
> Nun spreng mich Herr mit Ysop gut,
> > So wird all sünd verderbet.
> Schneeweiss und rein: als helffenbein,
> > Wird ich dan wider werden.

where the sins are red and God's grace turns them white as ivory, which is a clear reference to Psalm 50. Brightness as a symbol of grace and strength has been pointed out above under the image-category of light. The Holy Spirit is called "gülden Regen / gülden-Fluss" (TN 29:31,1) and "gülden stral / gülden-schuss"

---

22 Lüers, *Sprache der Mystik*, p. 187.

23 E. Rosenfeld states: "Bei Spee ist die 'braune Nacht' ein Abbild seelischer Verzweiflung und Sündenbewusstseins, so dass die Seele keine Ruhe findet." *Neue Studien*, p. 71.

24 Jacobsen, *Metamorphosen*, p. 140.

25 Jacobsen, *Metamorphosen*, pp. 82—83.

26 For the influence of the Canticle of Canticles on Spee in general, cf. E. Rosenfeld, *Neue Studien*, pp. 72ff.

27 Similarities with such poets as Lohenstein, Stieler, Hofmannswaldau and Fleming can be seen by a comparison with the image-listings from these poets in Windfuhr, *Bildlichkeit*, p. 240.

28 Lüers, *Sprache der Mystik*, pp. 15ff.

(*TN* 29:31,3).[29] Golden is a favorite color for Spee. Because of its affinity with brilliance and luminosity, it aptly symbolizes grace, strength and divinity.[30] Through his varied use of colors and his application of them to paint "word-pictures," Spee stands within the mainstream of baroque imagery.

4. Water-Images

This category includes images of fountains, rain, snow, the sea, water, brooks, and streams. One group of these images functions as "compositions of place" as an aid in focussing our attention on the main theme within the poem itself. Metaphors, personifications, and similes structurally predominate in this group. Similes occur such as "Der schnee da kombt wie sanffte woll" [*TN* (28):12,1] (cf. Table 4.1, p. 129). Paraphrases occur (cf. Table 4.2, p. 130), and examples of personifications (cf. Table 4.3, p. 130).

Whereas this first category of images is subordinate to the central theme of the various poems and therefore stands more on the periphery of the poetic action, the next group of images is more directly involved in central themes such as: the praise of God, sorrow over Christ's suffering, contrition, love for the Spouse and the beauty of creation. Mary Magdalen's "marck in beinen wallet" [*TN* (11):57,1] when Christ speaks directly to her and calls her by name. The ocean's ceaseless movement and its abrupt changes from calm to fury are a symbol for the restlessness of the spouse in her yearning for union with Christ:

> Dass Meer wans wüht ohn massen
> Mags doch nit lang bestahn:
> Pflegt bald sich niderlassen
> Nimbt ruh begierlich ahn: [*TN* (6):7,1–4]

Later, in *TN* 19:33–36, the ocean is symbolized as an obstacle to Xavier's desire for souls. In other instances Spee uses these images to show praise of God: "hagel weiss / auch flocken greiss // Von schnee und eiss entzogen" [*TN* (24):5,5–6]; "die stolze wasser-wogen" [*TN* (25):5,6]. In *TN* 50:7,1–8 the brooks are paraphrased as:

---

29   The notion of the Holy Spirit as a stream is found in the thirteenth-century hymn of uncertain origin *Veni Sancte Spiritus*. "The authorship of the Pentecost Sequence *Veni sancte spiritus*, still used in the liturgy, is a debated subject; it is likely that the author was Stephen Langton, Archbishop of Canterbury (d. 1228)." J. Szöverffy, "Hymnology," *New Catholic Encyclopedia*, VIII, 294.

30   Cierlot, *Dictionary*, pp. 114–115.

> Lieblich alle bäch / und bächlen /
>   (Krum geführtes wasser-glass.)
> Auff den grünen wiesen lächlen /
>   Und befeuchten laub / und grass.
> Zierlich wider kombt gekrochen
>   Manches rauschend wässerlein /
> So mit steinlein underbrochen
>   Sausend lobt den schöpffer sein.

Rivers weep at Christ's sufferings: "Dich all flüss beweinen" (*TN* 40:23,3); also 49:321,19—20 and 45:284,18—18.[31] The brook Cedron, an Ovidian allusion,[32] first "stralet sein bintzen-haar" (*TN* 41:2,6), then seeks to escape Christ's captors in the garden of Gethsemane; a clear allusion to the disciples of Christ fleeing, in Mark's account of the Passion (Mark, XIV, 50). The flight of Cedron is expressed in the simile: "wie die pfeil von bogen zihlen" (*TN* 41:6,5). Later the brook Cedron sorrows: "traurig hub er an zu klagen" (*TN* 41:8,1).

In a third category comprising mainly brooks, the sea, and fountains Spee uses theological and religious motifs. The ship-motif which is such a popular notion in seventeenth-century literature[33] and was one of the most popular themes in Renaissance works[34] is found only once in Spee in *GTB* 191 : 29—36. However this is one of the poems in the *GTB* which he did not transfer to the *TN*, but because of its contemporary frequency is worthy of note (Gryphius uses the ship-motif more than seventy times):

> Und wan dan schon thut sausen
>   Der wind auff disem meer;
> Wan schon die wellen brausen
>   Rund umb mein schifflein her;
> Will ich doch nie verzagen,
>   Gott wird mein hülffer sein;
> Den ancker will ich schlagen
>   Zu seinem hertzen ein. Amen.

In Christian symbolism the ship is a symbol of human existence.[35] In the troubled waters of life Spee anchors his ship to God's heart (*GTB* 191.35—36).

---

31 This is but one of many examples to be found in Spee of the "Motiv der mitfühlenden Natur," a common seventeenth-century motif *(natura compatiens)*. For a full discussion of this motif, cf. Adelheid Beckmann, "Motive und Formen der deutschen Lyrik des 17. Jahrhunderts und ihre Entsprechungen in der französischen Lyrik seit Ronsard," *Hermaea. Neue Folge*, Bd. 5, pp. 61 ff.

32 Discussed in Rosenfeld, *Neue Studien*, pp. 165—166.

33 Lüders, "Auffassung," pp. 8—9.

34 Fricke, *Bildlichkeit*, p. 48.

35 Jöns, *Das Sinnen-bild*, p. 196.

A variation of this image is found also among the Pietists. The soul is pictured as anchored to Jesus' wounds.[36] Among the mystics of the Middle Ages and Renaissance, to be anchored to God is to be recollected, to live in deep union with God through a special, infused gift of grace.[37] Anchor, in classical writers, was a symbol of stability. This was adapted in Christian iconography of the second century as a symbol of hope.[38]

When the soul weeps and tears flow because of her sinfulness, Spee uses the term "bächlein" [TN (15):17,1−4]. This metaphor occurs later in Spee but in the context of tears of joy. The wounds suffered by Christ in His passion are also called "bächlein" [TN (42):1,7−8; 49:320,21−26].

Spee also applies the fountain-metaphor to the wounds of Christ (TN 46:8,1−8). In GTB 522.37 they are called "klare brünlein." Mystical language applies the fountain-metaphor to express the fullness of grace.[39] Christ Himself is called the "Brunnen aller lust und lieblichkeit" [TN (42:11,1−2]. (This notion also occurs in the GTB 324.3 and 360.21. Tauler and Angelus Silesius use it in the same context.)[40] The image of Christ as "Brunnen" is another example of the interaction between the GTB and the TN. Likewise, the Eucharist is referred to as a "Brunnen" (GTB 519.2). In explaining the relationship between the Father and the Son in the Trinity, Spee continues to use the fountain-metaphor.[41] The Son is "der bronn von seinem bronnen" (TN 29:18,4). The metaphor "deep fountain" as an image to describe the profundity of the divine nature is an ancient notion.[42] Elsewhere Brunnen occurs in Spee as an image of worldliness and vanity [TN (16):5,5]. The original context for this image is the prose text in GTB 324.3 in the context of Bk. III, chapter 9 "Noch andere Werck der liebe, und ist zerknirschung dess Hertzens."

The sea-image likewise has a theological application in the GTB. Its previous use as a symbol of the spouse's restlessness was noted [TN (6):7,1−8]. In TN 47 the kindness of God is compared to an ocean. Silesius and Kühlmann have been

---

[36] A. Langen, Wortschatz des Pietismus, p. 164, makes the following citation from Joh. Andreas Rothe, "Ich habe nun den grund gefunden, der meinen anker ewig hält; wo anders, als in Jesu wunden? ..."

[37] Cf. Maximilian Sandaeus, Pro Theologia Mystica Clavis (Köln, 1640 rept. Louvain: Editions de la bibliothèque S.J., 1963), p. 78, under the rubric "anchoratus." Sandaeus' mystical terminology and their correspondences in Spee indicate a common application of related terms among seventeenth-century Jesuits. Sandaeus' relationship in this regard has not been sufficiently treated by authorities on Spee.

[38] Jerusalem Bible, p. 377, footnote g, a commentary to Hebrews, 6.19.

[39] Sandaeus, Mystica Clavis, p. 217, under the rubric "fons." Note the fountain in the frontispiece of the GTB. Cf. Van Oorschot, op.cit., p. 568.

[40] Windfuhr, Bildlichkeit, p. 210.

[41] For a prose version of this trinitarian relationship between Father and Son, cf. GTB 412.4−11.

[42] Sandaeus, Mystica Clavis, p. 217. Pseudo-Dionysius, Jeremias, and Ruysbroek use it and it is also one of Mechthild's favorite motifs. Lüers, Sprache der Mystik, pp. 140ff.

known to use this image.[43] Spee's adaptation of Psalm 129 in *GTB* 124.1—4
contains the following application of the ocean to God as the source of grace:

> Ein gnaden Meer verschlossen
> In deinem hertzen ligt,
> Das komt mit hauff geflossen,
> Wan uns die noth anficht.

A practically identical use of this image occurs in Gryphius.[44] In *GTB*
519.19—20 the Blessed Sacrament is called "Unendliches Meer aller süssigkeit."
In *TN* (15):6,5—8 the soul asks God to cast her sins into the sea. This image
occurs likewise in the prose text accompanying this poem in *GTB* 325.33ff.
Finally, the traditional image of the Holy Spirit as "gnadenguss" (*TN* 29:32,3)
can be found also in Tauler.[45] The image "gülden Regen / gülden-fluss // Von
beiden gleich ergossen" (*TN* 29:31,1—2) is used to explain the procession of the
Spirit from the Father and the Son.[46] Spee's mystical and religious imagery
stemming from fountains, rains, the ocean and sea embodies traditional medieval
and baroque modes of expression.[47] Words such as: *Brunnen, fons, Bach, Anker,
Gnaden-Meer* have long histories among mystical and religious writers. Spee's
tendency to use paraphrase and personification in the first two functional
divisions above shows an affinity with the decorative mode of style. The second
division, however, shows more affinity with the affective than the decorative
baroque style.

5. Fire, Heat, Flame, Burning

Images of fire, heat, burning, flames, and hot coals occur with great
frequency in both the *GTB* and the *TN*. Spee uses them almost exclusively as
metaphors to describe the force and the intensity of love. Most of these images
are common to many seventeenth-century French and German poets.[48]
They also have a long literary history beginning with Latin love poetry.[49]
Not only the poems in the *TN* but the prose and poetic text of the *GTB*
are replete with images of this type. Those in the *GTB* are also metaphors

---

43 Windfuhr, *Bildlichkeit*, p. 209.
44 Fricke, *Bildlichkeit*, p. 51.
45 Lüers, *Sprache*, p. 192.
46 Cf. Parente, *Dogmatic*, p. 231, for notion of procession.
47 The fountain which appears in the fontispieces to the editions of the *TN* originates
most probably from a medieval motif. Cf. Rosenfeld, *Fr. Spee*, p. 200. It contains the blood
shed by Christ on the cross and purifies the soul of sin.
48 Cf. Beckmann, "Motive und Formen," pp. 36ff., cites examples from Weckherlin,
Opitz, and Czepko. Cf. also Windfuhr, *Bildlichkeit*, p. 56.
49 Jacobsen, *Metamorphosen*, p. 125.

expressing the intensity of the love of God for the soul and for the soul towards God. Several of these images in the *GTB* recur in similar contexts in the *TN* and indicate how prevalent these images were in Spee's writings (cf. Table 5.1, p. 130). The flame-image also occurs (cf. Table 5.2, p. 131). The image "feuer und flamm" is used for the stars [*TN* (28):4,1–2]. *TN*(28) was originally taken from the *GTB*, and the same terminology occurs in the preceding prose text (*GTB* 300.30) with reference to the stars.

Nominal and verbal metaphors for love and its effects from this image-field are frequent (cf. Table 5.3, p. 131): "brennen zu Kohlen" [*TN* (2):4,5–6] seems to be a reference to Zeus-Semele and has Petrarchan parallels.[50] The verbal forms in this category show more affinity with the affective-pathetic mode than with the decorative mode because of their destructive nature. This was also true of the verbal forms in the color-category.

Spee uses fire-metaphors likewise to express his religious ideas. Thus, "reiner augen-brandt" is an image used to express the effect of Christ's love on the soul since He is the bright mirror of the Trinity [*TN* (42):10,6]; "flammen" [*TN* (14):83,10] refers to the wiles of Satan, obstacles to the soul's relationship to God. The inner trinitarian love-relation between the Father and the Son is described in *TN* 29:21,7–8 as: "Mit aussgespannter flammen gross // Sich beyde gleich verlieben." Father and Son share intimately the same fire of love: "Der Sohn ihm wider seufftzet zu // Sich gleichem feur ergibet" (*TN* 29:23,3–4). (Cf. also *TN* 29:28,7; 29,4.)

Mystical language has traditionally employed antithetical and oxymoronic image-structures to express the effects of the love of God in the soul and the mystical union. This mode of language has also frequently used fire and heat-images to express its thoughts. These fire-images are likewise found in Sacred Scripture; for example, the Song of Songs 8,6–7 and Hebrews 12,29: "For our God is a consuming fire." The German mystics were influenced to a considerable degree by Pseudo-Dionysius with regard to images of this nature. Eckhart, Mechthild, Ruysbroek and Tauler frequently use "brennen" to express the action of God on the soul in the mystical state.[51] Whether Spee was influenced more by traditional mystical metaphor, or by the increased rhetoricization of poetry in the baroque age, or by a combination of these factors is still a question at this stage of inquiry. However, an analysis of the structure of the images in this category to express the effect of the love of God on the soul reveals an abundance of metaphors, paradoxes, antitheses and

---

50   Jacobsen, *Metamorphosen,* p. 125.
51   Lüers, *Sprache der Mystik,* p. 147.

oxymorons. In this respect one would have to conclude that there is an increase in rhetoricization in Spee.[52]

There is but one simile in this category, the comparison of the soul's love for God to a candle which is inextinguishable:

> Die lieb in meinen hertzen
>   Ein flämlein stecket an;
> Dass brint gleich einer kertzen
>   So niemand leschen kan. [TN (3):1,5—8]

This same simile occurs in the GTB 181.23 where Spee is attempting to turn the spiritual daughter from the love of earthly things to the love of God. Emmy Rosenfeld, in commenting on the symbolic meaning of the candle-simile, equates the eternal candle to the immortality of the soul.[53] In the context indicated above, the fire of the candle is indeed enkindled in the soul, but it seems rather a symbol for the reflection of God's uncreated grace in the soul. Theology explains grace as the presence of God's love in the soul. It is this presence which is inextinguishable (from a theological point of view) when true love of God is present.[54] The soul is eternal, but Spee is speaking here of a love-presence in the soul and not the soul exclusively. Elsewhere Spee uses the burning candle-image as a symbol for the transitory nature of life on earth (GTB 181.23ff.).

Spee calls the love which the soul experiences both fire and water simultaneously and this love causes pain and sorrow:

> Die lieb ist feur
>   O abentheur!
> Ist wasser auch im gleichen:
>   Bringt hertzen leid
>   Bringt hertzen freud
> Muss eins dem andern weichen. [TN (7):17,1—6][55]

---

52 Windfuhr, Bildlichkeit, p. 216, expresses the opinion that in general among the seventeenth-century mystics rhetoricization was on the increase: "Die meisten barocken Mystiker bemühen sich um virtuose Behandlung ihres Stoffes."

53 Neue Studien, p. 133.

54 For further discussion on the presential nature of this grace cf. Rahner, Theol. Wörterbuch, pp. 138ff.

55 This image seems to have been found by Spee in Conrad Vetter's translation of the thirty-second verse of the hymn, Jubilus de nomine Jesu:

Hic amor ardet jugiter. Eins brennens brinnt der Liebe Fewr.
Dulcescit mirabiliter. Wird wunder süss und abenthewr,
Sapit delectabiliter, Im kosten hat sie grossen Lust,
Delectat et feliciter. Im Lust ein Himmelsüssen Gust.

Cf. Rosenfeld, Neue Studien, p. 87.

The "Flämlein" of love is both bitter and sweet [TN (3):6,1—2]. It is a "bitter-süsser glut" [TN (11):27,5—6]. Even more striking is its secondary effect: it both cools and heats up at the same time [TN (3):6,5—8]. It is a "kühle Feuer und Flammen" [TN (11):27,5] which "wärmt und kühlet" [TN (11):59,1—3]. Finally, this love-experience cannot be described to anyone who has not himself experienced it [TN (6):2,7—8]. For further paradoxical structures compare: (TN 2:3,5—6 and 10:3,7—8). One final note: TN 33:4,1—4 contains the image of the half-frozen Christ-child with the fire of love burning in its heart and seems to have been a familiar theme among Jesuits. Spee's fellow Jesuit poet, Robert Southwell, uses the same motif in his poem, "The Burning Babe."

Stylistically, Spee's imagery in this category vacillates between the affective and mystical modes.[56] When the images of fire are applied to the effects of love, the affective mode predominates. When Spee attempts to describe the experience of love by means of anthithesis and paradox, the use of these structures indicates an affinity with the mystical mode.

6. Stars

The cosmic images in this category include the stars, the moon and the sun. They occur with considerable frequency in Spee, and all but a few of the poems in the TN contain at least one or more images based on the heavenly constellations. Some of these cosmic images have already been discussed, but only insofar as they functioned as images of light and darkness.

Many of the cosmic images found in the poems in the TN, especially those poems which originally existed in the GTB before being transferred to the TN, show an affinity with the prose expressions of the GTB. To point out some of the more obvious correspondences that show the influence of Spee's thought and style from the GTB on the poems of the TN, the following are cited: in GTB 173.17—20 and TN (38):14,1—4 the moon and the stars suffer and weep with Christ as He faces his oncoming passion. This theme, *natura compatiens*, also appears in TN 39 where the moon, "der himmlisch Sternen-Hirt ... kläglich betrauret," mourns Daphnis, who is a figure representing Christ in the later poems of the TN in numbers 39, 40, 41, 44, 45, 47, and 48. The moon weeps, her heart breaks, she tells the stars to clothe themselves ". . . pur in kohlen // Pur in lauter schwartzes wand" (TN 39:14,4—6). This theme occurs again in TN

---

56 Jacobsen, *Metamorphosen*, p. 127, makes the following point: "In der TN hält sich die Feuermetapher im grossen Ganzen innerhalb des Ausdrucksvermögens des zierlichen Stils; nur im GTB lodern Gefühl und Sprache zu mystischen Höhen empor. . . ." We disagree with his option for the decorative style here.

(15):12,1—8 where the soul calls on the stars and the moon to weep with her, to cease shining, to mourn together with her over her sinfulness. In *TN* 41.14,1ff. the brook Cedron commands the sun and the moon to mourn the fact that Christ has been captured by his enemies. In *TN* 44:2,1—8 Christ's mother calls on the moon and the stars to mourn the death of her son and to be sympathetic with her own sorrow. In *TN* 45:292,2—5 the moon calls on the stars to weep at Christ's death.

These same themes and images occur under similar circumstances and contexts in the *GTB*. In *GTB* 199.22ff., Spee wishes the soul to assume an attitude of prayer before the crucifix. This is reflected in a following poem that occurs in *GTB* 204.33ff. Within the context of this same chapter the soul prays to God, scolds the sun for looking on the death of Christ, and is told to cover the cross with darkness: "O ihr Element, wie mögt ihr solches leiden? O du unverschämte Sonn, wie magstu solchem jämmerlichen tod länger zuschauen können? blase auss dein freches liecht; uberziehe das Creutz mit dicker finsternuss..." (*GTB* 204.24—27). A variation of this theme occurs in *TN* 39:14,4—6 where the moon tells the stars to wrap themselves in darkness. In *GTB* 395.10ff., which begins: "S. Franciscus betrachtete seinen gecreutzigten Herren Jesum wie er so gar verlassen wurde; und er umbfinge das Creutz, und redete..." Francis compares himself to the sun in the following words: "... aber ich will bleiben, und die Sonn sein: will verlieren meinen schein, all reichtumb, schöne, kleider, zier unnd herrlichkeit der welt von mir verwerffen, und von meines gecreutzigten Herren wegen immer trauren" (395.16—19). In *GTB* 523.22ff. the soul again calls on the moon, sun, and stars to weep and mourn the death of Christ. It is obvious that Spee has transferred many of the images which first appeared in the *GTB* to a similar context in the *TN*, specifically in poems 39, (15), 41, 44, and 45.

Another instance where Spee's religious ideas in the prose chapters of the *GTB* undoubtedly influenced the *TN* is the theme of praise offered to God by the heavenly constellations. In Bk. III, chapter 7, Spee proposes to his spiritual daughter a journey through all of creation as a means of offering fitting praise to God:

> Mein kind, was duncket dich? Ich zwar empfinde in mir einen lust, dass ich einmal mit dem könig David in die höhe und tieffe, durch den lufft, durchs meer, und durch die Welt spatzieren gehen, und die Creaturen Gottes gleichsam auffwecke, und zu seinem lob ermahne, wiltu dass ich dich bey der hand nehme, und mit mir führe, damit du mir auch helffest alle zum lob Gottes antreiben? (299.7—12)

Spee closely identifies praise of God with the practice of charity and the love of God which he practiced so well in his own life and is the subject of the third Book (cf. also Bk. II, p. 64). As a matter of fact, all the poems which treat the theme of praise in the *TN* (Emmy Rosenfeld considers these poems to be the basis of what she calls the second cycle of poems in the *TN*)[57] were taken from the third section of the *GTB,* which is devoted to the awakening in the spiritual daughter of *amor benevolentiae.*[58] Furthermore, in *GTB* 297.13—21 Spee states:

> Wer aber Gottes lob gern höret, der liebet ihn gewisslich: dan zwar wan ich jemand hasse, kan ich ja sein lob durchauss nicht hören; . . . wan aber ich jemand liebe, da höre ich also gern dass man ihn lobe. Also das weil ich verstehe dass du so gern Gott loben hörest. . . .

It is for this reason that the theme of praising God is a constant theme in the third Book. In *GTB* 294.25—32 Spee wishes that the Lord's name be inscribed in each star so that His praise be all the greater:

> Wünsch ich, der nahm des Herren wer
> In iedem Stern geschrieben:
> Und weil der Himmel eilet sehr,
> Mit ihn wurd umbgetrieben:
> Damit doch immer tag, und nacht
> Thet leuchten also prächtig,
> Voll herrlichkeit, und ehren pracht
> Der Gottes nahm allmachtig.

In *GTB* 300.19—36 Spee points out to his spiritual daughter how the stars and the firmament praise God. He concludes: "Eja lasset uns auch zu ihnen schreyen, sie zum Gottes lob erfrischen, und also mit freuden singen . . . ." Thereupon the third and fourth strophes of what later became *TN* (28) follow and these lines provide us with an interesting insight into the poetic technique of Spee. Many of the prose expressions for the stars find their way into the poem: "schöne licht und sternen" (4,6); "fackel-pracht" (4,5); "Mit feur, und flamm besaamet!" (4,2). The identical process is operative after the prose section beginning in *GTB* 301.22—32, where the next two strophes of *TN* (28) follow. A comparison between the prose and poetic versions indicates several images related to the stars as the poetic versions: "Du silber-glantz," "du gülden-schein," and "gemacht zu klaren liechten."

Another example of correspondence between images in the *GTB* and the *TN* occurs in *TN* (25):2,1—8 and 3,1—2. Here, again, the stars and the moon praise their Creator. When this poem is read in the context of *GTB* Bk. III, chapters 7 and 8 (the poem actually occurs in the *GTB* at the beginning of Bk. III, chapter 8) we have another example of how Spee's poetic technique functions.

---

57 *Neue Studien,* pp. 136ff.
58 Cf. *GTB,* 29ff., for an explanation of these scholastic terms in Spee's own terminology.

In the *GTB* 310.20—30 the prose sentences are imperative statements: "Lobet ihn Sonne und Mond: lobet ihn alle sterne und liechter." In the poetic version, the imperative statements take the form of a question: "Wer hat in golt uns silber-stuck // Die Sonn und Mon gekleidet? " (312.5—6) and [*TN* (25):2,1—2].

Consequently, when the theme of the stars and the firmament praising God is encountered in Spee, its function and origin within the *GTB* must be recalled if its full significance in the *TN* is to be grasped. By demonstrating to the soul the praise-significance of the elements, Spee hopes thereby to bring the soul more easily to the love of God. Perhaps this is the reason for their position in the middle brace of poems in the *TN* from poems 20 to 28. These poems are placed in context between poems *TN* 1—19, where the dominant theme is the ardent yearning of the spouse for her beloved, Christ, and the later poems of the *TN* which are concerned with the contemplation of the suffering and the passion of Christ. This produces the following general thematic sequence in the *TN:* Christ appears first as the sought-for Lover, then as Creator deserving of the praise of creation and the soul and, finally, in His death He is an object of compassionate love.

In addition to the stars' functional role as instruments of praise to the Creator, it is interesting to note their overall function in the *TN*. In the earlier poems (*TN* 1—19) where the theme is more sorrowful love and the desire of the soul for union with her beloved, Christ, the cosmic-images serve a more decorative function. They occur as background motifs.[59] Later, when the themes of praise and contemplation of the passion and death of the Spouse become operative, Spee places these cosmic images more within the central action of the poems. Here their poetic function becomes more explicit. The stars are asked to mourn with the soul at the sight of Christ suffering [*TN* 39 *passim;* (38): 14,1—4; 44:18—508; 45:292,2—5]; or they proclaim the creative love of the Father [*TN* (25):2,1—8; 31:185; 188; (42):7,1—8].

Structurally, such cosmic-images abound in paraphrases and neologisms. This is characteristic of the decorative mode among baroque poets (cf. Table 6.1, p. 131). Spee also has many mythological paraphrases for the stars based for the most part on Ovid[60] (cf. Table 6.2, p. 132). In *TN* (11):1,1—4, the sun rises late in a striking example of the grotesque mode:

> Die Sonn sampt ihren Rossen
> Späth Oesterlich bezecht
> Mit schlaff noch ubergossen
> Wolt früh kaum wachen recht.

---

[59] Compare *TN* (6):3,1—4; (8):3,5—10; 9:1,1—8; (11):1,1—4 and 10:1,1—4.
[60] Jacobsen, *Metamorphosen,* pp. 137ff.

Spee shows likewise a striking variety of verbal personifications (cf. Table 6.3, p. 132).

The moon is given special preference by Spee, particularly in *TN* 39. Whereas Gryphius uses the moon in his imagery only sparingly, Spee shows his predilection for moon-images in his use of the moon as the compassionate "Seelen-freund der Liebenden," which is characteristic of the more subjective religious poet in the seventeenth century.[61]

Spee's characteristic use of paraphrase and personification in his cosmic-images is logically connected with both their decorative and *natura-compatiens* role in the *TN*. When these images are not directly involved in the central action of the poem, they occur predominantly as paraphrases. When, however, they are more involved with the soul as it mourns, weeps, and sorrows, personifications abound.

Other poetical figures of speech occur less frequently in this image-category. The head of Christ in the garden of Gethsemane is "Viel weiss and bleicher dan der Mon" [*TN* (38):3,3]. In Gryphius just the opposite process is operative. The moon pales before the beloved.[62] In a suppressed simile the stars "Zucken ihre stralen ein" after they are outshone by the splendor of the Risen Christ(*TN* 50:11,5—8).[63]

In *TN* 49, Spee composes a medieval allegory on *Heilsgeschichte*. Spee professes this in the title to this poem: "Eckloga oder hirtengespräch uber dass Creutz, und aufferstehung Christi, darin / wass der eine hirt Damon genant von seinem vorhaben vorspielet, der ander Halton genant, allweg nachspielend auff dass Geistlich deutet und ziehet." In this poem there is a series of twelve images, each with a corresponding interpretative strophe. Damon and Halton, two popular shepherd figures in Spee (they appear in *TN* 30-32, 34, 36, 45, 48—49)[64] act out this "medieval allegory." Damon sings, as it were, the *sensus litteralis* of the images and Halton in reply discloses either the *sensus moralis, allegoricus* or *anagogicus*.[65] Of the twelve images which are presented in this poem, seven of them are derived from the sun, moon, or the stars. In *TN* 49:316,5—12 Damon sings the following to the accompaniment of his violin:

---

61 Cf. Fricke, *Bildlichkeit,* p. 39 for examples.

62 Fricke, *Bildlichkeit,* p. 40.

63 A related notion occurs in the *GTB* poem "O Jesu Jesu Wunder Nahm 226.9—12 where the spouse prefers to look on God's Son rather than the sun, stars and the moon. In *TN* 50:13,5—8 the wounds of Christ are compared to the stars.

64 With the exception of *TN* 40 in which Damon appears alone, Damon always appears together with Halton. Nowak, "Versuch," pp. 161ff., discusses the origin of these figures and their occurrences in the context of seventeenth- and eighteenth-century Shepherd poetry. He claims that they represent Spee's "ganz im Gefühl aufgehendes Ich."

65 For a discussion of these four senses, cf. Friedrich Ohly, *Vom geistigen Sinn des Wortes im Mittelalter* (Darmstadt: Wiss. Buch., 1966). This is a *Sonderausgabe* of an article which originally appeared in the *Zeitschrift für deutsches Altertum und deutsche Literatur,* 89 (1958/1959), 1—23.

> Wan von heisser Sonn verwüstet
> Kalt und winter ligen todt
> Man den sommer wider grüsset
> Wider bricht man rosen roth.
> Thal und felder schön verblümet
> Grün sich wider legen an:

Halton, in response, sings in *TN* 49:316,14—21:

> Wan die sünder zeitig büssen
> Und mit ihren hertzen-eyss
> Sie sich neben Jesu füssen
> Legen zu den wunden heiss:
> Werdens wider bald entzündet
> Wider leuchtet sommer-schein
> Heyl unss wider wird verkündet
> Straff sich wider zäumet ein.

Thus God's grace is compared to the hot sun burning away the sins of the repentant sinner. If the repentent sinner throws himself at the feet of Jesus, the "sommer-schein" of His grace will bring salvation (tropological sense). In *TN* 49: 319,2—9 Damon presents the following scene as he begs the sun not to leave: "Schöner fuhrmann halt den wagen // Lass die Ross verschnauffen doch," while he lies in the shade of the oak tree. Halton, in response, says in *TN* 49:319,11—18:

> Wan auch ich die sünd will meiden
> Zu dem Creutz mich setzen thu:
> Ruff O Jesu wolst nit scheiden
> O nit thu dein äuglein zu:
> O nit weiche nit verfahre
> O nit wöllest undergahn;
> Unss noch deine stralen spahre
> Bleib zu dieser frist doch stahn.

The sun is compared to Christ and the rays of the sun to God's grace for the sinner (tropological sense). In the next scene (*TN* 49:319,20—320,1) Damon sings that the sun has disdained his request and has set, so he takes his herd home. Halton gives his interpretation in 320,3—10, comparing the setting sun to "Jesu wares Liecht und fackel // als verlohrest deinen schein." Thus Jesus has died and Halton compares the herd of sheep to man lost in darkness and sorrow through the death of Christ.[66] This last interpretation is, of course, in the allegorical sense.

---

66 There is no evidence here for the disciples fleeing Calvary after the death of Christ, as Emmy Rosenfeld maintains. *Neue Studien*, p. 178.

The remaining four allegories can be summarized briefly as follows: in *TN* 49:321,4—11 the setting of the sun and the onset of night when the world "gantz erstummet" is interpreted by Halton, in 321,12—20, as an allegory for the darkness and confusion that resulted after the death of Christ on the cross. In the next strophes the moon and the stars put their beloved sun to bed: "Mon und sternen abends wachen // Legen ihre Sonn zu beth," until he arises again in the morning (*TN* 49:321,22—322,3). So, too, the pious people of the Gospel prepare Jesus for burial, and Mary, Christ's mother, has a premonition of his coming resurrection (322,5—12). In the next image, 322,14—21, the sun prepares to rise, "Geht zu wagen sitzet drauff" (322,17) and Damon puts his flock to pasture. This is interpreted by Halton as the descent of Christ into Hell and the freeing of the souls who have been captive there (322, 23—323,4). The final image (323,6—13) pictures Damon greeting the rising sun: "Sey mir wilkom liebe Sonn." In the interpretation of Damon's verses, Halton greets the rising sun as the Risen Christ, triumphant over death: "O wie wilkom bist entstanden // Jesu zu gewünschter zeit!" (323,15—22).

Thus we discern in these seven interpretative stanzas a compendium of the early Christian *kerygma* allegorized by means of the sun, moon, and the stars. Christ is the sun, night is death and suffering, the moon and the stars are the followers of Christ, dawn is the symbol of His resurrection and the light of the sun is His grace. By considering Damon's strophes in this poem analogously as the literal sense, we have an extended medieval allegory constructed by means of cosmic symbolism. The use of such imagery for Christ and His divine grace is characteristic of the mystical style among baroque poets.[67] This type of imagery is also employed by Spee with considerable frequency in the *GTB*. Christ's face is called: "du heller morgenstern," "du schöner Mon," "du heitere Sonn" (*GTB* 523.8ff.). Other examples can be found in *GTB* 525.38 and 226.9—12. This transferral of cosmic imagery to describe the beloved is also found among such poets of the decorative mode as Opitz, Weckherlin, Fleming and the Nürnberg Shepherd-poets.[68]

A final but significant use of cosmic imagery in Spee occurs in the metaphorical application of the sun and the stars to the greatest and most profound of the Christian mysteries, the Trinity. In describing the generation of the Son from the Father, Spee writes: "Ein Stern von eben seinem Stern // Die Sonn von seiner Sonnen" (*TN* 29:18,1—2). In his penchant for using cosmic nature to express the love of the soul for the beloved, to portray the inner states of the soul in its pursuit of the love of God, and in his description of the power

---

[67] Similar usages can be found in Silesius, Kuhlmann and Rosenroth. Cf. the list presented by Windfuhr, *Bildlichkeit*, p. 225.

[68] Cf. Beckmann, "Motive und Formen," p. 40, and Windfuhr, *Bildlichkeit*, p. 250. For similar uses among the Pietists, cf. Langen, *Wortschatz*, p. 347.

and grace of God, Spee exhibits many characteristics common to the baroque mystical mode. Medieval mystical language also used the sun as a symbol for God and His grace, but for the most part the medieval mystical gaze was more introspective.[69] It was turned more inward upon the soul itself, rather than upward and outward to God Himself. This also holds true for the language of the Pietists. A casual reference to the occurrence of such terms as *Seelengrund* and other composites with *Grund,* in addition to the superabundance of verbal prefixes with *hinein,* and a corresponding lack of images taken from the cosmos, indicates many of the common characteristics shared by both the Pietists and the medieval mystics.[70] On the other hand, Spee, together with other baroque poets of the mystical mode, turned his gaze outward and upward to the stars and to cosmic nature to express through these images his deepest religious feelings and his own theological beliefs.

7. Firmament

Images derived from the heavens and the surrounding firmament occur with less frequency than those of the stars and the moon. There are approximately sixteen such images in the *TN* and two others occur in the *GTB*. For the most part these images are ornamental or descriptive in function. Occasionally their function is to offer praise to the Creator as in *TN* 27:3,1—4; (28):4,1—3 and 3,1—8. In one instance they occur in a context where Mary Magdalen is sorrowing over the loss of the beloved [*TN* (11):20,1—8].

Spee's conception of the firmament is both biblical and scholastic in origin. Many of the images of heaven and the firmament are Spee's own adaptations from Caspar Ulenberg's translation of the Psalms.[71] In addition, Spee himself composed entire poems based on the psalms. *TN* 24, "Anders lob Gottes; und ist der 48. Psalm Davids Poetisch auffgesetzt," is one such poem. Spee was deeply imbued with their spirit, as many of his other poems testify (cf. *GTB* 68.31—38; 123.30—124.23 and 129.24ff.). As a priest, Spee would also have had an intimate acquaintance with the psalms since he was bound to daily recitation of them from the *Breviarium Romanum.*[72] That his conception of the firmament was also strongly influenced by the Church Fathers and the scholastic tradition can be gathered from a passage in the *GTB,* Bk. III, chapter 7, "4 Frag" (*GTB*

---

[69] Lüers, *Sprache der Mystik,* p. 15.
[70] Cf. Langen, *Wortschatz,* p. 515, and "Deutsche Sprachgeschichte," p. 1142.
[71] For a discussion of Ulenberg's influence on Spee, cf. Rosenfeld, *Neue Studien,* pp. 77, 136, and Van Oorschot's editorial comments on *GTB* 51.31 in his notes on p. 588.
[72] Spee was Professor of Sacred Scripture in Köln and Paderborn. Cf. Rosenfeld, *Neue Studien,* p. 67.

300.19—35). Spee's marginal notations to this paragraph indicate his sources. This passage is quoted in full since it not only offers valuable information for the origin of Spee's cosmology but is another excellent example of the influence of his prose thought in the *GTB* on the imagery in the *TN*. In addition, *TN* (28), as it stands in the Arlt edition, is actually found interspersed within the seventh chapter of the *GTB* between the prose passages. To demonstrate this, *TN* (28):4,1—8 will be cited after the prose passage of the *GTB*:

Wolan, so last uns weiter gehen: Siehe da die schöne Himmel, wie sie sich so Circkel-rund hinumb gezogen, und wie ein reines gläsernes gewölb vill tausent mahl tausend meilen aussgespant den grossen lufft in ihre arm gleich auffgefasst, und eingeschlossen haben? wie haben sie stäts ihren lauff so ordentlich und bestendig? wie seind sie mit einer unsterblichen, immer-glüenden blauen farben, gleich einer Crystallinen gefarbten kugell, zärtliche angeblasen? wer wilt ihre schöne gnugsam aussprechen können, wan sie nächtlicher weil nach art stoltzen pfauen ihre spiegell auffgesetzt, sich mit den allerscheinbaristen carbunckelen und demanten der himmlischen Feur und Sternen auff das prechtigste geschmücket haben? O wie schöne kertz und fackel? wie so prachtige und weit aussgebreite zelten des allerhöchsten?

Wer will aber auch ersteigen die hohe wässer, so im anfang der erschaffung Gott der Schöpffer auch noch uber die himmel aussgegossen hat, zu erkühlung der so hitzigen vill tausen flammen des gestirns? Eja lasset uns auch zu ihnen schreyen, sie zum Gottes lob erfrischen, und also mit freuden singen

> Nun lobet Gott ihr himmel klar,
>   Gewölbet von crystallen
> Mit sampt den wässer allegar,
>   Welch uber euch noch wallen:
> Dan ihr mit wasser wurd bedeckt
>   Mit wellen hoch bezogen,
> Als Euch der Schöpffer aussgereckt,
>   Und in die ründ gebogen.
> Ey wie so weit und breites feld,
>   Mit feur, und flamm besamet!
> Ey wie so gross und reiche zelt,
>   Die doch auss nichten kamet!
> Ey wie so schöner Fackel-pracht!
>   Wie schöne liecht und sternen!
> Wan ihr euch zeiget in der nacht,
>   Im bestem schmuck von fernen!
> [300.1—16; *TN* (28):4,1—5,8]

Next to this prose passage just quoted the following marginal notations appear in the *GTB:* "Ita S. Chrysostomus. Theodoretus. Gregorius Nyssenus. Procopius. Anastasius Sinaita. Arnobius. S. Anselmus. apud Salianum. ita Theodoretus in Genesim q. 11; Procopius in Genesim." As Van Oorschot has indicated, Spee did not read the above-mentioned authors in the original. He read them in Salianus' book: *Annales Ecclesiastici Veteris Testamenti.*[73] Also of interest here are Spee's marginal notes to the verses that indicate additional biblical sources for his poetry: "Gen. 1,v.6; Ps. 103,v.2; Ps. 148, v.4; Dan. 3,v.60; Vide Cornelium à Lapide in Genesim. Salianum & alios." In addition to having read Salianus' *Annales,* Spee also read Cornelius à Lapide's commentary on the book of Genesis. Thus Spee's marginal notes clearly indicate as the sources of his cosmology the Bible and the Scholastic philosophers. Note, too, the influence of the ideas in the prose text on the shaping of his poetic images. Many of these firmament-images in *TN* (28):4 and 5 occur again either verbatim or with slight changes in *TN* 27:3,5–8; (28):3,2–8, *GTB* 59.32ff.; and (24):2,6–9.

Structurally, Spee's cosmology is characterized by an abundance of paraphrases. God's dwelling place is called: "gülden Tempel" (*GTB* 121.5); "runde Tempel" [*TN* (11):19,6]; "Ihr tempel wol gezieret" [*TN* (24):2,6]. These paraphrases are undoubtedly taken from the Psalms, where God's dwelling place in the heavens is frequently referred to as a temple.[74] God's dwelling place is also called a tent: "ihr zelt" (*TN* 27:3,4); "gross und reiche zelt" [*TN* (28):4,3], which is also a biblical notion.[75]

Paraphrases for the surrounding firmament occur as follows (cf. Table 7.1, p. 132). Also interesting is Spee's description of the area surrounding the heavens as being glazed, and constructed of glass or crystal: "Von aussen verglasiert" [*TN* (24):2,8]; "Gewölbet von Crystallen" [*TN* (28):3,2]; and "zelt von glas geblasen" (*TN* 27:3,4), which are all adaptations of Spee's cosmology expressed in the *GTB* 300.

In summation, this image-category is strongly influenced by scholastic and biblical ideas. The images function both to decorate and to praise. They do not manifest any of the qualities of either mystical or theological modes of expression. Unlike the cosmic images in the previous section, which occur partly in the mystical mode, their metaphorical extension is limited to purely poetic description and paraphrase in the baroque decorative mode.

---

[73] Cf. Van Oorschot's note to this passage, pp. 607 608, and also "GTB II," p. 99.
[74] Cf. also Psalm 48,9; 65,4 and *passim.*
[75] Cf. Psalm 104,3.

8. Air, Wind and Clouds

Images of the wind, air and clouds occur frequently in the *TN*. They express a rather wide range of poetic feeling. They symbolize the vanity and the transitory nature of life [*TN* (12):2,7 and *GTB* 181.16—20]; depict the beauty of nature [*TN* (21):11,7—10]; describe the soul's pain and sorrow at her lover's absence [*TN* (6):6,1—8] or simply praise God [*TN* (28), (24), and 27].

The *GTB* has influenced the wind-imagery in the *TN* in several instances. In the poem which immediately precedes *TN* (13) in the *GTB*, "Halt, halt mein hertz; nit eylen thut" (*GTB* 181.7), the following simile occurs:

> Lass dich zur welt nit binden:
> Nach kurtzer weill: sie wird in eil
> Wie rauch im lufft verschwinden.
> Gleich wie der lufft: und oder tufft
> Wird alles bald zerfahren. (181.16—20)

This expresses, in poetic form, Spee's purpose in Bk. II, chapter 9, to which this poem belongs:

> Weil die hoffnung in sich begreifft ein verlangen und begierd, auch grossschetzung der himmlischen, hingegen aber verachtung der irrdischen sachen, sollestu dise woch anfangen, und dir eine schöne gewonheit machen, durch welche du hernacher mehr und mehr wirst angezündt werden in begird der himmlischen ding, und in kleinschetzung der irrdischen. . . . (179.3—8)

TN (13) also occurs in the context of this chapter of the *GTB* and likewise its purpose is to indicate the transitory nature of earthly existence through the allegory of the wilted flower. Although there is no image from this wind-category in *TN* (13) which shows an immediate correspondence to the prose text, Spee does use the following image to show a related idea: the initial beauty of the flower which contrasts sharply with its later dying state [*TN* (13):3,1—8]. Another related image occurs in a poem originally in the *GTB*, *TN* (12):2,7: "Dein starck verschwind / Als wie der wind" which is closely related to the ideas expressed in *GTB*, Bk. II, chapter 9,[76] In this same chapter of the *GTB*, the seventh, eleventh, and twelfth questions posed by Spee to test the reactions of his spiritual daughter emphasize a key notion that occurs in the *Spiritual Exercises of Ignatius Loyola:* "I neither desire nor am I inclined to have riches rather than poverty, to seek honor rather than dishonor, to desire a long life rather than a short life, provided only in either alternative I would promote . . . the salvation of my soul."[77] From this Ignatian background, Spee continually

76 Weckherlin has a similar image, cf. Beckmann, "Motive," p. 65.
77 *Spiritual Exercises*, p. 69.

represents the world, its riches, its vanity, and pomp as a transitory phenomenon in comparison with eternal salvation and eternal life, and wind-images are employed for this purpose.

GTB Bk. III, chapter 5: "Noch etliche Werck der liebe zu Gott" (280.8) is an exercise in the love of God through the praise and beauty of His creation. Several statements have been made above on the relationship between these two notions in Spee. In typical Spee fashion, the poem included in this chapter, TN (24), contains images of the wind and air which have directly evolved from the prose text of GTB 285.1—8.

In GTB, Bk. III, chapter 7, 299.7—11, Spee proposes a leisurely walk through creation with King David to sing the praise of God. This same theme is expanded into the poetic version in TN (28):7,1—8; 8,9 and 10:

> Nun lobe Gott du reiner lufft
>   O web gar zart gespunnen!
> Zu nacht bist du ein schwartze klufft
>   Biss zu der morgen-sonnen:
> Da zeigest dich in klarem schein,
>   Vil weisser als die schwanen,
> Wan schon gleich aussgespannet sein
>   Ihr breite feder-fahnen. (GTB 302.35—303.4)

This notion of the air, clouds, and wind giving praise to God is found frequently in other poems of the TN as well.

With regard to the functions which these images have in the TN, the vast majority are involved directly in the praise of God (cf. Table 8.1, p. 133). Some of these images function as introductions or "compositions of place" to the main themes such as: TN (4):1,3—4; 1:4,1—8; 23:14,5—8. Others serve to heighten the main theme. For example, in the "Wiegenlied" (TN 35:1,1—8), the wind stretches forth her wings and grasps the ". . . glieder // Dem frisch vermenschten Gott" and helps to portray the impoverished conditions surrounding the incarnation of Christ. Here the wind becomes: "schnöder wind" (TN 35:2,2). Later in the same poem, the breath of the oxen warms the Christ-Child with its "süssem Rosenwind" (TN 35:4,1—4).

The images in TN (8):4,1—4 serve a contrasting function: the cool, peaceful summer wind, paraphrased as: "All jüngling still von sitten," contrasts with the spouse's lament at her lost and distant beloved. In TN (18):2,4 the image "Lufft und wetter wider lacht" contrasts with the sorrowful context of Book II, chapter 8, and is intended by Spee to lift up the spirits of his spiritual daughter after her protracted and sorrowful contemplation of her crucified lover (GTB 168.10—20).

Other images in this category pertain directly to the action of the poems on Christ's passion. In TN 40: "Andere Eckloga oder Hirtengespräch von der gefangnüss Christi," Damon first relates how nature formerly stood at the service of Daphnis (Christ)[78] and His flock: "Wind und wetter feld und wiesen // Freundlich dienten deiner herd" (22,1—2), but now nature sorrows with Him over His capture: "Dich beseufftzen alle wind" (23,4). In *TN* 41 the brook Cedron, mourning over Daphnis' capture in the Garden of Gethsemane, recalls the reaction of nature to Daphnis and His flock. When Daphnis blew on his flute:

> Auch die wind sich gundten legen
> Banden ihre flügel ab
> Kaum den athem thäten regen
> Wie den offt gespüret hab. (11,1—4)

In *TN* when Mary, the mother of Christ, laments at the grave of Christ, all of nature is *compatiens*, even the wind and the air: "Schlaffen waren lufft und wind" (1,4).

In the next poem, *TN* 45, the air and the wind share in the "klägliches hirten-gespräch" between Damon and Halton. When Damon recalls how Daphnis played the harp and the lyre in the peaceful days before His capture: "Lufft und wetter thäten feyren // Wind und regen blieben stahn" (286,18—19). But now that Daphnis no longer plays his lyre, Damon tells us how the air mourns and the clouds weep:

> Schau nun lufft und wetter trauren
> Daphnis nu nit spielet mehr
> O der viehlen regen schauren
> Schau die wolcken weinen sehr. (287,22—25)

As shown above, this is a characteristic structural trait in Spee, where his nature-images participate in the main action and theme of the poems by means of frequent personification.

The wind is given an additional metaphorical extension on yet a third level of function. Spee uses wind-images to express the inner relationships within the Trinity. The notion that the Holy Spirit is a force resembling the wind is found in both scripture and Catholic dogma. An explicit reference to the Holy Spirit in Scripture is found in the Acts of the Apostles, 2,1: "A powerful wind from heaven."[79] Dogmatically He, the Holy Spirit, is the *pneuma* of the Father and

---

[78] The name Daphnis originated with Theocritus. Spee combines this figure with the *Pastor Bonus* of the Gospel; cf. Rosenfeld, *Neue Studien*, p. 73. The Daphnis figure does not appear in the *GTB*. Nowak, "Versuch," pp. 156ff., discusses the Daphnis-figure in the context of sixteenth- and seventeenth-century pastoral poetry. He claims that Spee borrowed the name from contemporary secular poetry.

[79] Cf. also Psalm 33,6.

the Son.[80] Thus Spee is both dogmatically and scripturally on solid traditional
ground when he calls the Holy Spirit: "O süsser Wind, o süsser Blast! // Von
beiden her geblasen" (TN 29:30,1−2). The actual process whereby the Spirit
proceeds from the Father and the Son is likewise described by Spee in
pneumatic imagery: "Von beiden kompt der hertzenwind // Von beiden gleich
gewindet" (TN 29:38,1−2). Here "hertzenwind" equals the Holy Spirit and
"gewindet" verbalizes the act of procession from the Father and the Son.
"Wind" is also used to express the union between the Father and the Son in
addition to their role in the procession of the Holy Spirit.[81] Spee expresses this
trinitarian vitality as follows: "Aha der Sohn auch seuffzet gut // Mit eben
selbem winde" (TN 29:24,1−4).

Spee also uses the term "hertzenwind" as a metaphor for Mary Magdalen's
sighs of love at the foot of Christ's cross:

> Beym Creutz mich hab lan finden
> Hab ihm die purpur Füss
> Gekühlt mit hertzen winden
> Mit meinem Athem süss. [TN (11):32,1−4]

Later in TN 46:10,3−6 the soul loses her breath when she sighs continually at
the sight of Christ's wounds. Wind metaphors occur elsewhere among medieval
poets in the mystical mode.[82] "Hertzenwind" as it occurs in TN (11):32,1−4
and TN 46:10,3−6 expresses the overwhelming effect of the soul's love for God
and as such approaches the mystical mode of language.[83]

Images of the air, wind, and the clouds abound structurally in personifications
and paraphrases. Similes and comparisons occur less frequently (seven times) (cf.
Table 8.2, p. 133). As similes and comparison in TN (6):6,3−8 Spee uses the
wind (an animal personification) and its restlessness to exemplify the restlessness
of the spouse in her sorrow. Just as the wind never ceases to blow, so pain and
restlessness are a part of the spouse's inner disposition. Here the more
complicated image-structure reflects the tense restlessness of the theme of the
poem. On two occasions Spee uses similes in comparing the swaying cedars to
the clouds [TN (26):7,3−4 and (24):6,7−8]. These are biblical images. TN 24 is

---

[80] Cf. Rahner, Wörterbuch, p. 64 and Henricus Denziger, Enchridion Symbolorum
Definitionum et Declarationum, 26th ed. (Freiburg im Breisgau: Herder, 1946), nos. 19, 83,
277, 460, and 691.

[81] On the notion of precession discussed from a theological point of view, cf. Gerard
S. Sloyan, The Three Persons in One God (Englewood Cliffs, N.J.: 1964), pp. 90ff.; and
John L. McKenzie, Dictionary of the Bible (Milwaukee: Bruce, 1965), pp. 840ff.

[82] Lüers, Sprache der Mystik, pp. 302ff., gives examples from Mechthild, Tauler and
Seuse.

[83] According to the Deutsches Wörterbuch, Bd. IV, 2, p. 176, this word occurs only in
Spee.

an adaptation of Psalm 148 which is a cosmic hymn of praise to God.[84] In *TN* 10:5,5—6 Christ the beloved "... sprang durch feld und wisen // Frisch fertig wie der windt." This is an adaptation of an image found in the Song of Songs 2,8—9. The simile in *TN* (12):2,7 has already been discussed above.

In summary, the majority of these images of wind and air are used in praise of God. Less often they express either the theme of vanity or operate as "compositions of place." Structurally, personification and paraphrase coincide with the main function: nature's praise of God in the decorative mode of style. To express the theme of vanity, Spee uses simile in the decorative mode; to depict the restless character of the love of the spouse, extended personification is used. When wind as an image is used theologically to symbolize the process of the Holy Spirit from the Father and the Son, it assumes the mystical mode of language.

Up to this point eight image-categories based on inanimate nature have been investigated. Now an analysis of Spee's imagery from the aspect of organic nature follows.

B. Organic Nature

Nature-images in Spee can be centered around five basic categories from organic nature: flowers, trees, animals, the hours of the day and the seasons of the year. While the hours of the day and the seasons of the year are not organic in the same sense as trees and animals, in an extended sense, however, they reflect vital nature and her changes, and as such they are included under this main heading of organic nature.

1. Flowers

Flower-images occur frequently in the poems of the *TN*, approximately thirty-five times. Spee uses flowers in a variety of ways which include such metaphorical applications as occur in *TN* (18):8,6: "Nirgend besser blumen sein," a reference to the lips of Christ the Spouse, as well as in the lengthy flower-allegory in *TN* (13). The flower-allegory in *TN* (13) dominates the entire poem and forms the basis for the transitory nature of human existence compared to the life and death of a flower. This is a logical use since, by its very nature, the flower is symbolic of transitory nature, and of spring and beauty.[85]

---

84 Cf. *Jerusalem Bible*, p. 929.
85 Cirlot, *Dictionary*, p. 104.

TN (13) "Conterfey des menschlichen lebens" originally occurred in *GTB* II, chapter 9, "Andere Werck der Hoffnungh." The purpose of the *GTB* chapter is to lead the soul to a greater desire for heavenly things: "Weil die hoffnung in sich begreifft ein verlangen und begierd, auch grossschetzung der himmlischen, hingegen aber verachtung der irrdischen sachen . . ." (*GTB* 179.3—5). Spee has chosen the image of the wilting flower to indicate the transitory nature and the fragility of human existence and thus lead the soul to grow in the desire for God:

> . . . will ich dir auch dise jetz folgende mittheilen, darin ich durch eine gleichnuss newlich einem frommen kind vorgemahlet habe die eitelkeit dess menschlichen lebens. Es schicket sich zwar nicht so gar zu unserer jetzt vorhabenden materi, aber doch dieweil ichs jetzt also bey der hand habe, und auch etlicher massen zur verachtung irrdischer schöne dienen mag, nime es hin, und singe es, wan dirs gefellt. (*GTB* 182.18—24)

He uses these words to introduce the poem in the *GTB*.[86] However, Spee's verbal images describing the process of the flower's disintegration differ from that of poets of the affective mode of style. They lack the destructive force which Gryphius' verbal forms manifest.[87]

Interestingly, both Spee and Gryphius employ the *Weitzenkörnlein* simile which, like the flower-image above, is also biblical in origin.[88] Spee has written a brief poem on the *Weitzenkörnlein,* which occurs in the first part of the *GTB,* in the sixth chapter, where he is expounding upon certain articles of faith for his spiritual daughter. In this instance, the grain of wheat and its dying and rebirth is compared to the death and the resurrection of the soul (*GTB* 64.9—16). Gryphius uses the same image in his sonnet: "Auf den Tag Laurentii / Joh 12," and it occurs elsewhere with considerable frequency in seventeenth-century emblem literature.[89]

As stated above, flower images in the *TN* exhibit a variety of functions. In *TN* (17):2,5—8 the beauty and the abundance of flowers stand in direct contrast with the penitential spirit of the soul in sorrow. The poem's position in the *GTB* Bk. II, chapter 8, "Noch andere Werck der Hoffnung und vertrawen zu Gott in einer sehr grossen betrübnuss und betrangnuss dess hertzen," follows Spee's

---

[86] This particular image was widespread among baroque poets of the affective-pathetic mode such as Gryphius, Männling, Treuer and Tscherning, and it is ultimately biblical in origin. Cf. Fricke, *Bildlichkeit,* p. 68; Windfuhr, *Bildlichkeit,* p. 190; Lüders, "Auffassung," pp. 12—13, and Beckmann, "Motive," p. 65. Cf. also Psalms 102,103 and James 1,11.

[87] Compare: *weichen, verlieren, einschlaffen, hinfahren* and *verwelcken,* Spee's verbal forms, with those of Gryphius: *abhauen, krachen,* and *entzweibrechen,* which typify the affective style. Cf. Windfuhr, *Bildlichkeit,* p. 189.

[88] Cf. John, 12,24 and I Corinthians 15,36—44.

[89] For a discussion of this poem cf. Jöns, *Sinnen-bild,* p. 215.

discussion with the soul when she finds herself in a state of desolation and how she should conduct herself while she is in this state of depression. This, for the soul, is a period when God is absent and the knowledge of her own sinfulness in comparison with God's goodness and majesty leads her to despair. The poem is basically an attempt to lift the soul from her depression and help her adhere to the good spirit. Spee uses the beauty of flowers to raise her spirits, and throughout this entire chapter in the GTB Spee shows heavy dependence on Ignatius' discussion of spiritual consolation and desolation in his book, *The Spiritual Exercises*. In particular numbers 317 and 318 of the *Exercises* are pertinent in the present discussion:

> In time of desolation we should never make any change, but remain firm and constant in the resolution and decision which guided us the day before the desolation, or in the decision to which we adhered in the preceding consolation. For just as in consolation the good spirit guides and counsels us, so in desolation the evil spirit guides and counsels. Following his counsels we can never find the way to a right decision.
>
> Though in desolation we must never change our former resolutions, it will be very advantageous to intensify our activity against the desolation.
>
> I call desolation what is entirely the opposite of what is described in the third rule, as darkness of soul, turmoil of spirit, inclination to what is low and earthly, restlessness rising from many disturbances and temptations which lead to want of faith, want of hope, want of love. The soul is wholly slothful, tepid, sad, and separated, as it were from its Creator and Lord.[90]

Spee also applies these Ignatian principles and Ignatius' philosophy to TN (8):1,7–10 where the smiling flowers are used to contrast not only with the passing phase of winter but also with the soul in its dejected state. All of nature is joyful: "Schwebt alles fast in lüsten" (GTB 235.8), while the soul is in sorrow: "Nur ich, O Jesu, bin allein//Mit statem leid umbgeben" (GTB 235.13–14). But the sorrow of the soul is transitional. She must adhere to her resolve to love God above all, and Spee offers her TN 8: "Zu einer geistlichen erquickung" (GTB 218.22).

On a second level of function flower-images help set the stage for coming poetic actions. Here the images are mainly decorative and involve poetic "compositions of place" as preludes to the soul's experience of her bitter-sweet love for Christ as in TN (5):4,4; or wonder at the mystery of the Eucharist in TN 51:1,1–2,8; or lamentation at the passion of Christ as in TN 9:4,7–8; 6,7–8.

On a third level of function, flower-images serve directly to elicit themes

---

[90] Cf. *Spiritual Exercises*, nos. 317–326, where Ignatius expounds in full detail his thoughts on consolation and desolation.

which, for the most part, are religious in nature and either praise the goodness and the power of God the Creator [TN 50:4,1—4; 26:6,1—4; 27:6,3—4; 9,2—6; 10,3—4; 23:7,1—8; (21):5,1—6; (22):8,1—8; 10,1—8]; or show nature as *compatiens* with Daphnis' death in TN 45:289,24—26; or as in TN 49:316,7—10 where Damon's verses on the appearance of red roses in the springtime after the winter has gone are interpreted allegorically by Halton as the proclamation of salvation to the sinner who repents in TN 49:316,14—21.

The following structural variations occur according to the image-functions, as discussed above. When flower-images serve a contrastive function, as in TN (8):1,7—10, Spee uses both simile and personification. However, the contrastive function of the image in TN (17):2,5—8 exhibits a simple metaphorical statement. On the other hand, when flower-images serve as mood-setters, as "compositions of place," personification frequently results, as in TN 51:1,1—2. Finally, when this image category is involved in a religious theme such as the praise of God [TN (21):12,7—8; (22):10,1—8; 27:9,2—6], once again personification predominantes. In TN 45:289,24—26, where the flower-image reflects the death of Christ *(natura compatiens)*, then the flowers "Todt zur Erden sie sich lenken" *(TN* 45:289,26). An extended allegory, based on the "vanitas vanitatum" motif, occurs in TN (13).

In TN 10:11,1—6 and 13,3—4 the image of Christ in the wine-press appears. Christ is compared to the pressed grape:

> O mägdlein wir dich fragen /
> Ist er dan roth / und weis?
> Thut er die farben tragen
> Von rothem trauben-schweiss?
> Hat er händ / füss gefarbet
> In aussgepresstem wein?
> Hat er in roth verarbet
> So weisses helffenbein? *(TN* 10:13,1—8)

This so-called *vitis-mystica* metaphor[91] is based on several passages in the Old Testament: Isaiah 63,2ff.; Jeremiah 25,30; 48,33 and Lamentations 1,15. The same metaphor occurs in St. Bonaventure and in medieval hymns.[92] In the Old Testament the trading of the grapes is a figure for the punishing wrath of Jahweh. As the wine press is filled with grapes, ready to be trodden down, so, too, sinners are ripe for God's punitive action.[93] Christian writers place Christ in the wine-press as a substitute for sinners in order to demonstrate his action as mankind's Redeemer. The Church itself has adapted this metaphor and it occurs

---

91   Cf. Rosenfeld, *Neue Studien,* p. 130.
92   Cf. Rosenfeld, *Fr. Spee,* p. 248, and Jacobsen, *Metamorphosen,* p. 141.
93   Cf. McKenzie, *Dictionary of the Bible,* pp. 928—929.

in First Vespers in the Roman Breviary for the Feast of the Most Precious Blood which falls in the Church calendar on July first: "Why then is your apparel red, and your garments like those of a wine-presser? I have trodden the wine-press alone, and of my people there is no one with me." Spee's application of the wine-press metaphor stands within this tradition, and this metaphor also appears in emblem literature of the baroque period,[94] and among the Pietists.[95] Later in *TN* 48:313,9—16, Halton refers to Christ as "kelterman" in the context of this metaphor.

The verbal expression *verblümet* has an interesting theological application to the Holy Eucharist in *TN* 51:12,10. In strophe 12,1—10:

> Den Leib man leiblich niessen thut /
> Nur nichts in Leibs gestalten:
> Und blütig nimbt man wahres blut /
> Kein sinn für blut kans halten.
> Es alles ist verduncklet gar;
> Und wie die kirch unss rühmet /
> Mit fremder form / und schein fürwar,
> Gantz obenhin verblümet.

Spee describes in poetic terms what for Catholic theology is one of its deepest mysteries, the presence of Christ in the Holy Eucharist, the mystery of transubstantiation.[96] The problematic involved in explaining this mystery is as follows: after the words of consecration in the Mass, when the priest repeats the command of Christ at the Last Supper to change bread and wine into His body and blood,[97] traditional theologians explain the ensuing change according to the Thomistic philosophical concepts of substance and accidence.[98] After transubstantiation has taken place the accidents of bread and wine remain, but the substance of the bread and wine has become Christ's body and blood.[99] In the strophe quoted above in *TN* 51:12,1—10 Spee describes the theological mystery in his own poetic fashion. His chief concern in these verses, where he uses the

---

[94] Cf. the emblem in Jacobsen, *Metamorphosen,* p. 103, which clearly depicts the wine-press metaphor.

[95] Cf. Langen, *Wortschatz,* pp. 347—348.

[96] Cf. Rahner, *Wörterbuch,* p. 363.

[97] Cf. Luke, 22,19; I Corinthians 11,23.

[98] Parente, *Dictionary,* p. 171, explains these terms at length.

[99] Spee discusses this mystery at length in the *GTB* as follows: "Dass auch in dem heyligsten Sacrament dess Altars warhafftig, leibhafftig, mit gantzer substantz, und wesen sey der wahre leib und blut mit der Seel und Gottheit unsers Herren Jesu Christi? Das auch ein warhaffte verwandlung der wesenheit, oder gantzen substantz des brots in den leib, und des weins in das blut geschehe, welche verenderung oder verwandlung die heilige Catholische kirch zu Latein nennet *Transsubstantiationem?* " (37.18—24); cf. also *GTB* 67.1—68.15; 476.9—32.

term *verblümet,* is the description of the accidents of bread and wine overlaying
the substance of Christ's body in the Eucharist after transubstantiation has taken
place. *Verblümet* refers to the adherence of these accidents in the substance of
the bread. The accidents veil and decorate the substance of Christ's body. Thus,
the image conjured up by the verb *verblümen* is a poeticization of the theological
concept of the accidents in the mystery of transubstantiation. Later this same
verb will occur, but in a strictly poetic application, in reference to the "thal und
felder" in *TN* 49:316.9.

Flower-images assume a variety of verbal and nominal personifications in the
TN (cf. Table 1.1, p. 134). Metaphors occur in the mystical-decorative mode of
style based on descriptions of Christ's wounds and body (cf. Table 1.2, p. 134).
The following paraphrase for the stars occurs (cf. Table 1.3, p. 134).

In this category, as noted above, Spee's verbal forms lack the destructive
quality of poets of the affective-pathetic mode. This was indicated specifically in
the analysis of the flower allegory in *TN* (13). Spee's verbal characteristics in this
category show a clearer affinity with the decorative and mystical modes of
expression. In the first two functional categories above, the decorative mode
predominates. On the religious level, in his description of Christ's wounds, Spee
shows a decided affinity with other baroque poets of the mystical mode such as
Silesius and Kuhlmann. His use of *verblümen* in the theological mode has already
been explained. Although the flower-allegory was used by baroque poets, such as
Gryphius, Männling and Treuer, in the affective-pathetic mode, it is preferable
here to place Spee's style in the decorative-mystical category, particularly in the
light of the overall function of the images within the *GTB* Bk. II, chapter 9, and
the Ignatian teaching on the "Discernment of Spirits" in the *Spiritual Exercises
of St. Ignatius* which influences Spee's style and thought in the same chapter.

2. Trees

This image-category of the *TN* includes trees, forests, mountains, and foliage.
There are approximately twenty-five occurrences of these images in the *TN*. The
TN poems taken from the *GTB* exhibit interesting characteristics when they are
compared with the surrounding prose text of the *GTB*, particularly in what
concerns their genesis into poetic images. As with tree imagery in the *TN* as a
whole, their collective use in the *GTB* poems can also be divided into two main
poetic categories; tree as tree and the tree as the symbol of the cross of Christ.

The cross, of course, has been a dominant motif in Christian symbolism.[100]
The Bible itself employs a two-fold tree symbolism: the tree of knowledge of

---

100 Cf. Cirlot, *Dictionary,* p. 329.

good and evil in Paradise and later the tree of life on Golgotha. Spee uses this latter notion in both the *GTB* and the *TN*. As would be expected of a follower of Ignatius of Loyola, the cross plays a central role for Spee's spiritual doctrine. Just as Ignatius places the exercitant before the crucifix for purposes of spiritual meditation and reformation of life in the *Spiritual Exercises,* so, too, the same methodology can be found in Spee. Bk. II, chapter 8, embodies, in succinct fashion, Spee's theology of the cross. In the text of the *GTB* Spee consistently repeats such phrases as: "Zum Fundament bilde dir vor Jesum an dem Creutz" (*GTB* 164.7); "Bleibe du bey mir, an meinem Creutz, in meinen armen" — these are Christ's words to the soul (166.26—27). In *GTB* 164.19—20 Christ appears as a "süsse Nachtigall auf disem Baum des Creutzes." This image also is found in Silesius.[101] Further examples of Christ on the cross in dialogue with the soul are: "Wan ich dich creutzigen will, stehet bey mir . . ." (*GTB* 166.38—39); ". . . so setze dich eine kleine weil zu meinen füssen, lehn dein haupt ans Creutz" (168.3—4). Spee instructs the soul: ". . . so werffe dich vor dem Crucifix nider auf die erde . . ." (*GTB* 168.18); "Etlich mahl im tag setze dich zum Creutz . . ." (168.11). Other examples occur in *GTB* 199.22—25 and 218.12—15. When these references to the cross in Spee are compared with some of Ignatius' statements in the *Spiritual Exercises,* the eleventh rule of the Summary of the Constitutions of the Society of Jesus, and the *Summa et Scopus nostrarum Constitutionum,* all of which were composed by Ignatius himself, then Spee's affinity with Ignatius' theology of the cross becomes even more apparent.[102]

Spee's spirituality of the cross in *GTB* Bk. II, chapter 8, can be summarized in the following paradox: the cross of Christ is both the source of joy and sorrow for the soul. The cross is a source of sorrow since the sins of the penitent soul have crucified her beloved, Christ (*GTB* 168.17ff.), and it is a source of joy since the crucified Christ is offering the soul not only the deepest union and love (*GTB* 166 *passim*) but also the most profound spiritual consolation: "ich konde dir dein hertz in lauter Rosen setzen" (*GTB* 166.2—3). Correspondingly, these spiritual concepts in the prose passages of *GTB* Bk. II, chapter 8, are reflected in *TN* (17):6,5—8; 9,1—8 where the cross brings joy, and in *TN* (38):11,1—4 where Christ on the cross speaks to the soul of His intense suffering.

In *GTB* Bk. II, chapter 18, which contains the famous "Clock-Tale" poem [*TN* (43)], Spee's theology of the cross is again articulated: "Ein trauriges

---

101 Cf. Jacobsen, *Metamorphosen,* pp. 15—16.
102 Cf. nos. 53 and 297 of the *Spiritual Exercises;* and the *Thesaurus Spiritualis Societatis Jesu* (Rome: 1948), pp. 419 and 484, for the eleventh Rule and the *Summa et Scopus.* No. 53 of the *Exercises* is as follows: "Imagine Christ our Lord present before you on the cross, and begin to speak with him, asking how it is that though He is the Creator, He has stooped to become man, and to pass from eternal life to death here in time, that thus He might die for our sins. . . . . A I behold Christ in this plight, nailed to the cross, I shall ponder upon what presents itself to my mind."

gespräch, so Christus an dem Creutz führet."[103] Parallels to the "Clock-Tale" occur in the prose text of the *GTB* (383.13–14) where the cross is termed the key to paradise and in 384.17–18, where the cross is the tree of life. In this context, no. 30 of the same chapter represents the cross by means of six metaphorical conceits reminiscent of the type of poem Harsdörffer wrote in his: "Was ist die Welt" (*GTB* 390.14–34). The cross for Spee is "ein Schifflein, ein Stab, ein Leiter, ein Thron, ein Schul, ein beth." These are extravagant baroque metaphors in the metaphysical mode. In no. 51 of the same chapter the "Heiliges Creutz" is again represented under a long series of metaphors: "Himmel, Abendstern, brunnen, garten, Weinstock, Rosenbusch, blumen, lilien, starckes feur, Edelgestein, Regenbogen, morgenröthe, and Schatz" (402.26–403.26).

The second division of tree-imagery, tree as tree *in se,* offers additional examples of correspondence between the *GTB* and the *TN.* This offers further enlightenment into the nature of Spee's poetic technique. The twenty-second stanza of *TN* (28) is an obvious poeticization of *GTB* Bk. III, chapter 8, ninth question (307.23–308.24). This proximity presents an obvious case of the prose text's influence on the poetic imagery. The relationship of the images in this second category between the prose text of *GTB* Bk. II, chapter 5, and the statements in *TN* (24):6,7–8 is notable. The poetic thrust here is praise to the Creator on the part of both organic and inorganic nature. Praise of God, for Spee, as indicated above, is the equivalent of loving *Him.* Thus, when the soul invokes the cedars to praise God, she is in actuality demonstrating her love of God the Creator. This also explains the poem's position in the third Book of the *GTB,* which is devoted primarily to a discussion and treatment of the virtue of charity. This notion will be expanded below to other examples where trees are involved in this praise-function. However, the tree as the symbol of man, his birth, death and life, that is found frequently is Gryphius, does not occur in Spee.

Before considering further the image-function and style in this category, it is important to explain the emblems found on the title pages in the various seventeenth-century editions of the *TN.* In these emblems the *Christus-Cupido* figure is crucified on a tree.[104] In the light of Spee's theology of the cross developed in the *GTB* Bk. II, chapter 8, and Bk. III, chapter 19, and the

---

[103] Cf. Max Lüthi, "Eine Ringerzählung (Clock-tale) bei Friedrich von Spee," *Fabula,* 4 (1961), 209–230.

[104] Cf. emblems reproduced in Jacobsen, *Metamorphosen* pp. 13, 14, 16 and 18. Jacobsen has indicated the relevance of these emblems towards a correct interpretation of the overall thematic of the *TN.* Cf. his discussion on pp. 22ff. However, he emphasizes the relationship between the *Cupido* figure and the *anima* in the emblems and the *TN* itself, but he omits any further comment about the significance of the tree (cross) in these emblems. For example, the fact that the figure on the tree is crucified goes unnoted.

influence of these ideas on the poetic images in the *TN*, the emphasis given the Christ-crucified figure — as *Cupido* — in these emblems should be noted. *Cupido* appears as crucified on all the emblems, and not only the fact that this figure is portrayed but the mode of the portrayal is illuminating. All the emblems picture the Christ-figure looking down upon the soul in a loving gaze while the soul is seated at the foot of the cross looking up at her beloved. Spee describes this dialogue posture in the *GTB* 337.10—11: "... und für das Creutz Christi zu seinen füssen niderlegen."[105] In these chapters, *GTB* Bk. II, chapter 8, and Bk. III, chapter 18, Christ crucified to a tree and the soul are in continual dialogue. Commentators on the *TN* have overlooked the central significance of the crucified *Cupido-Jesus* figure from the viewpoint, not only of the emblems accompanying the editions of the *TN*, but also of the relationship between the emblems themselves and the corresponding images of the tree as cross symbolized in the *TN* and the *GTB*.

The tree-images in the *TN* function in a five-fold manner. Two of these functions have been alluded to, in regard to the influence of the *GTB* on the *TN*: (a) the tree image offering praise to God; (b) the tree as cross or crucifix functioning on a religious-theological level. There is an additional three-fold function: (c) tree-images as "compositions of place" or poetic preludes; (d) tree-images as contrastive; and (e) their function in a *natura-compatiens* sense.

Examples of images functioning as poetic-preludes ("c," above) occur in *TN* 1:3,1—4; 4,5—8 where they are nothing more than simple poetic statements, and again in *TN* 49:315,16—17 which involves personification. Examples of images as contrastive ("d") occur in *TN* (8):2,4—8 and *TN* (8):5,1—10 where joyful nature under the guise of tree and branch stands in sharp contrast to the soul "Mit stätem leyd umbgeben" (7,2). On the concluding level of function ("e") nature reflects the main theme as *natura compatiens*. *TN* (18):3,5: "die grüne wiesen lachen," is in consonance with the joyous mood of the soul "nach uberwundener traurigkeit." In *TN* (4):19,3—4 the soul is jubilant over the fact that Jesus' name echoes throughout the forest and she calls on the trees to leap with joy: "Mit mir auch sollen uberal // Die Bäum und Stauden springe."[106] In *TN* 45 where Damon and Halton lament Christ's death the "schöne wiesen trauren" (288,5): "gras / und kräuter gar versauren // Saur und bitter alles wirdt" (288,7—8). The green sap flowing from the trees "seind wie truckner erden-staub" (289,15—21). The trees, nests, and branches weep "mit lauter leyd belastet" (290,16—21). Structurally, within this division ("e"), personification predominates, whereas only one example of simile occurs.

---

[105] The emblems are based on those in the *Pia Desideria* of Hermann Hugo. For the precise emblem in Hugo, cf. Jacobsen, p. 13. For Hugo's influence on Spee, cf. Jacobsen, p. 58, and Rosenfeld, *Neue Studien*, pp. 76, 88 and 147.

[106] A related expression occurs in *GTB* 281.32ff.

Functional category ("a"), praise of God the Creator, occurs in *TN* (21):11,5–8; (24):6,7–8; 26:7,3–4; (28):22,1–8 and 50:8,1–8. The cedar is a favorite image in Spee, which he undoubtedly found in Scripture and the Psalms in particular. In *TN* 26:7,3–4 God crowns the rocks with cedars: "Das gleich den wolcken schwebet." This is a favorite image-form for Spee. In *TN* (24):6,7–8 the cedar is again compared to the clouds, and in *TN* (21):11,5–8 the trees "klimmen in klaren lufft hinauff" and swim like the clouds. In functional category ("a"), simile and personification predominate.

Category ("b") functions on the spiritual and theological levels. The symbolism of the tree in the *GTB* and the *TN* as a theology of the cross and its relationship to the emblems of the editions of the *TN* has been detailed in the discussion above on *GTB* Bk. II, chapter 8, and Bk. III, chapter 18. In addition, there are further examples of tree-images in the *GTB* and the *TN* which are related to this theological function. In *TN* (38):11,1–4 Christ dreams of His coming crucifixion: "Ein Creutz mir für den augen schwebt // O wee der pein und schmertzen." In *TN* (17):6,5–8; 8,4–6 and 9,1–8 the soul replies in colloquy as she addresses the cross on which Christ was crucified: "In Creutz allein mag sagen // Ist freud und fröligkeit" (6,5–6). These two citations reveal a distinctly Ignatian technique. The colloquial dialogue between the soul and Christ appears in Ignatius Loyola's *Spiritual Exercises* at all the critical meditations.[107] For Spee the dialogue technique also occurs in the *GTB* and the *TN* at critical points in the evolution of his own spiritual doctrine. The fact that this dialogue involves both Christ on the cross and the soul in dialogue with the cross is indicative of the emphasis Spee places on the theology of Christ's death and crucifixion for the spiritual life of the penitent. The cross brings joy and peace to those who embrace it, as explained in *TN* 49:317,26–318,7. The cross is sweet (*GTB* 403–7–8; good (*GTB* 175.18); and lovely [*TN* (17):9,1].

The wine-press motif also occurs in this context. In *TN* 48:313,4–16 Halton and Damon speak of the harvested red grapes which will bloom again, a reference to the resurrection of Christ. The motif is closely allied with the *Herbergsmotiv* in *TN* 48:307,11–19:

> Alss ich newlich auff der reysen
> Ware worden müd und matt /
> Mich der Daphnis thäte speisen;
> Und von früchten machet satt.
> Stieg auff einen grünen palmen /
> Warff der schönen früchten ab /
> Sang zu gleich wol sieben psalmen /
> Ich mit lüsten gessen hab

---

107   Cf. nos. 53, 54, 61, 147 and 156 in the *Exercises*.

> Alss ich newlich auff der reysen
> Wolt zum weinhauss kehren ein /
> Thät man mich zur herberg weisen /
> Hiess zum rothen lämmelein /
> Auff dem schilde stund gemohlet
> Daphnis in der kelter sein.
> Jeder dort zu trincken holet /
> O was roth- und guter wein!

The *Herbergsmotiv* has a long history.[108] Earlier in a somewhat outlandish metaphor bordering on the grotesque mode, the dead Christ is called a "matt und falbe pflaum" (*TN* 47:302,10).

The imagery of the cross and the wine-press exhibits a simple structural type of metaphor. However, the mystical mode predominates stylistically with Spee's constant references to the cross and the shedding of Christ's blood in the wine metaphor.[109] In the remaining three levels of function (*natura compatiens*, contrast and poetic prelude) the decorative mode is operative.

3.*Seasons of the Year, Hours of the Day*

Within this image-category are some fifty images that involve the seasons of the year or hours of the day. However, investigation into the relation between the *TN* and the poems of the *GTB* offers no direct correspondence between the prose text of the *GTB* and the development of the imagery in the *TN* within this category. It is significant that by far the greater majority of the images from this category which are intended to reflect the sadness of the soul or to indicate her change from sorrow to joy originate in the *GTB* poems which Spee later incorporated into the *TN*. The images in this category basically arise from a context in which Spee attempts to lead the soul to a state of spiritual joy. Thus he provides her with exercises which keynote sorrow for sin, dejection due to her lack of gratitude to God [*GTB* Bk. II, chapter 8, and *TN* (38), (17), and (18)], or where he cautions against too great a concern for earthly creation [*GTB* Bk. II, chapter 9, and *TN* (13)]. The titles of these poems indicate Spee's intention. *TN* (17): "Ein Christliche Seel muntiert sich auff im abgang ihrer traurigkeit," *TN* (18): "Jubel einer Christlichen Seelen nach uberwundener traurigkeit," and *TN* (13): "Conterfey des menschlichen lebens."

---

108 It occurs in Mechthild von Magdeburg and in the *Theologia Deutsch*. Cf. Lüers, *Sprache der Mystik*, pp. 296—302. Jacobsen has reproduced emblems based on this motif. Cf. Jacobsen, *Metamorphosen*, pp. 128 and 130.

109 Cf. Lüers, *Sprache*, pp. 296ff., under the rubric *win* for similar images among the medieval mystics.

In general the seasons are frequently used in literature to symbolize the four stages of man's life.[110] In the Bible dawn is a propitious time for the soul (Psalm 5,3), and a time for deliverance (Canticle of Canticles 2,17). Night in the Canticle of Canticles indicates painful waiting (3,1). The baroque poet and the Pietists use dawn to characterize Christ and Mary in the mystical mode.[111] For Gryphius the seasons and the periods of the day are symbols of the ages of man. Morning and springtime signify youth, noon, the prime of life, evening, the aging process, while dawn stands for the Last Judgment.[112] Apart from their function as poetic preludes and images of praise, Spee uses images in this category in a more introspective manner than Gryphius. In this respect he shows greater affinity with the sixteenth-century tradition, which had not yet become so estranged from nature and its manifestations as had the period in German literature from 1620–1700.[113] Spee's season-images reflect varied interior states of soul such as: joy, sorrow, dejection, relief, and consolation. In analyzing the function of these images in the *TN* and the *GTB,* a further subdivision of the seasons and hours of the day into winter, summer, spring, dawn, day, and night follows. Fall- and noon-images do not occur in the *GTB* or in the *TN.*

Winter-images in the *TN* generally accompany the soul as she passes from a period of interior sorrow and dejection [*TN* (17):1,3–4; 11,1–2], to a period of joy [*TN* (18):2,5–8]. In *TN* (8):1,1–8 winter gives way to spring. Spring in turn contrasts with the soul's sorrow over her separation from God.[114]

Summer-images function as poetic preludes and as "compositions of place" (*TN* 48:307,21–24). However, in *TN* 49:316,5–19 summer is used in a religious context to represent the time of repentance and to indicate the need of conversion to God. In *TN* 48:308,13–16 the flowers of summer are compared to Daphnis' wounds.

Dawn-images are the most prolific in the diurnal category. Purple dawn rising from her bed is not nearly so red as Daphnis' bloody side (*TN* 48:311,16–23). Other dawn-images play a more subordinate role relative to the main action as they introduce or act as preludes to the main thematic [*TN* (13):2,1–4; 51:1,1–4]. The dawn is also referred to within the context of praise to God [*TN* 32:191,8–11; 30:179,8–9]. Occasionally dawn either reflects the soul's consciousness of her sinfulness [*TN* (16):1,1–2]; or signifies her attentiveness to

---

110   Cf. Cirlot, *Dictionary,* p. 269.
111   Langen, *Wortschatz,* pp. 347 and 350, for examples from Tersteegen and Spener. However the poet of the decorative mode tends to apply the dawn to the face of the beloved, as in Weckherlin, Hofmannswaldau and Schwieger. Cf. Windfuhr, *Bildlichkeit,* p. 251.
112   Cf. Fricke, *Bildlichkeit,* pp. 71–72.
113   Cf. Beckmann, "Motive und Formen," pp. 55ff.
114   This is a common Petrarchan trait. Cf. Jacobsen, *Metamorphosen,* p. 76.

God's presence [*TN* (7):1,1–6].[115] For Gryphius dawn is a symbol of the resurrection of Christ and the soul.[116] Finally, in *TN* 10:10,1–4, the beloved's "wänglein roth" are compared to the dawn. In comparison with the beloved dawn pales and becomes like mud:

> Die Morgenröth erbleichet /
> Und scheinet gleich dem koth /
> So nur man sie vergleichet
> Gen seine wänglein roth. (*TN* 10:10,1–4)

The expression for day in the *TN* has, for the most part, a univocal significance in the following statements which refer to the soul: it finds her "in stätem last," in a state of sorrowful love and ardent yearning for her lover [*TN* (6):4,3–4; 5,7–8; 9,7–8; and (3):1,1–8; 3,1–8].

Images of springtime function either as:

a) poetic preludes in the decorative mode [*TN* (4):2,1–2; (11):2,1–4].
b) as a means of showing God's praise [*TN* (22):3,3–4].
c) to indicate the beauty of the beloved, Christ. He is more beautiful than the dawn in springtime (*TN* 2:1,1–2,1); the Christ-Child's cheeks rival springtime in their beauty (*TN* 33:3,5–8).

This latter image is an excellent example of what has been termed "Geistlicher Petrarkismus," an aspect of the baroque mystical mode.[117] The Petrarchan school frequently compares the beloved to flowers and spring. However, baroque religious poets incorporate these images and apply them to either God or Christ.

Allusions have already been made to images of night in their functional role as "compositions of place" and their role within a context of religious contemplation. In the present category it is useful to recall their function in portraying a mood of penitence [*TN* (15):1,1–2; 12,7–8], and in expressing the idea of spiritual desolation [*TN* 49:324,4–5 and (18):2,1–2]. To the extent that these images indicate a slow transition from a state of sorrow to a period of peace they show a strong affinity with the images of winter [*TN* (18):2,5–8; (17):1,3–7; 11,1–2].

The following structural variations occur according to image-function. Personifications predominate when this image category functions as poetic preludes and as "compositions of place" [*TN* (11):2,1–4; 27:6, 3–4; 51:1,1–4; 1:1,1 and (13):2,1–4]. When these images are related to the wounded Daphnis, to the Christ-Child, or to the beloved as spouse, we find either suppressed or

---

115 This notion is also present among the medieval mystics. Cf. Lüers, *Sprache*, pp. 227–228.
116 Cf. Beckmann, "Motive," p. 60.
117 Windfuhr, *Bildlichkeit*, pp. 228ff.

explicit similes (*TN* 48:311,16—23; 10:10,1—4; 2:1—2,1). In each instance where the seasons and the hours praise God, then, personification is the rule [*TN* 32:191,8—11; 30:179,8—9; 183,17—18; (22):3,3—4; 4,1—2]. In portraying introspective states of the soul Spee uses winter, March, "braune Stunden," and dark night as metaphors for sorrow and depression; spring and summer represent the soul's consciousness of God's presence or are occasions for a *conversio animae.*

Adjectives modifying the seasons and hours occur mostly in the decorative mode (cf. Table 3.1, p. 134). Verbal personifications of the seasons and the hours are (cf. Table 3.2, p. 135). In his application of adjectival and verbal modifiers, and where the images function as poetic preludes and as praise of God, Spee has many characteristics common to other German baroque poets of the decorative mode. When the images are applied to interior states of soul and to the beloved, Spee exhibits traits characteristic of "Geistlicher Petrarkismus."

4. Animals

The *TN* contains a wide variety of animal-figures. Spee's favorite images involve sheep, birds, the nightingale, bees, horses, reindeer, and swans, respectively. However, fish, doves, and the falcon occur less frequently. Although the nightingale is given the pre-eminent position both in the title of Spee's work and in the "Vorrede dess Authoris:" "Truz Nachtigall wird diss Büchlein genandt / weiln es trutz allen Nachtigalen süss / unnd lieblich singet / unnd zwar auffrichtig Poetisch: also dass es sich auch wol bey sehr guten Lateinischen unnd anderen Poeten dörfft hören lassen," the nightingale makes an appearance in only a limited number of the fifty-two poems of the *TN* [nos. 1, 5 (20), 22 and 45]. However, nightingales, used collectively, occur in *TN* 52, the final poem.

Scholars, among them Jacobsen and Rosenfeld, have indicated that the nightingale is, in reality, a guise for Spee himself. They base their opinions on interpretations of the emblems in the frontispieces of the various editions of the *TN*.[118] The nightingale is a spiritual chanteuse offering poetic rivalry to the nightingale of worldly love. Spee states this objective in his "Vorred" Derohalben hab ich solchen zu helffen understanden / und befliessen mich zu einer recht lieblichen Teutschen Poetica die baan zu zeigen / und zur grösseren ehren Gottes einen neuen geistlichen Parnassum / oder kunstberg algemach anzutreten."

---

[118] In these emblems both the nightingale and the soul are gazing toward the *Christus-Cupido* figure who is crucified on a tree. Jacobsen reproduces these emblems on pp. 14, 16, 18 of the *Metamorphosen,* and cf. Rosenfeld, *Fr. Spee,* pp. 104, 192 and 128.

The spiritual nightingale had become a poetic favorite for many Jesuit poets of Spee's time. Conrad Vetter's *Paradeissvogel* which had a considerable influence on Spee, particularly on *TN* (18), is a translation of Bonaventure's *Philomela*.[119] Bonaventure employed the nightingale to express his religious thought. John Pecham, also a Franciscan, in his *Philomena*, likewise adopted a nightingale as the subject of his poem. The nightingale is the type of pious soul which longs for the heavenly country.[120] It seems plausible not only to assume the nightingale's specific role within the volume as a mask for Spee himself but also to interpret, on the basis of what Spee states in his "Vorred," the entire volume allegorically as the nightingale, since all fifty-two poems are fundamentally oriented toward one purpose: singing God's praise and searching for His love. Further evidence for this symbolism may also be derived from the nightingale's function in *GTB* Bk. III, chapter 21, 442.20–30. In this chapter Spee recommends that the spiritual daughter offer her heart-beats in praising God in imitation of the nightingale's song to God.

The mystics of the Middle Ages use the nightingale as the chanteuse of man's union with God. For Mechthild von Magdeburg, she is "die allersüsseste nahtegale der getemperten einunge ... die vogel der heiligen bekantnüsse."[121] For Bonaventure (1221–1274), the nightingale is "animam virtutibus et amore plenam" who sings of Christ's passion and death.[122] For the German baroque poets of the decorative mode the nightingale is a special favorite, but not in the religious sense. Rather the nightingale helps create the ornate effect so essential to baroque rhetoric. On the basis of the individual appearances of the nightingale in the *TN*, particularly in *TN* 1,(5), (20), and (22), she possesses characteristics as follows (cf. Table 4.1, p. 135). Although the role of the nightingale in these poems seems at cursory glance to be a limited one, nonetheless, from the point of view of the overall theme of the *TN* and the *GTB*, the bird participates in most of the major themes: praise of God, desire for Jesus unto death, and rejection of what the world holds dear. Thus, when Spee gives his volume the title *Trutznachtigall*, there is justification both in the light of its theme and in

[119] Cf. Rosenfeld, *Neue Studien,* p. 78. A hymn of Spee's from the collection of Catholic hymns published in 1625, *Catholische Kirchengesang,* reproduced in A. Schoene, *Das Zeitalter des Barock. Texte und Zeugnisse* (München: Beck, 1962), pp. 154–159, contains the title: "Friedrich Spee von Langenfeld. Die geistliche Nachtigal gezogen auss der Nachtigal des H. Bonaventurae" (p. 154).

[120] F. J. E. Raby, *A History of Christian-Latin Poetry,* 2nd ed. (Oxford: Clarendon, 1953), pp. 425ff. Jacob Blade also imitated Bonaventure's *Philomela* in his *Paraphrasis lyrica in Philomelam.* Cf. Ernst Reichert, "Einflüsse und Anregungen auf die Dichtung Friedrichs von Spe. Ein Beitrag zur Kennzeichnung eines jesuitischen Dichters," *Programm Neuruppin,* 1913, 26. Dominicus Nugent wrote a collection of poems entitled *Christliche Nachtigall* based on Spee's *TN,* in 1675. Cf. Rosenfeld, *Studien,* p. 79.

[121] Cf. Lüers, *Sprache,* p. 273.

[122] Cf. Jacobsen, *Metamorphosen,* p. 13.

the nightingale's traditional function in this type of religious poetry since the time of Bonaventure and other spiritual writers of the Middle Ages.

In the *GTB* poems the nightingale is referred to infrequently, only in *TN* (5) and (20). Christ Himself is called "süsse Nachtigall auf disem Baum dess Creutzes" (164.19ff.). St. Agnes also compares Christ to a nightingale: "Jesus ist mein bräutigam: dann er auff dem baum dess Creutzes, wie ein Nachtigal gar lieblich singet" (*GTB* 404.31–32). The nightingale is called blessed: "O wie viel seeliger als ich, ist dises Vögelein? " (*GTB* Bk. III, chapter 18).[123]

The nightingale is but one of Spee's favored animal figures. Birds used collectively occur twenty-one times, and sheep rank high in frequency of occurrence in the *TN* (twenty-three times). References to bees (eight occurrences), horses (six), and reindeer (four) are less frequent. Spee employs his animal-figures in the following manner (cf. Table 4.2, p. 135):

a) in a *natura compatiens* role.
b) as poetic preludes and "compositions of place."
c) in praising God's creation.
d) in symbolizing joyful consolation after the passage of a period of spiritual desolation: the bees [TN (18:4,7–8; 5,1–8 and 8,1–8].

The topos involved here, the "Bienenkuss," is used by Petrarch and is classical in origin. Bees collectively gathering honey from the beloved's lips, mouth, and eyes occur also in secular Latin poetry.[124]

e) in calling out to the beloved as the soul's emissary: the nightingale [*TN* (5):2,1–6 and 3,5–7].
f) on the level of religious symbolism Christ is called the "Lamb of God." The *agnus Dei* motif occurs in *TN* 33:5,5–6; 48:310,24–311,5; 312,26–313,7. This symbol is found also in the *GTB* Bk. II, chapter 13, where Christ is called "O du schönes lamb, du schöner Jesus" (208.28–30).

Christ as the sacrificial lamb is a traditional Christian notion found in the Bible (John 1,29–36 and Isaiah 53). St. John the Evangelist lends great theological importance to the title "Lamb of God." This springs from the fact that the Johannine Gospel account centers around this proclamation of Jesus as Lamb of

---

123 In the *GTB* Spee does not call the nightingale "Creutznachtigall" as Rosenfeld, *Studien,* p. 78, and Jacobsen, *Metamorphosen,* p. 10, assert. Brentano is responsible for this incorrect insertion into the text. Jacobsen used this edition of the *GTB* in his study. Rosenfeld apparently copied this.

124 Cf. Jacobsen, *Metamorphosen,* p. 88. Angelus Silesius uses this motif in connection with the wounds of Christ (cf. Jacobsen, p. 88). E. Rosenfeld maintains that in its application to the Christian soul conceived of as stealing grace from the lips of Christ, and as used by Spee, this topos appears for the first time in German literature. *Neue Studien,* p. 131. This motif is also found in the *GTB* 524.4–6.

God and the evocation of the prefigurative lamb of sacrifice in John 1,29 and 19,36. It occurs in the Roman liturgy texts of the mass as early as the fourth century. Spee employs this liturgical symbolism in GTB 5–11 and 402.14–22.

The lamb in the TN stands for Christ: "Lämlein ohne flecken" (TN 33:5,5–6) and "schäfflein wund gemacht" (TN 48:311,1); "Wurd getödt ein Lämlein zart" (TN 48:313,5). In TN 48:307,11–19 the agnus Dei motif is linked up with the Herbergsmotiv which was discussed above under the tree category. (The "Herberg" is named "zum rothen lämmelein.")

Finally, two other animal figures occur that have theological and religious implications: the falcon and the roe, both referring to aspects of Christian salvation-history. The falcon with wings outstretched (TN 48:311,7–12) is compared to Christ crucified on the cross. The slain roe, a symbol for Christ (TN 47:303,26–304,7) reminds the sorrowing Palaemon of Daphnis' death. Thus Spee uses both the roe and the lamb as symbols of gentleness and sacrificial innocence.

g) *The Pastor-Bonus* motif, Christ as the good shepherd caring for His flock, occurs frequently [TN 9:14,3–8; (24):10,1–4; 37:1,1–8]. The sheep represent mankind and the shepherd is Christ.

This motif is also biblical in origin and is found in Matt. 18,12–24; Luke 15,4–7; John 10,1–18. It influences most of images contained in TN 27: "Der Evangelisch gute hirt sucht das verlohren Schäfflein" (221,10–11). The good shepherd seeks the lost sheep and desires its return to the fold.[125] This notion is also expressed at length in GTB Bk. II, chapter 4, pp. 131–134 from which Spee has taken his poetic images in TN 37. Christ speaks as follows:

Ich habe schon angedeutet, dass weder ich noch mein Herr Vatter einigen nutzen von disem Schäfflein haben: allein begeren wir, es solle leben, und solle nicht in dieser wüsten umbkommen.

Die lieb allein, die ich zu disem Schäfflein trage, macht mir das Schäfflein werth: die lieb zwinget mich, und machet mir alle diese müh und arbeit süss; und wan ich nur mein Schäfflein finde, frage ich nach keinen thieren. Die lieb stärcket mich, die lieb wapffnet mich, die lieb macht mich unerschrocken und sonsten suche ich keinen anderen nutzen: ich suche nur das Schäfflein. (GTB 134.6–15)

The following image-structures occur according to the functional categories listed above. In category ("a") personification [TN (38):15,3] and paraphrase (TN 45:282,25–283,2). In category ("b") mythological paraphrase [TN (6):3,3–4]; and personification (TN 49:315,21–316,2). In category ("c") personification predominates [*TN* (18):4,4; 5,1—8; 8,1—8]. In ("e") paraphrase and in the last two categories: ("f") and ("g"), allegory and simile. This schema illustrates Spee's imagistic structural progressions. When Spee moves to those themes which are more theologically oriented, the poetic structure shifts from personification and paraphrase to simile and allegory.

Other similes in the animal image-field which show affinity with the decorative style occur (cf. Table 4.3, p. 136). The *TN* abounds in colorful and decorative paraphrases and personifications from the animal-category (cf. Table 4.4, p. 136).

These paraphrases and personifications link Spee closely with the tradition of the German baroque decorative poet. On the other hand, Spee's use of animal-images lacks the ponderous and pessimistic aspects of the affective-pathetic style that tends to compare men's sins and foibles with the more vicious type of animal characteristics. The dog, lion, tiger, ass, vulture, viper, and snake do not appear in the *TN* but they do in Gryphius, an exponent of the affective-pathetic style.[126] Nor does the poet of the affective-pathetic style employ animal characteristics to proclaim God's praises or as mystical qualities of the soul yearning for God. These characteristics, however, are found in the animal-images of the *TN*, as was demonstrated above under functional category ("c").

C. Human Existence

In the previous two sections image-categories in Spee based on inorganic and organic nature were analyzed. In this section image-categories based on human existence, emotion, and interpersonal life are analyzed. Those image-categories from human existence have been selected which are noteworthy for their frequency of occurrence in the *TN* and which encapsulate distinct themes prominent in the *TN*. Their point of origin in the *GTB* will be indicated for a fuller understanding of Spee's theological premises and for greater insight into Spee's own personal character.

1. Love

Spee's poems in the *GTB* and the *TN* are replete with metaphors and images based on the love-relationship between the spouse (or soul) and her beloved, Christ. These *TN* love-images are an outgrowth and product of Spee's philosophy

---

126   Cf. Fricke, *Bildlichkeit,* pp. 72ff.

and theology of love that he has expounded at length in the *GTB*. Of the three theological virtues in the *GTB* Spee gives greatest emphasis to charity, the highest of the three. If the *GTB* is related to the *TN* in the way potential poetry is to actual poetry,[127] Spee's love-imagery will become clearly intelligible only through a complete review of the relationship between the two works.

Spee's methodology in the *GTB* undergoes a gradual development in which the exercises he presents progress from the more theoretical to the more practical, from the ideal to the real, from intellectual expression to a more emotional type of language.[128] In this respect Spee follows a methodology similar to that used by his spiritual father, Ignatius of Loyola, in the *Spiritual Exercises*.[129] The structure of the typical Ignatian meditation shows a development from discussion of a topic such as sin, death, creation, or an aspect of the life of Christ, to an affectual and personal reply by the exercitant in the all-important concluding colloquy.[130] Ignatius' meditation on the Incarnation of Christ, which is presented on the first day of the "Second Week,"[131] is a good example of this typical progression.[132] In this instance, Ignatius proposes that the exercitant beg ". . . for grace to follow and imitate more closely our Lord, who has just become man for me."[133] In like manner, Spee in his chapters in the *GTB* frequently begins with a speculative discussion of some spiritual topic and concludes with an affective response for the daughter to whom he is addressing his exercises.

GTB Book III, chapter 18, section 56, provides an excellent example of this lyrical response in the poem "So offt ich mir bild Jesus ein" (*GTB* 408.20ff.). Spee's introduction to this section contains a discussion on the love of Christ crucified, comparing His love to that of a mother for her child. Spee clearly intends a personal, emotional reaction as he states in his introduction to this exercise: "Derohalben soltu dise anstehende woch an statt deiner gewöhnlichen übung, alle tag, am bestimpten viertelstündtlein, auss diesem Capitel etliche stücklein lesen, wenig oder viel, wie dir geliebet; damitt du also versuchest, ob

---

127 Van Oorschot, "GTB II," pp. 166—167, makes the point: "Das GTB ist die Knospe, die sich in der TrN in voller Pracht entfaltet."

128 Van Oorschot, "GTB II," p. 121.

129 Forthcoming references to the *Spiritual Exercises* are based on the new translation by Louis J. Puhl, S.J. (Westminster, Md.: Newman, 1952). Spee, a member of the Society of Jesus, was thoroughly schooled in Ignatian spirituality. Cf. also, M. R. P. McGuire, "Friedrich Spee," *The New Catholic Encyclopedia*, XIII, 558—559.

130 For Ignatius' definition of the colloquy cf. no. 54 in the *Spiritual Exercises*.

131 The Ignatian *Exercises* are divided into four "weeks": the first "week" is concerned with death and sin, the second with the life of Christ, the third with His passion and death, and the fourth and last with a contemplation on the love of God.

132 Cf. *Spiritual Exercises*, nos. 101—109.

133 Cf. *Spiritual Exercises*, no. 109.

nicht auch du zu besagten unterschiedlichen affecten, durch solches lesen, mögest angereitzet werden" (*GTB* 381.11−16). The soul pours out her response in the poetic colloquy in *GTB* 408.20−31. Thus many of the poems of the *GTB* and the *TN* are emotional responses in imitation of the Ignatian colloquy in the *Spiritual Exercises*.

It is necessary, therefore, to place the lyrical love-images in the *TN* into proper perspective against their philosophical and theological contexts in the *GTB*, if the functional manifestations of Spee's love-imagery are to be clearly understood. At first glance Spee's love imagery seems not much different from that of the secular love poetry of his age. Petrarchan, classical and medieval motifs and images abound. But these motifs, once they are placed into proper perspective in the *GTB* and the *TN*, illustrate that Spee is not describing a worldly secular love but the love of the soul for God by means of poetic *Kontrafaktur*. In this *Kontrafaktur* the secular theme or motif is absorbed and finally "canonized" within the context of religious poetry. Spee defines this love of the soul for God at great length in his introduction to the *GTB* in "3 Erinnerung, ohnewelche dises Buch nicht soll gebraucht werden" (*GTB* 19.26−27). Here the "Beichtvatter" answers the daughter's question: "Was ist die eigenschafft und natur der liebe? " (*GTB* 21.7):

> Es seind zweyerley Liebe: die eine wird genennt *Eine liebe der Begierlichkeit*, die andere wird genennet *Eine liebe der Gutwilligkeit* oder *der Freundschafft*. . . . *Die Lieb der Begierlichkeit* wird genent, wan ich mir, oder für mich etwas begere, wünsche, und haben will, oder, so ichs habe, mit einer liebreichen neigung und affect umbfange, und mich darin ergetze, als etwas das da mir nutzlich oder bequemlich, annemlich, gut, schön, wollustbarlich, lieblich anmütig, und behäglich ist. . . . *Die liebe der Gutwilligkeit* aber, oder *Die liebe der freundschafft* wird genennet, damitt man den jenigen liebet, deme man etwas dergleichen begeret, das ist, deme man etwas gutes günnet oder wunschet. (*GTB* 26.18−27.7)

These two types of love are based on Aristotle's *Nicomachaean Ethics*, Bk. 8, cc. 2−3. Thomas Aquinas makes a similar distinction, by calling "Die Liebe der Begierlichkeit" *amor concupiscentiae* and "Die Liebe der Freundschaft" *amor benevolentiae*. Spee is well aware of Thomas Aquinas' distinction between *amor concupiscentiae* and *amor benevolentiae, seu amicitiae*, since he makes immediate reference to these Thomistic terms and to the *Summa Theologiae* in the marginal gloss to *GTB* 26.18−21.

When these two types are related to man's relationship with God within the Christian dispensation, the love of concupiscence becomes the theological virtue of hope, the love-friendship toward God becomes the theological virtue of charity or love. Within this context Spee offers his discourse on the nature of love. Theologically, however, Spee has made too sharp a distinction between the theological virtues of hope and charity in his introductory explanation in the "3 Erinnerung" (*GTB* 26–27). Spee makes the theological virtue of hope contradictory in itself since the one who longs for God with the love of concupisence desires his own happiness and does not directly desire God.[134] God is the source of happiness, but the soul primarily desires its own advantage over God. The common opinion among Catholic theologians is that for the soul possessing God's grace, hope and love exist concomitantly.[135] The essence of the virtue of hope is not primarily a longing for its own happiness. For the justified, hope is the desire and the longing that God will grant him a greater share in His love. For the sinner, hope is the desire that God will give him the grace of repentance. Thus, hope is really the beginning, the inception of love.[136] Having made too sharp a distinction between the two types of love, Spee has overemphasized the egocentricity of hope and the total selflessness of charity. The essence of true love, seeking only the good of the beloved, he has highlighted.[137]

These two elements in love, egocentric desire and total self-giving (*GTB* 270.33–35; 272.30–33 and 333.26–29), are reflected in Spee's images of love in the poems in the *TN* and the *GTB*. However, the overly precise distinctions which Spee has made on the theological level are intermingled indiscriminately in his poetic imagery and, in addition, are overladen with secular and religious motifs. Spee describes the *effects* of this love on the soul and on Christ more frequently than he does the *nature* of this love. This is a logical consequence of his general tendency to emotionalize the philosophical and theological aspects of the *GTB* in the lyrical sections of the *GTB* and, consequently, in the *TN*. In order to understand clearly these love-images, we must first focus our attention on the nature of this love in the context of the *GTB*. With an understanding of that love as a fundament, we can better discuss the affective and effective functions as manifested in Spee's love-imagery in the *TN*.

There can be no doubt that the highest function of love for Spee is the selfless, total love exemplified by Christ in his love for the soul.[138] The soul tries to exemplify this love, even though her love lacks the purity and the fullness of Christ's love. Furthermore, Spee clearly distinguishes love of God from love of the world. This is a definite characteristic of Ignatian and Jesuit Spirituality. In the *Spiritual Exercises* Ignatius places a consideration of these two loves at a crucial point, at the beginning of the "Second Week" immediately preceding the

---

134 Cf. *GTB* 30 and 31 *passim*.
135 Cf. Ludwig Ott, *Fundamentals of Catholic Dogma* tr. Patrick Lynch, 5th Ed. (St. Louis: Herder, 1962), p. 160.
136 Cf. Van Oorschot, "GTB II," p. 61.
137 Cf. discussion in Van Oorschot, "GTB II," p. 62.
138 Cf. *GTB* 134.10–15; 188.9–10; 273.4ff.; 397.10–16.

all-important moment of decision for the retreatant in the Election.[139] This
distinction between the love of God and the love of the world helps Spee clarify
further the necessity for total giving to the Other, Who is God, that true love
demands. Worldly love, in Spee, appears under the image of "O Venus Kind, du
blinder Knab." The love of God appears under the image of "O Jesus mein, du
schöner Knab." Spee expresses this distinction in the *GTB* 198.8—16 as follows:

> O Jesu mein, du schöner knab,
>   Nim hin Cupidons waffen:
> Reiss ihm die pfeil und kocher ab,
>   Und leg ihn ewig schlaffen.
> Nur du bitt ich: du zihl auff mich:
>   Von dir will sein getroffen:
> O reines gifft: wan Jesus trifft.
>   Alssdan ist heil zu hoffen.

The love of God, "O Jesus mein," is triumphant over worldly love, "Venus
Kind."

In *GTB* Bk. II, chapter 18, the destruction of "die liebe der welt" by "die
liebe Gottes" is described as follows:

> Auff einen Sontag begegneten ein ander *die liebe Gottes* und *die liebe der
> Welt:* die Welt Lieb sagte: Schwester, wie bistu also traurig, est thut dir,
> glaub, ich, schmertzlich wehe, dass mich die menschen einlassen, und dich so
> gar ausschliessen.
>   Da nam die Liebe Gottes, die welt lieb mit gewalt, und band sie an das
> heilig Creutz. Da starb alsbald die welt lieb: und es schwure darauff die liebe
> Gottes, so offt ihr die welt lieb begegne, so wolle sie dieselbe fangen, und an
> das Creutz binden: sie habe nicht gewisst, dass die welt lieb sterbe, so man sie
> ans Creutz anbinde. (383.23—31)

Much of this description contains basic ascetical principles characteristic of
Spee's theology of the cross and suffering. Worldly love brings a false joy; the
love of God brings true joy. The cross is sweet (*GTB* 403.7—8); good (*GTB*
175.18); and lovely *TN* (17):9,1. The triumph of the love of God over worldly
love is reflected in the poetic imagery of the *TN* 2:3,5—4,2. Here the secular
love-god, *Cupido,* is transformed into *cupido divinus:* "O keusche Lieb / Cupido
rein." It seems in this instance that Spee received his inspiration from his fellow
Jesuit, Hermann Hugo, who employs the *Christus-Cupido* motif in his *Pia
Desideria.*[140] The *Christus-Cupido* figure crucified on a tree which appears on the

---

139   Cf. *Spiritual Exercises,* nos. 91—100.
140   Cf. Rosenfeld, *Studien,* p. 45; and Jacobsen, *Metamorphosen,* pp. 100ff., and the
Cupido emblems on pp. 29 and 30, cf. also Dimler, "The Genesis and Development of
Spee's Love-Imagery," *Germanic Review,* March, 1973, 93.

frontispieces of the Strassburg manuscript, the *Pariser Abschrift* and the *Erstdruck* of the *TN*, demonstrates the importance of this motif in Spee. This poetic *Kontrafaktur* is carried out further as Spee canonizes other Petrarchan and classical love-images and employs these images to describe the love-union between the soul and her beloved, Christ. The images are divested of their "wordly" function and assume a spiritual function within the context of the poems in the *GTB* and the *TN*.

The basic two-fold aspect of love which Spee defines and upon which he bases his exercises in the *GTB*, Books II and III, illustrates the egocentric, self-centered aspect of love which corresponds to *amor concupiscentiae* and the total selflessness of charity which corresponds to *amor benevolentiae*. These distinctions are clearly reflected in Spee's love-imagery in the *GTB*. Correspondingly, the poems that are contained in the second part of the *GTB*, where Spee treats of the "liebe der begierlichkeit," (= hope), have a general tendency toward images in which the self-centered, subjective, and introspective aspects of love are present [*TN* (3), (6), (7), (11), and (16)]. Images in the poems from the third part of the *GTB*, where "die liebe der freundschaft" (= charity) predominates, tend to be of a more altruistic, selfless, other-oriented nature. Here the spouse is more concerned with going out of herself, forgetting her sorrow and sinfulness and focusing her attention and sympathy on Christ. This is particularly true where the praise of God the Creator, Christ's passion, the soul's sorrow for sin, or the wounds of Christ become central themes [*TN* (43), (12), (15), (16), and (11)].

Applying this basic two-fold division of love to the *TN* and the *GTB*, the introspective, self-centered aspects of love are manifested (cf. Table 1.1, p. 137). The selfless, altruistic, sympathetic nature of love, on the other hand, is reflected in those images which show the soul's love for Christ (cf. Table 1.2, p. 137).

The question now arises: what type of images functions in the description of Christ's love? Does His love for the soul also contain both the concupiscent and altruistic aspects? In the *GTB* Christ's love is described as total (151.33); He dies for the soul (197.20); His love is inexpressible (412.14–15); He loves with His whole heart (273.4ff.); His love is compared to that of a mother for her child (*GTB* Bk. III, chapter 18, no. 56). These images are basically altruistic and perhaps they find their best summation in the *GTB* 134.10–15:

> Die lieb allein, die ich zu disem Schäfflein trage, macht mir das Schäfflein werth: die lieb zwinget mich, und machet mir alle dise müh und arbeit süss; und wan ich nur mein Schäfflein finde, frage ich nach Keinen thieren. Die lieb stärcket mich, die lieb wapffnet mich, die lieb macht mich unerschrocken und sonsten suche ich keinen anderen nutzen: ich suche nur das Schäfflein.

In *TN* 40, Daphnis (Christ) is described as suffering, confused and blinded in His selfless pursuit of the soul (*TN* 40:4,4—5; 9,2; 11,1—2; 13,3).[141] In *TN* (42) love has driven Him (Daphnis) from heaven to suffer for the soul. Christ's heavenly Father in *TN* (43):42,1—8 remarks that it was Christ's love for men which caused Him to leave heaven and to save mankind. His supreme love was the cause of His own death and crucifixion, *TN* (43):46,1—4. From these examples in Spee it is clear that Christ embodies for Spee the highest form of love. In His selflessness and altruism Christ is the highest analogate of "die liebe der Gutwilligkeit oder der Freundschafft."

Spee's love-imagery reaches a theological climax when he describes the love-relationship between the Father and the Son and the mystery of the Trinity. The love between the Father and the Son is described as: "hoch- und hoch gespante lieb" (*TN* 29:22,7); "Ohn Anfang / End / und Zeiten" (*TN* 29:22,8); it is "unermessen" (*TN* 29:25,2); Father and Son love one another "Mit aussgespanter flammen gross" (*TN* 29:21,7); their love achieves a peak of intensity because, as Spee describes it, their eternal love-embrace, "Sich ewiglich umbfassen" (*TN* 29:29,6); their love kiss, "Dess Sohns / und Vatters einig kuss" (*TN* 29:32,1); their joy in communion: "O wollust in gemeine" (*TN* 29:26,8); is in reality the Person of the Holy Spirit. This mystery is expressed in *TN* 29:29,1—8:

> Der Sohn / und Vatter ewiglich
> Mit gleichem hertzen inniglich
>   In gleicher Lieb erbrinnen.
> Sie beyde zween / und eines beyd
>   Sich ewiglich umbfassen
> So sauset auch in Ewigkeit
>   Der Geist / ohn underlassen.

The trinitarian union between the Father and the Son is so intense, unique, and selfless that it results in the procession of another Person with the Trinity, the Spirit. Spee here follows Catholic theology which teaches that the Holy Spirit proceeds from the mutual love of the Father and the Son.[142] The Holy Spirit is the common love of the Father and the Son;[143] he is the result of the total

---

141   The name Daphnis originated with Theocritus. Spee combines this figure with the *Pastor Bonus* of the Gospel; cf. Rosenfeld, *Neue Studien*, p. 73. The Daphnis-figure does not appear in the *GTB*. Nowak, "Versuch," pp. 156ff., discusses the Daphnis-figure in the context of sixteenth- and seventeenth-century pastoral poetry. He claims that Spee borrowed the name from contemporary secular poetry, cf. also my article on Spee, *Classical Folia* XXVI, (Dec. 1972), 279—288.

142   Cf. Ludwig Ott, *Fundamentals of Catholic Dogma*, pp. 66—67.

143   Cf. M. J. Donnelly, "The Holy Spirit, *"The New Catholic Encylclopedia*, VII, 96—97; and Denziger, *Enchiridion Symbolorum Definitionum et Declarationum*, no. 527.

altruism of the Father and the Son. Thus, Spee in *TN* 29:1—8 has embodied traditional Catholic dogma in the images he uses to express the love-relation between the Father and the Son in the mystery of the Trinity, the highest analogate of love.

Within the image-category a wide range of verbal forms can be found in the *GTB* and the *TN*. Many of them show a kinship with classical, Petrarchan, and above, all, mystical and pietistic metaphor (cf. Table 1.3, p. 137).

The image of the burning fire of love is found among the German mystics to express the mystical state.[144] It is also found in Latin love poetry[145] and among the Pietists.[146] Verbal forms such as: *zerschmeltzen, durchreissen, durchstecken, einnehmen, brennen, erfüllen,* and *verwunden* are used in Pietistic language, which indicate common mystical sources for both Spee and the Pietists.[147]

Adjectival forms modifying love are (cf. Table 1.4, p. 138). The *Liebesflamme,* and the interchange between heat and cold to show the effect of love, are common motifs among seventeenth-century French and German poets.[148] The similarity of expression among Spee, the German mystics and Pietists becomes even more apparent upon comparison of the metaphorical expressions listed above and the analyses of Lüers, Langen, and the love terminology of the mystics listed in Sandaeus.[149]

The rhetorical structures which occur most frequently in the love images of Spee are antithesis and oxymoron. They are employed to describe the impact, force, and destructive effect of love (cf. Table 1.5, p. 138). Seuse and Mechthild describe their mystical experiences under the formula "liep und Leit."[150] This formula occurs in the GTB 133.20—23 where Christ addresses the lost sheep: "Ach Schäfflein Schäfflein, wie bringestu mich in grosse angst und noth! Ich habe dich viel zu sehr geliebet. Nun spüre ich erst, das lieb mit leid vermischet ist, und dass keine lieb ohn leid gefunden wird."[151] Antithesis was always a common

---

144 Cf. Sandaeus, *Pro Theologia Mystica Clavis,* pp. 237ff., "ignis mysticus"; Lüers, *Sprache der Mystik,* pp. 147ff. for examples from Tauler, Ruysbroek, and Mechthild.

145 Jacobsen, *Metamorphosen,* pp. 125ff.

146 Langen, *Wortschatz,* p. 336.

147 Langen, *Wortschatz,* p. 421, states: "Sie *(TN)* enthält Spuren einer dem mystisch-pietistischen Wortschatz verwandten Sprache im Ausdruck der Jesusminne oder in der Schilderung der Dreifaltigkeit. ... Dieses Wortfeld weist zurück auf die Spee und den Pietisten gemeinsamen mystischen Quellen."

148 Beckmann, "Motive und Formen," Bd. 5, pp. 36—38, lists the occurrence of this motif in Czepko, Opitz, Hofmannswaldau, and Fleming.

149 Cf. Lüers, *Sprache,* pp. 148ff.; Langen, *Wortschatz,* pp. 518ff.; and Sandaeus, *Clavis,* pp. 50ff.

150 Cf. Lüers, *Sprache,* pp. 78—79.

151 Beckmann, "Motive," p. 106, makes the following point in this regard: "Bei der barocken Vorliebe für Gegensätze aller Art ist es nur zu verständlich, dass Antithesen zu den beliebtesten Formelementen der Barockdichtung gehören. Von den antithetischen Gegen-überstellungen einzelner Worte in Oxymoron bis zu den antithetischen Gedichtpaaren reichte die weite Skala ihrer Anwendungsmöglichkeiten, die in der Antithesenhäufung gipfelt."

rhetorical characteristic among mystical writers.[152] In the *TN* simile occurs but twice in this image-field. In *TN* (3):1,7—8, love burns in the Spouse's heart like a candle which is inextinguishable. In *TN* 34:205,3—10 Halton is as eager to kiss Christ's cheeks as a suckling lamb is eager when it leaps toward its mother's dugs.

In his use of love-imagery Spee's style and terminology show remarkable similarities with the medieval mystics and the Pietists. However, more recent research on the relationship between Spee's terminology and the medieval mystics rejects any direct immediate influence of the medieval mystics on Spee. Jesuits who were contemporaries of Spee were encouraged *not* to read the writings of the medieval mystics. The fourth General of the Society of Jesus forbade their persual for all practical purposes.[153] Thus, when Spee uses what appear to be mystical terms, as he does frequently in his love-images, he is merely reflecting contemporary literary usage which was strongly colored with these terms.[154] Sandaeus' dictionary of mystical terms is a good example of how contemporary terminology in the poetry of the seventeenth century was a compendium of many sources.[155] It is clearly evident that Spee has "spiritualized" many Petrarchan love-motifs (the sweetness of love and its bitterness, its heat and its cold, its debilitating effect) and intermingled these motifs with a heritage of mystical terminology. But Spee has done so fundamentally within the context of his theological discussion in the *GTB* and within the basic two-fold structure of the egocentricity of love and its altruism.

2. Heart

Closely associated with the love-images in the previous category are those images that concern the heart. The heart has traditionally been a symbol of both physical and spiritual love.[156] In emblem literature the heart frequently signifies love as the center of happiness, and this is the reason why it is frequently surmounted by flames in many emblems. Secular seventeenth-century German poets frequently employ various motifs based on the symbolism of the heart. Gryphius and Opitz used the motif of the heart as a "Fackel," lighting the lover on his path to the beloved.[157] The motif of the exchange of hearts between

152 Cf. Lüers, *Sprache*, pp. 107—108; and Josef Quint, "Mystik und Sprache," *Altdeutsche und Altniederländische Mystik, Wege der Forschung,* XXIII, ed. Kurt Ruh (Darmstadt: Wiss. Buch. 1964), 135ff.

153 Cf. Josef Stierli, "Devotion to the Sacred Heart from the End of Patristic Times down to St. Margaret Mary," *Heart of the Savior,* tr. Paul Andrews (New York: Herder, 1957), p. 98; and Van Oorschot, "GTB II," p. 102.

154 Cf. Van Oorschot, "GTB II," p. 103; Windfuhr, *Bildlichkeit,* p. 228; and Reichert, "Einflüsse und Anregungen," *Programm Neuruppin,* 1913, 13.

155 Cf. also Langen, *Wortschatz,* pp. 402ff.

156 Cf. Cirlot, *Dictionary,* pp. 135—136.

157 Cf. Beckmann, "Motive," p. 42.

lovers also occurs in Weckherlin.[158] Spee himself uses a wide variety of heart-motifs. Some of these motifs bear close resemblance to those used by Mechthild, Tauler, and Seuse.[159]

The image of the burning-heart occurs in the GTB 216. 12–13; 219.21–22; 224.34–35. In GTB 216.11ff. the soul asks Christ to enclose His love in her heart and then ignite it so that it will burst into a thousand pieces: "Ich bitte dich verschliesse doch in mein eysenes hertz ein wenig deiner liebe, zünde sie an, und mache dass es in tausend stück zerspringe; nichts solle mir liebers seine auff erden." A variation on the burning-heart motif (TN 29) occurs regarding the trinitarian relationship between the Father and the Son: "Mit gleichem hertzen inniglich // In gleicher Lieb erbrinnen" (TN 29:29,3–4). Verbal uses occur likewise such as: brinnen, entzünden, zünden, brinnend; paraphrases are: "brand der liebe" (GTB 200.2–3); "feuer meines hertzens" (Christ) in GTB 200.25; "hertzen-brandt" [TN (6):2,6; and TN 10:6,4] that offer further variations on the motif. The motif of the wounded heart is found in GTB 199ff.: "Schöne weiss das Hertz Jesu zu verwunden." This motif is found in connection with the arrows of love wounding the lover's heart (further discussed below). Other variations on this motif are found in the GTB and TN: "verwunden" (TN 2:2,5); "verwundtes hertz" (Christ in GTB 202.7–8).

Devotion to the Heart of Christ, commonly known today as the Sacred Heart devotion, came into vogue among Jesuits in the early part of the seventeenth century. Wilhelm Nakatenus,[160] Philip Kiesel, and Spee follow Peter Canisius' lead in propagandizing this devotion that later became a special concern among Jesuits.[161] This motif occurs in Spee in the GTB 392.32–393.27 and 406.30–37. Surprisingly there are but few references to this devotion in the TN. Only traces of the wounded heart of Christ as a motif occur (TN 46:12,1–8).

The image of the stolen lover's heart occurs in the TN (7):22,1–8 and 44:12,7ff. In this instance Christ is characterized as "hertzen-dieb" (TN 7:22,2). This motif occurs in the Petrarchan school, in Herrick, and among religious writers such as Balde and Bonaventure.[162] There is no evidence for this motif in the TN. The image of the beloved enshrined in the lover's heart occurs in the GTB 60.11–15 and in the TN 10:8,5–8. The name of Jesus burning in the heart of the spouse is developed as a motif in the poem in the GTB 224.34–35: "O

---

158 Cf. Beckmann, p. 42.

159 Lüers, Sprache der Mystik, pp. 196–197.

160 Cf. Ludwig Koch, Jesuitenlexikon (Louvain: Bonifacius, 1932), p. 1270.

161 Stierli, "Devotion to the Sacred Heart," pp. 97ff. Angelus Silesius employed the motif of Christ's wounded heart.

162 Cf. Jacobsen, Metamorphosen, pp. 110–111. Fleming, Zesen, and Silesius also use this motif (cf. Jacobsen, pp. 112ff.). It occurred frequently in emblem literature of the fifteenth to the seventeenth centuries (cf. the emblems in Jacobsen, pp. 89 and 91, which portray this motif).

Jesu, Jesu Wunder Nahm // Wie brinnest mir im hertzen!" However, Spee does not transfer or expand upon this motif in the poems of the *TN*. On the other hand, the heart melting from the heat of love is an explicit motif in Spee. This is based on the biblical image found in the Canticle of Canticles 5,6. In the *GTB* and the *TN* God's heart is pictured as melting when the soul repents of her sins [*TN* (16):13,8 and *GTB* 145.39–40].

A medieval motif, the *Burg-Allegorie,* occurs in connection with the imagery in this category in *TN* 12:1,1–2. The poem is entitled: "Ermahnung zur buss an den Sünder dass er die Burg seines hertzens Christo auffmache und einraume." This is found also in *GTB* Bk. III, chapter 9, which is basically an exercise to help lead the soul toward true contrition and sorrow for sin. To do this she must open the "feste burg deines verstockten hertzens" to the grace of God. "O Sünder und O Sünderin! . . . was haltest so hart versperret und verriglet die feste burg deines verstockten hertzens? Warumb offnest nicht dem Himmel Fürsten Jesu Christo, der so freundlich dich von Creutz ermahnet, und zur buss erwecket? " (327.12–16).[163] The German mystics used the image of the "bürgelin der sele."[164] A variation of the *burg*-motif occurs in Spee, where God is referred to as "burg"; "Du bist mein burg, mein festes hauss, // Kein ding soll mich bewegen" (*GTB* 129.34–35).

In this image-category Spee's uses of verbal formations are striking not only for the variety of their emotional expression and affectivity, but also for their close resemblance to verbal forms found among the Pietists. The following forms, common to Spee and the Pietists occur (cf. Table 2.1, p. 138). Based on a combination of their affective and pathetic impact, plus their almost exclusive application to religious themes, these verbal forms can be termed a combination of the mystical and the pathetic modes. (For verbal forms that occur in both the *GTB* and the *TN* cf. Table 2.2, p. 138).

Paraphrases occur in this category (cf. Table 2.3, p. 139). Heart-images in Spee function in a variety of ways. As in the preceding analysis of love-imagery, there are also heart-images which emphasize the soul's introspection and inward reflection on its love-state which corresponds to the *amor concupiscentiae* of the *GTB* (cf. Table 2.4, p. 139).

Of an introspective nature, but with the accent on interior sorrow and lamentation over the state of interior sinfulness, are the following images which express:

a) great distress of soul due to the soul's sinful state [*TN* (15):1,4];
b) the broken heart as a sign of interior renewal and revulsion at the former sinful state [*TN* (15):4,3–4];

---

163 This motif also occurs in contemporary seventeenth-century emblem literature. Cf. Jacobsen, *Metamorphosen*, p. 63.
164 Cf. Lüers, *Sprache*, p. 195, for an example from Seuse.

c) sickness of heart in asking God to grant purity of soul [*TN* (15):7,6];

d) a heart broken in pieces by God's grace [*TN* (15):8,7—8];

e) pain because she has tormented Christ's "treues hertz" [*TN* (16):7,5—6]. In *TN* (16):13,7—8 Christ answers that His heart has melted because the soul has repented.

Heart-images which are of a more altruistic nature and which correspond to *amor benevolentiae* (= love) in the *GTB* occur in *TN* (5):8,1—8 where the soul through her representative, the nightingale, breaks her heart in singing out the name of Jesus; in *TN* (7):5,1—2 the soul yields to Christ who is her only consolation; in *TN* (11):23,3—4 Mary Magdalen ardently desires Christ, and, finally, in *TN* 46:12,1—8, the soul enters the wound in Christ's side and takes delight in resting next to His heart. A similar image may be found in *GTB* 407.14ff.

A third category of heart-images reflects the compassion of Christ, nature, Mary, or the soul. The soul's heart breaks at the sight of Christ being taken captive (*TN* 9:13,5—6). In *TN* (38):8,6 Christ tells His mother her heart would be torn in sorrow if she knew His pain. In *TN* 39:6,2 the moon's heart breaks at the sight of Christ suffering in Gethsemane. In *TN* (43):27,8 the blood runs to Mary's heart because her Son is suffering so intensely.

In the *GTB* Spee includes a chapter demonstrating a new method of offering praise to God: "Eine ausserlesen schöne und lüstige Weiss wie eine andechtige Seel Gott loben könne tag und nacht, und mit den Engelen ohn einige unterlass singen Heylig, Heylig, Heylig" (*GTB* 435.2—4). After a rather extensive philosophical discussion on the nature of signs and symbols in *GTB* 436ff., Spee proposes human heart-beats as an excellent way of praising God: "nur lautere ehr- und lobzeichen" (438.40—41).

> Dann siehe da, lasset [uns] auss allen disen schlägen lautere zeichen machen, und ihnen dise bedeutnuss aufflegen zwischen Gott und uns, dass ein jeder solcher schlag, hinfurther so vill by Gott und den heiligen bedeuten und heissen solle, als vill bedeuten und heissen dise wort der Engelen: Heilig, Heilig. . . . (438.28—33)[165]

However, this praise symbolism based on the beats of the heart, which is given such emphasis in the *GTB*, does not appear in the *TN*.

The greater emphasis on interpersonal aspects regarding heart-images in the *GTB* is noteworthy. In the *GTB* the images manifest greater intensity of intimacy, union, and deep friendship between the soul and Christ than in the *TN*.

---

165 Cf. also *GTB* 447.7—10; 15—17; 25—27. The following references to the *GTB* are illustrative of this deeper intimacy: 166.8—9; 208.31—32; 215.34—216.1; 152.35—36; 393.4—11 and 515.38—39.

Heart images assume a distinctly theological function in the trinitarian poem, *TN* 29: "Das geheimnuss der Hochheiligen Dreyfaltigkeit / so wol Theologisch als Poetisch, wie viel geschehen können entworffen." The first trinitarian process, the generation of the Son from the Father,[166] is described by Spee as: "Das hertzen wort / und hertz-concept // Von ihm / gleich ihm gezeuget" (*TN* 29:15,5—6). Spee's poetic terminology reflects the traditional scholastic concept of the generation of the Son that is based on the analogy of human knowing. Scholastic theologians build their analogy on the ideas of Augustine in their attempt to explain the mystery of the procession of the Holy Spirit and the generation of the Son. They consider the human psychology of knowing and loving as analogous to the trinitarian procession.[167] The procession of a mental word within the intelligence of man was likened to the utterance of the Word by the Father.[168] Actually the prologue to John's Gospel speaks of the Son as the Word *(Logos)* of the Father. Spee's terminology: "hertzen wort und hertz-concept" together with the term "gezeuget" reflect these traditional Scholastic notions on the Trinity. In *TN* 29:15,5—6 "das hertzen wort" reflects Christ the *Logos,* as the Word from the Father. "Hertz-concept" reflects the process of intellection analogously considered in the Trinity. His term, "gezeuget," is the completed process of generation. However, the use of the term "hertz" in combination with "wort" and "concept" from the theological standpoint is a poetic accretion, since the procession described here, when applied to the generation of the Son, is a process of intellection. Spee's genius, in this instance, is his inclusion of the love element involved in the generation process through the word "hertz" in combination with "wort" and "concept." The Son is indeed beloved of the Father. The generative act on the part of the Father involves an intellectual act of love, and the final term of this process results in the Father's "hertzen-wort" and "hertz-concept" who is none other than the Son.[169]

The second procession in the Trinity, the spiration of the Spirit, is founded on the concept of the Spirit as used in the Gospel of John 3,8: "The wind blows wherever it pleases; you hear its sound, but you cannot tell where it comes from or where it is going. That is how it is with all who are born of the Spirit." Scholastic theology, in attempting an explanation of this deep mystery of the spiration of the Holy Spirit, considered the procession of the Spirit as analogous to human loving. St. Augustine sees the second procession in the Trinity as a product of the mutual love of the Father and the Son.[170] The Catechism of the Council of Trent says that the Holy Spirit proceeds from the divine will inflamed

---

166 Cf. Parente, *Dictionary,* pp. 230—231.
167 Cf. J. Peter, "Generation of the Word," *New Catholic Encyclopedia,* VI, 323.
168 *Summa Theol.* 1a, 27.2—4.
169 For further reference to the notion of generation in Spee, cf. *GTB* 35.25—28.
170 Cf. G. M. Greenewald, "Spiration," *New Catholic Encyclopedia,* XIII, 567—568.

with love.[171] To indicate this intimacy of love involved in the spiration of the
Holy Spirit, Spee uses the image of the unified Heart of the Father and the Son
in TN 29:27,7–8: "Auss einem hertzen her und her // Der athem süsslich
rauchet." To show the intensity of the love (TN 29:28,7–8): "ist beyder Glut
und hertzenbrand // Ohn mass und ziel gezündet." To indicate both intensity
and intimacy: "In gleicher Lieb erbrinnen // Mit gleichem hertzen inniglich" (TN
29:29,3–4); to show the actual procession: "aus einem hertzen her und her"
where the particle "her" is repeated.[172] Thus Spee has again based the
heart-imagery in his poem on the Trinity (TN 29) on traditional Scholastic
teaching regarding the Trinity. However, he has reformulated and beautified the
description of the trinitarian process through his poetic genius.

Apart from the verbal and paraphrastic metaphors illustrated above, the
image-category of the heart exhibits basically simple image structures. There are
only two instances of personification in the TN: (a) TN 41:8,8 where the brook
Cedron's heart is broken in compassion for Christ; and (b) TN 39 where the
moon's heart is pictured as splitting out of compassion. There is but one simile:
in TN (7):8,5–6 the soul's heart will become like soft wax if she does not soon
find Christ.[173] Stylistically, aside from TN 29 where heart-images function in the
mystical mode, the other functional categories involving heart-imagery combine
similarities with the mystical and the affective-pathetic styles.

3. Pain and Sorrow

Images of pain, sorrow, desolation and lamentation play a strong role in the
TN. The basis of these emotions and their function in the TN become more
apparent when they are examined against the background of Spee's philosophical and theological thought in the GTB. As so often the case in Spee, the
poetic form which images of pain and desolation assume in the GTB is often
determined by the specific function Spee gives them in the particular chapter in
which they occur. The following examples are offered to show this interrelationship between function and image in the GTB, with particular attention to
those which later occur in the TN.

In GTB Bk. II, chapter 8, Spee presents an exercise to help bulwark and
strengthen the soul's courage in time of severe desolation and temptation:
"Noch andere Werck der Hoffnung und vertrauen zu Gott in einer sehr grossen

---

[171] M. J. Donnelly, "Holy Spirit," New Catholic Encyclopedia, VII, 96–99.
[172] For further reference to the procession of the Holy Spirit in Spee, cf. GTB 50.26ff.
and 54.12ff.
[173] For further motifs based on the notion of God's heart melting like wax, cf. GTB
145.39–40.

betrübnuss und betrangnuss dess hertzens" (162.17–18). Spee's aim is to turn the soul's attention away from herself by means of a detailed meditation on the suffering which Christ underwent on the cross. Christ's sorrow, caused by the soul's sins, is portrayed in the most picturesque and vivid images. Following this exercise (*GTB* II,8) he appends several "Trauergesänge"; "magst sie zunzeiten lesen oder klaglich singen, oder singen lassen, wie dirs gefallen wird" (*GTB* 170.25–28). Here the images of pain and sorrow are:

1) the soul's pain of desolation at God's absence (*GTB* 170.30ff.);
2) the pain suffered by Christ in the Garden of Gethsemane [*TN* (38):11,1–2];
3) the soul's pain out of compassion for Christ on the cross [*TN* (18):6,1–4];
4) the soul's passage from pain to joy through union with Christ [*TN* (18):7,1–8].

These images of pain and sorrow correspond directly with their prose context in the *GTB*. This relationship continues throughout the *GTB*, both with regard to the *TN* poems taken therefrom, and with other poems which are preserved in the *GTB*. A summary will be made of these relationships, with special attention to those poems which eventually were included in the *TN*. In this manner, when the overall classification of pain-images by function in the *TN* is formulated below, some of the more dominant themes which correspond with the *GTB*'s philosophy and theology will become more evident.

In *GTB* Bk. II, chapter 10: "Noch andere werck der Hoffnung oder Begierlichen liebe zu Gott," Spee presents the classical conflict between the worldly way of life (188.27ff.) and the manner of life for the soul that desires God above the riches and pleasures of this life.[174] Correspondingly in *GTB* 190.23–30, the poem "Ade, fahre deine strassen," images occur which portray the soul's pain because of her renunciation of the world and its "Pracht, ehr, und herrlichkeit" (190.20). *GTB* Bk. II, chapter 12 (this chapter has the same title as Bk. II, chapter 10) is an exercise in wounding the heart of Christ with sighs of love and longing. Correspondingly, the verses in *GTB* 201.29–32 contain an image of the soul's painful longing over the absence of Christ.

The aim of *GTB* Bk. II, chapter 16, is to illustrate the "natur der begierlichen liebe" (220.5–6). "Begierliche Liebe" corresponds closely to *amor concupiscentiae,* which is the introspective, self-centered movement of the soul (*GTB* 26.22ff.). The painful, subjective effects of love are described in *TN* poems: (7), (3), (6), (5) and the pain of absence in *TN* (8). These *TN* poems were written within the context of *GTB* Bk. II, chapter 16. The titles of these poems transferred to the *TN* indicate the soul's state of introspection: "Die

---

[174] Ignatius Loyola stresses this notion in the *Spiritual Exercises,* in the "Meditation on Two Standards," nos. 136–148.

Gesponss Jesu klaget noch ferner ihre lieb" [TN (7)]; "Die Gesponss Jesu klaget ihren hertzen-brand" [TN (3)]; "Die Gesponss Jesu beklaget sich dass sie nimmer ruhen könne" [TN (6)]; "Liebgesang des Gesponss Jesu, im anfang der Sommerzeit" [TN (8)].

GTB Bk. III, chapter 9, is an exercise on "zerknirschung dess Hertzens" or *contritio*. Spee attempts to lead the soul to true and complete sorrow for her sins. Previously in his "gemeine Unterrichtung" (31.28–32.19), Spee has clearly defined *contritio* by distinguishing it from *attritio*. Contrition stems from the love of God *(amor benevolentiae)* or from some other supernatural motive:

> Es ist wahr; zerknirschung hat auch diese krafft; aber eben dieselbe rew und leid ist ein werck der liebe.
>
> Damitt du solches verstehest, ist zu mercken, dass die rew, und leid herfliessen oder enstehen kann auss unterschiedlichen motiven oder ursachen. Dan entweder kompt sie her, auss der dritten Göttlichen Tugend, das ist auss der liebe der gutwilligkeit gegen Gott: oder aber auss einer anderen ursach, als nemlich auss liebe der Tugend, abschewlichkeit der sünden, forcht der hellen, hoffnung der belohnung, und dergleichen guten, heiligen, ubernaturlichen motiven. (*GTB* 31.32–41)

Attrition, on the other hand, is not motivated primarily by the love of God:

> Wan dan nun sie herfleusst nit auss einem affect der Liebe, oder dritten Göttlichen Tugend, sonder auss einer anderen obgezelten ubernaturlicher ursachen, so wird ein solche rew, und leid genennt, eine unvolkommene Rew, auff Latein *Attritio* . . . . (*GTB* 32.1–4)

Only contrition has the power to obtain God's forgiveness for serious sins outside of confession: "Dan sie warhafftig ein werck ist der liebe . . ." (*GTB* 32.16 and cf. also 51.30ff.). Thus a discourse on contrition logically belongs in Book III, which is devoted to charity, and this Spee has done.

In *GTB* Bk. III, chapter 9, "Noch andere Werck der liebe, und ist zerknirschung dess Hertzens," Spee, through his frequent question and answer method, shows the soul, in succession: (a) the horror of sin, (b) the majesty of God compared with the ingratitude of man, and (c) the need for true contrition and for renewal of spirit. The pain-images which occur in the following poems reflect:

a) The danger to the soul of meriting eternal pain for her sins [TN (12):3,3–4];
b) the pain of the sinful state in which the soul finds herself [TN (15):3,1–6];
c) the soul's desire for sorrow and agony because of her sins [TN (15):16,1–4];
d) the bite of her sinful conscience [TN (16):1,3–8];
e) her painful realization that she is responsible for tormenting Christ's heart [TN (16):7,5–6; 8,4].

These images are arranged according to the following general schema. The criterion for the seven divisions in the schema is based on the diversity of image-function within the context of the present image category.

1. There are frequent instances where nature is in sorrow out of compassion *(natura compatiens)* (cf. Table 3.1, p. 139).

2. Not merely nature but humans show sorrowful compassion towards Christ (cf. Table 3.2, p. 140).

3. Christ Himself sorrows in His passion and death (cf. Table 3.2).

4. Nature either contrasts or reflects the soul's inner mood of sorrow (cf. Table 3.3, p. 140).

5. The pain of contrition and the pain of repentance from sin have already been analyzed on the basis of their context in *GTB* Bk. III, chapter 9.

6. Pain-images occur according to the following three-fold aspects of the soul's relationship to Christ (cf. Table 3.4, p. 141): (a) The painful effects of Christ's love in the soul; (b) the soul's love-yearning expressed in her pain and her absence from Jesus; and (c) there is also the pain which results from actual union with the beloved.

The verbal forms associated with images in this category exhibit certain similarities with images of the heart and love. The verbs show characteristics proper to the affective-pathetic mode of style having destructive force and vivid action such as (cf. Table 3.5, p. 141).

The following nature personifications occur [these are all identical with category (1) above]:

Perhaps the most striking structural image-form within this category is the (17):3,5 where "qual und pain" are called "schnöde wahren." This paraphrase is included in an unusual Spee-image: the soul tells wagons and cars to load up her trouble and care and carry them far from her heart [*TN* (17):3,1—6]. Simile occurs in *TN* (15):7,1—8 where the soul, in a spirit of true contrition, speaks to God of her sorrow and tells Him that her sorrow is intense: "Und ich von leyd fast jederzeit // Zerfliess gleich einer kertzen."

Perhaps the most striking structural image-form within this category is the frequent use of oxymoron and paradox to describe the soul's pain and sorrow. The following occur (cf. Table 3.6, p. 141). "Süsser Schmerz, süsses Weh, zuckersüsse Pein" are terms found among the Pietists with probable origins from the Petrarchan bitter-sweet antithesis.[175] Damon proclaims: "Gantz wol mir ist bey solcher pein," when he speaks of the effect of Christ's love in his heart (*TN* 34:206.27—207.1).

When image-structure and image-function are correlated, the following facts emerge:

---

[175] Cf. Langen, *Wortschatz*, pp. 374—375.

a) The oxymorons and paradoxes listed above occur exclusively in the category of the painfulness of the love-experience either as effect, as yearning, or as union (cf. functional categories 6a, 6b, and 6c above). The majority of these figures of antithesis (nine of eleven occurrences) seemingly function to indicate the painfulness of love as effect. The occurrence of love and pain together has long been a characteristic of both religious and secular poetry. "Liep und leit" as a religious love-formula occurs among the Mystics, in particular Seuse and Mechthild. The two emotions placed in such antithetical relationship are used to describe the mystical relationship between God and the soul.[176]

b) The majority of the personifications listed above occur in the category of painful-compassion ("1" above) where nature, the soul, and the mother of Christ mourn over His suffering and death.

Stylistically, this image-category shows considerable similarity in both vocabulary and function with the mystical-pietistic mode of expression. A comparison between Spee's verbal forms to express the effect of God's love on the soul and those of the Pietists makes this evident.[177] Moreover, the use of oxymoron and antithesis to express the subjective state of the soul in her relationship to God is traditional among Mystics and Pietists. Similarities also exist with the pathetic mode, particularly regarding the power and the intensity of the verbal expressions relating the painful love-experience. This mixture of pathos and religious feeling is a dominant trait in Spee's imagery.

4. Wounds

In this category images of the spouse of Christ wounded by the effects of love, which play a strong devotional role in both the GTB and the TN, are analyzed as well as images pertaining to the wounds of Christ. The cult surrounding the wounds Christ suffered in His passion is found in Book III of the GTB and in the later poems of the TN: 46, 48 and 49. Spee's cult of the wounds of Christ in these poems is attributed to his latest creative period as a poet, the years 1632 and 1633.[178] TN poem 46 is the locus classicus for Spee's poetic treatment of this motif. In this poem devotion to the wounds of Christ is formulated in the poem's title: "Eine Christliche Seel redet von dem Creutz, und Wunden Christ."

---

[176] Cf. Lüers, Sprache, pp. 78–79. The terms Liebespein and Liebesschmerz are found in Gottfried Arnold in the context of the soul's yearning for union with God. Cf. Langen, Wortschatz, p. 135.

[177] Cf. Langen, Wortschatz, pp. 218–293, 77, 377–378, 420–421.

[178] Cf. Rosenfeld, Studien, pp. 91ff. and 168ff.

Special devotion to the wounds Christ suffered in His passion began in the Middle Ages. The devotional emphasis in the medieval liturgy was directed primarily to the passion of Christ rather than to His resurrection and ascension. Christ's earthly existence took precedence over His divine origin and being in the minds of the medieval worshipper.[179] Medieval man desired to follow the history of Christ's passion and death in all its vivid and explicit detail. In monasteries the passion became a favorite subject for pious meditation. However, it is St. Bernard of Clairvaux, above all others, who is responsible for setting the trend toward devotion to the five wounds of Christ.[180] There actually existed a liturgical feast in the Church's calendar to commemorate the five wounds of Christ which was celebrated in solemn fashion in the Dominican monasteries of Germany in the Middle Ages.[181]

It is not surprising to find that the main source for much of Spee's inspiration and imagery surrounding the wounds of Christ in the GTB is the Dominican, Georg Munzius. In GTB Bk. III, chapter 18, Spee reveals his source:

Es pflegt zu geschehen, das unter dem lesen etwan geistlicher und schöner concepten, ein fromme andächtige Seel jeweilen nicht wenig erwecket, und entzündet wird in der liebe gegen Gott, und anderen Tugenden: und derohalben habe ich etliche schöne, bewögliche, kurtz- und ausserlesene geistliche Einfall zusammen gesucht, so ich bey Georgio Müntzio Prediger Ordens hin und wider gefunden, in die ordnung gesetzt, gebessert, und vermehret: welche sehr tauglich sein die einfeltige, andächtige, und sonderlich zarte reine hertzen zu allerhand wercken der hoffnung, liebe, zerknirschung dess hertzens, andacht, mittleyden, und dergleichen liebreichen anmutungen zubewegen, wan man sie in der stille mit auffmerksamkeit und mit etwas nachdenckens uberliset: in massen es etliche versucht, und also befunden haben. (GTB 381.9−21)[182]

Two other Catholic poets of the seventeenth century, Jakob Balde and Angelus Silesius, use this motif in their poetry.[183] But Spee is the first poet in the

---

[179] Josef Jungmann, Pastoral Liturgy (New York: Herder, 1962), p. 78, states: "It is significant, however, that meditation stops beside the sepulchre, or, if it does go on to the Resurrection ... it scarcely ever reaches the mystery of the Church. Christ glorified, who lives on in His humanity as Redeemer, is hardly ever seen."

[180] Cf. J. P. Bruni, "Devotion to the Five Wounds of Our Lord," New Catholic Encyclopedia, XIV, 1036.

[181] Cf. Stierli, "Devotion to the Sacred Heart," p. 106.

[182] Van Oorschot has shown it is the two books of Muntzius upon which Spee in this chapter bases his treatment: "Der Geistliche weiss gilgenstock" and the "New Gülden Berckwerck." GTB, 613. Van Oorschot offers selections from these two works in his commentary on the GTB. They indicate the presence of this cult of the wounds of Christ as those from which Spee derived his inspiration. GTB, 615ff.

[183] Cf. Jacobsen, Metamorphosen, pp. 142ff.

German language to give such emphasis to the cult of Christ's wounds, and thereby had a great influence on the entire religious poetry of his age, in particular Angelus Silesius.[184]

In *GTB,* Bk. II, the theme of Christ's wounds is still relatively infrequent in comparison with the manifold occurrences in Book III of the *GTB.* The emphasis in *GTB* Bk. II is on the soul's subjective state, which is a result of her being wounded either by desire for Christ [*GTB* 227.30 and *TN* (7):20,2–3]; by Christ's love [*TN* (7):15,1–2]; or through the soul's desire that Christ wound her heart with His love (*GTB* 202.7–9 and 202.16–17). In addition, the notion that sin has wounded the divine merciful heart appears (*GTB* 323.21–24). There are but three instances where the wounds of Christ are referred to: in *GTB* 201.16ff., the soul desires that its heart dwell in Jesus' wounds; in *GTB* 204.5, she desires to be refreshed within the wounds of Christ and, finally, in *GTB* 215.38 she asks to be buried in His wounded side.

The predominance given to that state, being wounded by love, and the soul's corresponding subjective reflection on that state rather than an objective contemplation of Christ's wounds, is in consonance with the overall thematic thrust of Book II which is basically a consideration of the nature of hope and "die liebe der begierlichkeit." In Book III, however, which is devoted mainly to the more selfless aspects of love, where the soul loses consciousness of self and becomes more aware of the beloved, the wounds of Christ become a more consistent and obvious object of contemplation. Spee presents these images of Christ's wounds repeatedly with the following goals in mind:

a) "zu erweckung aller-hand lieb-reichen affecten" (*GTB* 381.7–8);
b) "Gott zu loben" (*GTB* 431.6 and 432.1–3);
c) as helps to prayer before the receiving of Communion (*GTB* 521.21ff.);
d) to increase true sorrow for sin in the soul (*GTB* 521.28–29).

The following schema of the wound-motif in the *GTB* indicates both its function and relevance for the *TN.* Christ's wounds appear (cf. Table 4.1, p. 142). Whereas, on the one hand, there is a predominance of wound-images in which the soul is wounded in a passive manner by the force of love or in which she indicates her desire to be wounded by Christ, on the other hand, there is a heavy concentration of images portraying Christ's wounds. A similar thematic division is also reflected in the poems of the *TN.* The earlier poems in the *TN:* 2, (3), (7), and (11), show the soul as wounded with love. On the other hand, the later *TN* poems: (42), (43), 46, 47, 48, and 49, are replete with references to the wounds of Christ. *TN* poems 2, (3), (7), and (11) are love-songs of the so-called

---

184 Cf. Rosenfeld, *Fr. Spee,* p. 104. It should also be pointed out that Spee's own spiritual father, Ignatius Loyola, emphasized devotion to the passion and the suffering of Christ in his book, *The Spiritual Exercises.* Cf. Nos. 195 and 196 on p. 82.

"Sponsa-Zyklus."[185] In these poems the soul sings of her love-relationship with God. *TN* poems (42), (43), 46—49, however, are mainly meditative poems on Christ's passion and death.

The influence and/or similarity of the *GTB* with the *TN* regarding devotion to Christ's wounds is demonstrated by an analysis of *TN* images according to their function. When this schema is compared with the schema given above for the *GTB,* striking resemblances become apparent (cf. Table 4.2, p. 142). The notion that the sins of the soul wound Christ occur: [*TN* (16):7,5—8 and *GTB* 323.21ff.; 328.25ff.]. This is a biblical notion, based on the idea that man's sins were removed through Christ's passion and death.

In this image—category the poems of the *TN* exhibit a wide variety of metaphor applied to the wounds of Christ (cf. Table 4.3, p. 143). The wounds are made into constellations: "Seine gross- und kleine wunden // Er in himmel setzet ein" (*TN* 50:13,5—6). The presence of so many wound-images based on flowers and precious jewels in this category shows traits characteristic of the baroque decorative mode.

Spee's predilection for antithetical and oxymoronic expressions is also evident in this category. In *TN* (3):7,7—8 the soul experiences complete joy even though she is wounded with love. In *TN* (7):15,1—8 the soul is both wounded, and swoons in death, and is healthy and full of life in the same instance. In *TN* 34:206.24—207.1 Damon says he feels quite well despite the pain and wounds of love. In *TN* (43):47.1—8 Jesus says that, despite the burning pains and wounds of love, he desires to be extinguished through cold death. These antitheses in Spee demonstrate once again his affinity with the mystical mode of style.[186]

5. Joy

Images of joy and delight in Spee occur with less frequency than images of pain and sorrow. Interestingly, aside from isolated instances in *TN* poems: 1, 2, 29, 49 and 50, all of the images in this category originate in poems originally composed by Spee for the exercises of the *GTB*. To understand clearly the nature of these joy-images later transferred to the *TN* by Spee, examination again must be made of their environment in the *GTB,* since frequently the aim of the chapter in which they occur determines the form and function of these images.

The images of joy that Spee employs in Book II of the *GTB* are found in the poems which conclude chapters 8 and 16. In *GTB* Bk. II, chapters 1—8, Spee's

---

185 Cf. Rosenfeld, *Studien,* pp. 93ff.
186 For further examples among baroque poets, cf. Windfuhr, *Bildlichkeit,* pp. 230ff.

aim is to produce greater hope and trust in God's mercy and goodness within the soul of his spiritual daughter. No matter how great or many her sins may be, God in His mercy and love will forgive her and reconcile her to Himself. The source of her sinfulness and the sinfulness of mankind are rooted, basically, in man's desire for the transitory goods and pleasures of this world. But whatever exists in this world is "eitel und zergänglichkeit."[187] As Christ himself taught, whoever desires to follow Him to the heavenly Jerusalem, ". . . der müsse sich auff diser welt keiner mühe verdriessen; der müsse gern veracht und verworfen sein . . ." (GTB 152.24ff.).

But this commitment to Christ and to the things of eternity may produce spiritual aridity and desolation in the soul, which Spee describes at length in Book II, chapter 8, "Noch andere Werck der Hoffnung und vertrawen zu Gott in einer sehr grossen betrübnuss und betrangnuss dess hertzens" (GTB 162.17–18). To counteract this aridity and spiritual discomfort in the soul, Spee proposes a conversation with "Jesum an dem Creutz" (GTB 164.7ff.). As indicated above, a characteristic of Spee's spirituality is the cross of Christ as a source of joy. This basically involves a Christian and Ignatian paradox: to suffer with Christ is to experience the deepest type of spiritual joy.[188] This joy and spiritual consolation in the cross of Christ and His passion are reflected in the imagery in the poems accompanying this eighth chapter of Book II. In TN (17):7,5–8, the soul finds joy in the side of Christ:

> All meine freud verborgen
> In Jesu seiten ligt /
> Da find ich heut / und morgen
> Noch manches rein gedicht.

In TN (17):9,1–4 and 6,5–8 the soul cries out that all her joy lies in the cross of Christ:

> Im Creutz allein / man sagen /
> Ist freud / und fröligkeit:
> Wers wil mit Jesu tragen /
> Find endlich süssigkeit. [TN (17):6,5–8]

Joy also results when the soul is reconciled with God after her sins have been forgiven. This notion is reflected in TN (17):11,1–4 and TN (18):2,1–8. The soul's true hope lies in her rejection of earthly things and seeking her only joy in the heavenly Jerusalem which is reflected in TN (17):12,7–8 and 13,1–8.

---

187 In GTB 136.26–27 Spee says: "Ja freylich, freylich: Ich siehe wol, es ist doch alles eitel und zergäncklich, was auff diser erden ist." This actually is the answer Spee proposes for the daughter. Cf. also GTB 143.23ff.

188 Cf. Ignatius' formulation in the colloquy following the meditation on the "Kingdom" in the Spiritual Exercises, pp. 44–45.

Contempt for this world and joy in the things of the next world is a constantly recurring theme in the GTB.[189]

In the latter half of Book II, chapters 9—16, Spee concentrates not so much on "Gottvertrauen" as on "begierliche Liebe," its nature and its effects. Emphasis is again placed on the advantages to the soul if she will commit herself to heavenly riches rather than to earthly joys. Spee points out in GTB 181.7ff. that the things of this earth rapidly pass away and do not bring true joy. It is within this context that the long poem on the decaying flower was written [TN (13)]. The soul should seek after God and his heavenly treasures. This will bring her true satisfaction, fulfillment and advantage, "begierliche Liebe."

Moreover, God's goodness can cause the soul's heart "für unerträglichem lust und freud in stück zerspringen" (GTB 189.17—20). The last chapter within this grouping, Book II, chapter 16, that is concerned with "begierliche Liebe," consists almost entirely of poems which, as Spee writes in the GTB, have the following purpose:

> Damitt du dise woch noch etliche liebreiche begierden zu Gott jeweilen erwecken mögest, habe ich dir allhie etliche schöne geistliche Liebvers gemacht, darauss du sehen kanst die natur der begierlichen liebe: dieselbe magstu zu einer geistlichen ergetzlichkeit an statt gewöhnlicher ubung uberlesen. (GTB 220.3—7)

In conjunction with Spee's aim to turn the soul from earthly to heavenly realities: "Weil die hoffnung in sich begreifft ein verlangen und begierd, auch grossschetzung der himmlischen, hingegen aber verachtung der irrdischen sachen . . ." (GTB 179.3—5), the images of joy in the TN poems: (7), (3), (6), (8), (5), and (4) depict the soul in her love-union with Christ (cf. Table 5.1, p. 143).

The images of joy which were originally composed in the context of Book III are found in TN (24) from Book III, chapter 5; TN (20) and (22) from Book III, chapter 8; TN (15) and (16) from Book III, chapter 9; and TN (28) from Book III, chapter 7. Book III, chapters 4 to 8, have as their principal theme the appropriateness of praise to the Creator on the part of creation. Spee clearly equates the praise of God with the practice of "die liebe der gutwilligkeit." "Mein Kind, wan du hörest, dass Gott dein Herr gelobt, und gepriesen wird, empfindestu alssdann in deinem hertzen, dass dir solches recht gefalle, dass er also gelobet werde? Wan du nun solches empfindest, ists ein zeichen, dass du Gott liebest" (GTB 289.18—21). In all the poems which fall within this

---

[189] Cf. GTB 179.3—5; 212.32; 213.25ff.; 181.7ff.; and 341.9ff. God alone is the source of true joy and happiness. In GTB 249.19ff., Spee states: "Es vergehet alles gleich wie der schaum auff dem wasser: keine wollust ist hie bestendig. . . . Im himmel aber da ist alles; und kanst alles haben, alle lust und alle freud, in ewigkeit." Cf. also 217.22ff. and 189.2ff.

praise-context of the *GTB*, the soul finds joy in creation praising God [*TN* (22) and (24), *passim*]; in the beauty of nature in its praise-function [*TN* (22):5,1–8; 7,1–8]; and in the perfection of the angelic natures reflecting the perfection of their Creator [*TN* (24):1,1–8].

The remaining images of joy are clustered in *TN* (15) and (16) from Book III, chapter 9: "Noch andere Werck der liebe, und ist zerknirschung dess Hertzens." Contrition is a work of love, since the soul repents of her sins because she has offended God Who is all-good. In *TN* (15) and (16) a spirit of penitence brings joy because it brings about a reconciliation with God whom she has offended [*TN* (15):18,1–8]. The reconciliation with God causes the soul to exclaim: "Für wunder schier ich bleibe stumm // Die sprach ist fast ersessen" [*TN* (16):17,3–4].

The foregoing discussion of the mutual relationship and interaction between the text of the *GTB* and the poems of the *TN* verifies that images of joy in the *TN* can be summarized, in the following schema, according to their overall functional aspects (cf. Table 5.2, p. 143).

Structurally, the outstanding rhetorical figures in this image-category are oxymoron and antithesis, as shown by the following examples: when the soul dies of love she lives "in lüsten" (*TN* 2:7,6); the burning flame of Christ's love brings her both sorrow and delight simultaneously [*TN* (3):6,5–8]; the wound of love causes the soul to sway with pure joy [*TN* (3):7,7–8]; Jesus' love brings joy and sorrow [*TN* (7):17,4–5]. The love-experience itself causes her tears of both sorrow and joy [*TN* (7):21,4–6].

Stylistically, Spee's images of joy exhibit characteristics of both the affective and the mystical modes. The application of affective-pathetic imagery to the sufferings and to the passion of Christ and to the love-experience of the soul with Christ is a stylistic trait found frequently among religious writers of the seventeenth century. Moreover, the use of oxymoron and paradox is a traditional rhetorical feature among mystical writers and poets.

6. Sighs

Images based on sighs in the *GTB* and the *TN* occur with such frequency that a separate division has been made because of their important role in both works. Sigh-images frequently occur in conjunction with tears and weeping (nine times in the *TN* alone), but much more often they stand alone.[190] To understand fully

---

[190] The combined occurrences of tears and sighs is a Petrarchan motif found frequently in baroque pastoral peotry. Nowak, "Versuch," pp. 142ff., discusses this motif at length.

the role of sigh-imagery in the *TN*, their specific function in the chapters of the *GTB* must first be clarified. As will become evident from the following analysis, sighs, as distinguished from weeping, assume a more positive function in the methodology employed by Spee in the *GTB*. Tears are frequently but a passive reaction in the emotional part of the soul, whereas sighing frequently involves an effective, rational, and not merely emotional recollection of the soul's powers when she is confronted by a proposed course of action or program of life in the exercises of the *GTB*.[191]

In the *GTB* Spee gives extensive directions regarding the role of these "Seufftzer" in the soul's response to God and what he intends their function to be. The following are examples: "Erstlich, werden hie geübet zwölff unterschiedliche werck des glaubens; dan weil du auff jeden articul etwas still haltest, und dar zwischen seufftzest, . . ." (*GTB* 41.13–15); ". . . und wo ein solches * Sternlein steht, da thue einen tieffen Seufftzer; halte ein wenig still; und gehe darnach fort" (*GTB* 256.9–11). "Darumb wo dises Sterlein steht*, da soltu (allemahl ein wenig still halten / unnd betrachten / das ist / da soltu) das, was du gesprochen, etwas tieffer mit dem hertzen bedencken, . . ." (*GTB* 521.37–522.3). They also play an important role in the overall methodology of the *GTB*.[192]

This may be seen more clearly through an analysis of the basic structure of the *GTB* chapters. The basic structure used by Spee in each chapter of the *GTB*, is as follows:

a) A theoretical introduction and explanation of the particular goal (usually the practice of one of the theological virtues of faith, hope, or charity) of the ensuing chapter, occasionally in the form of a parable.
b) A series of questions posed by Spee based on the content of the particular chapter, usually formulated with a view toward a practical application or response from the soul.
c) The answer of the spiritual daughter to the question proposed by Spee, frequently concluded with the notation "Seufftzer."

These "Seufftzer"-notations occur so frequently that no attempt will be made at a quantitative enumeration for each chapter. Frequently the simple word "Seufftzer" stands by itself.[193] The full meaning of the term "Seufftzer" can be gathered by its other occurrences, in the form of phrases like the following:

---

191   For an analysis of the notion of "Recollection": in this sense, cf. the *Oxford Dictionary of the Christian Church,* ed. Frank L. Cross (London: Oxford Press, 1957), p. 1142.
192   For a more detailed discussion on this methodology, cf. Van Oorschot, "GTB II," pp. 113ff.
193   Cf. *GTB* 43:30; 44.3; 36.12,24,36 and *passim.*

"Nun sage dann ob du dieses alles glaubest? Bedencke dich allhie ein wenig, und dan antworte mir; also, dass du nach der antwort auch noch, mit einem tieffen Seufftzer beschliessest an statt einer pausen, und also auch hernacher" (GTB 36.8—11). "Seufftze, und ruhe, ein wenig: und also thue in allen articulen, wo dises Sternlein * steht; dan dass solle bedeuten, dass du allda etwas ruhen, und seufftzen sollest, an statt einer pausen: weil solches das gemüt ein wenig erquicket" (GTB 53.13—16). "Meinestu dises auch recht ernstlich, so thue widerumb einen tieffen Seufftzer" (GTB 251.17—18).

In these short directives Spee clearly intends a positive response, an act of recollection on the part of the soul. She is to collect herself, pause, consider, and reflect before making her personal commitment and response to the proposed question or challenge which Spee has made in the pertinent exercise. But the full potential of these "sighs," these positive acts of recollection and reflection unfolds with further reading of the GTB. After sighing, the soul frequently emits an aspiration (GTB 168.12ff.; 290.10); or a prayer to God or Christ (GTB 343.6ff.; 375.36ff.) The sigh then becomes an actual aspiration or prayer. The flowering and blossoming of these sighs into poetic form occurs frequently. The following TN poems are the end-result of this sigh-technique in the GTB. They occur in Book II, chapter 16: "Noch andere ubung der begierlichen Liebe," in a context where "die liebe der begierlichkeit" is the central theme. In this connection Spee, in his introduction, links up sighs with "begierliche liebe:" "Durch die Hoffnung seind wir Gottes begierig; wir warten, verlangen, seufftzen nach ihm: wir hoffen und begehren auch alles guttes von ihm: . . ." (GTB 20.27—29). The titles of the following GTB poems indicate the prominence given to the sigh-technique in Spee's methodology. "Seufftzen einer Gott-liebenden seel zu Gott, darin die eigenschafften einer volkommenen begierlichen liebe eigentlich abgemahlet seind" [TN (7)]; "Noch andere Seufftzen der Gesponss Jesu" [TN (3), (6)]; "Andere Seufftzen der Gesponss Jesu" [TN (8), (5)]; "Noch andere Seufftzen der andächtigen Seelen nach Jesum" [TN (4)]. The titles were later changed by Spee after he transferred them to the TN, although the title of TN (5) still expresses the sigh-notion in its caption: "Die gesponss Jesu seufftzet nach ihrem Bräutigam, und ist ein spiel der Nachtigalen mit einer Echo und widerschall." The content, however, of the poems has remained the same.

As a consequence of the interrelationship between the sigh-technique in the methodology Spee employs in the GTB, and the poems of the TN and the GTB as poetic expressions of these sighs, the following conclusions may be made: the poems in the TN taken from the GTB are, in many instances, actually lyrical outpourings of the soul determined in their formulation and imagery by their specific function as answers to the exercise-technique in the GTB; these TN poems are fundamentally acts of yearning, longing, and desire for union with God. These poems embody prayerful acts of recollection, the desire to practice the virtues of faith, hope, and charity, expressions of sorrow for sin, and sympathy with Christ suffering as in GTB 514.12 and 432.11. Such motifs, incorporated in the soul's sighs in the GTB, appear again in an identical functional-recurrence in the TN.

In this sigh-technique Spee once again shows the influence of Ignatian spirituality. Spee's direction to the soul that she recollect herself, pause, and consider before making her response, that she respond through prayers of longing and yearning under the rubric of "Seufftzer," is basically the application of a distinct Ignatian technique.[194] Again, Ignatius stresses the need for recollection: "I will remain quietly meditating upon the point in which I have found what I desire, without any eagerness to go on till I have been satisfied."[195] Ignatius directs the exercitant not to hurry through the meditations and considerations but to pause, reflect, recollect and relish the truths presented.

Another characteristic in the Spiritual Exercises of Ignatius is the colloquy, the intimate converse between the soul and God in the form of a prayerful response to the proposed exercise. A clear parallel between Ignatius and Spee in this regard can be found in the colloquy Ignatius proposes in the meditation on "Sin" in nos. 45–54 of the Exercises, with special attention to number 53, and the corresponding colloquy-form in the GTB 164–170. In those instances where Spee concludes an exercise with a lyrical poem of prayerful yearning on the part of the soul, the similarity between the GTB/TN poem and the Ignatian colloquy is striking, particularly where the GTB poems bear the title "Seufftzen."

Against the background of this sigh-technique and sigh-function in the GTB interesting conclusions can be drawn with regard to their occurrence in the TN. Twenty-one poems in the TN contain images of the soul or Christ sighing. The vast majority are the sighs of the soul. The majority of the sigh-poems of the TN which were taken from the GTB come from Book II, chapter 16 and Book III, chapter 9. Book II, chapter 16, is an exercise in "der begierlichen liebe." All of

---

194 Ignatius, in the Exercises, makes the following statements in his directions to the exercitant:

Let him adhere to the points and add only a short or summary explanation. The reason for this is that when one in meditating takes the solid foundation of facts, and goes over it and reflects on it for himself, he may find something that makes them a little clearer or better understood. This may arise either from his own reasoning, or from the grace of God enlightening his mind. Now this produces greater spiritual relish and fruit than if one in giving the Exercises had explained and developed the meaning at great length. For it is not much knowledge that fills and satisfies the soul, but the intimate understanding and relish of the truth.

Cf. Spiritual Exercises, pp. 1–2.
195 Cf. Exercises, p. 36. Apart from the "sigh-poems" listed above [TN (7), (3), (6), (8), (5), and (4)], the following poems also occur in the GTB in the form of colloquies and are actually called "Seufftzer": 211.19–213.4; 218.25–219.32; 224.33–227.16; 227.17–231.4.

these poems are entitled "Seufftzer." The sigh-images which occur in these poems embody the soul's yearning and desire for Christ the beloved [TN (4):2,3;8,2—4]; or the sighs are emitted because of the pain or sorrow involved in her love for Christ, an aspect of "begierliche liebe;" e.g., TN (5):11,1—2; (6):11,1—4.

Book III, chapter 9, is an exercise on "zerknirschung dess hertzens" (GTB 322.5ff.). The TN poems in this chapter embody sighs of contrition and penitence [TN (15):17,1—4; and (16):3,4]. The prayerful aspect of these sighs is maintained in TN (14):80,16—19:

> Nim auff von mir geringen
> Ja nim die seufftzer an /
> So mir von hertzen dringen
> Durch läre Wolcken-baan,

where the soul asks the heavenly Father to accept her sighs which will be sent to Him under the form of the petitions in the "Our Father." The vertical concept, of the sigh climbing up through the winds and the clouds to God in the form of prayerful aspirations, also appears in the simile in TN 9:2,5—8:

> Baldt JESU dir von hertzen
> Ich schickt ein seufftzer tieff /
> So gleich zum Himel-kertzen /
> Recht auff in lüfften lieff,

and in the verbal forms: (cf. Table 6.1, p. 144).

Based on the foregoing analysis and the function of sighs in the GTB, the religious aspect of these sighs in both the GTB and the TN is clearly evident. Even though they may not evolve into the explicit prayer-form in the strict sense of this word,[196] they nevertheless are basically profound movements of the soul to God embodying petition, contrition, and longing. The love-sighs in Spee are essentially distinct, by reason of their object and goal, from the love-sighs in secular poetry.

The religious, mystical nature of these sighs becomes more apparent through analysis of their function in the poem on the Trinity in TN 29. The sighs in the GTB previously have been demonstrated to be positive, effective responses to God's revelation, and to God Himself, through the soul's desire to practice the theological virtues. Their function in the GTB has shed light on their use in the TN, and, theologically speaking, they find their fulfillment and deepest significance in TN 29, vv. 23—30. In this poem God the Father sighs in love toward His Son: "Der Vatter seufftzet ohne ruh // Zu seinem Sohn verliebet"

---

196 Cf. the article on "Prayer" in the Oxford Dictionnary of The Christian Church, pp. 1096—1097.

(*TN* 29:23,1–2). God the Son sighs in return: "Der Sohn ihm wider seufftzet zu // Sich gleichem feur ergibet" (23,3–4). Their love-sighs attest to their mutual love: "Mit seufftzen hin / mit seufftzen her // Bezeugens ihr verlangen" (23, 7–8) and in *TN* 29:24,1–8:

> Aha der Vatter seufftzen thut
> Zu seinem Sohn geschwinde;
> Ahà der Sohn auch seufftzet gut
> Mit eben selbem winde.
> O schöner Sohn! du schönes Bild!
> Nun lieb ich dich so sehre.
> O schöner Vatter! Vatter milt!
> Zu dir mich eben kehre.

This mutual, inter-personal love-sighing between the Father and the Son results in the procession *(ab aeterno)* of God the Holy Spirit, who is the embodiment of the love of the Father and the Son:

> Schau da dan kräfftig windet ab
> Der seufftzer ihrer beyden.
> Der süsse Geist / die süsse gab /
> O freud / ob allen freuden!
> Der Sohn / und Vatter; der / und der
> Gar lieb- und freundlich hauchet
> Auss einem hertzen her / und her
> Der athem süsslich rauchet. (*TN* 29:27,1–8)

Spee has chosen the images of the mutual sighing of the Father and the Son to connote the mode of procession of the Holy Spirit in the Trinity. The close connection between the images of sighing and breathing applied to the Third Person of the Trinity, the Holy Spirit, stems from the usual connotation given to the words, sighs and breathing, and applied theologically. The Holy Spirit is called the "spirit," from the Latin *spirare*. The term is used, by analogy, with the manner in which we draw a deep breath or sigh, as expressive of the attraction of the will to some desired object.[197]

Throughout the *GTB* and the *TN* Spee has applied sighs and sighing in this sense of attraction, yearning, and desire of the will for some desired object [*TN* (4):2,3; 9:2,5–8; *GTB* 515.30; 20.28 and *passim*]. In *TN* 29:27,1–8 the sighs as the sign of mutual attraction between the Father and the Son, on the level of the trinitarian relations, results in the embodiment of all love and desire, the Holy

---

197 Cf. L. J. McGovern, "Processions, Trinitarian," *New Catholic Encyclopedia*, XI, 821–823.

Spirit. Here all human sighing and yearning finds its prime analogate and theological completion. The sighs of the soul in the GTB and the TN are ultimately ordained to this object, i.e., the longing for the final possession of the end-result of sighing, who is God Himself. Herein lies perhaps one source of Spee's mysticism and mystical imagery.

One concluding note: Spee's use of the expression "Da seuffzet ich von Seelen grundt" [TN (4):2,3; 8,2]; and similar phrases which appear in GTB 167.35ff., and 518.11ff., indicate a striking similarity to both mystical and Pietistic terminology.[198]

7. Tears

Within the sphere of human emotion, not only sighing but weeping, crying and the tearful-reaction are characteristic of Spee's imagery and spiritual technique. Previously, the soul's sighs have been demonstrated to be her attempt to make a positive, effective response to the challenge and the practice of the three theological virtues of faith, hope, and charity as presented by Spee in the exercises of the GTB. Entire TN and GTB poems are lyrical responses of love for God and yearning for the beloved, Christ, based on this sigh-technique. In analyzing images of tears and crying in Spee, another characteristic area of Spee's poetry emerges. Fourteen instances of tear-imagery are in the GTB poems, in addition to many more references in the prose text of the GTB itself. There are approximately forty-five tear image-occurrences in the TN.

Historically, tears and the gift of tears have been recognized as a characteristic trait among ascetics and mystics, particularly in monastic circles, from the earliest times into the late Middle Ages.[199] Teresa of Avila speaks of copious weeping in connection with her mystical ecstasies, although she is careful to warn that temperament may be a factor in this matter.[200] Tears are also characteristic of Ignatian mysticism.[201] In the first part of his *Spiritual Diary* Ignatius mentions the shedding of tears some 175 times, or an average of four

---

198 Langen, *Wortschatz*, p. 162, states: "Das Wort [Grund] ist in der Mystik einer der bekanntesten Termini. . . . Es ist hier Metapher für die Gottheit selbst, für die Seele und für den Vorgang der Unio mystica: im Seelengrund vollzieht sich die Vereinigung mit Gott. Die Zahl der Belege ist überaus gross. Für den Pietismus ist diese mystische Tradition ausschlaggebend."

199 Cf. R. Schulte, "Tränengabe," *Lexikon für Theologie und Kirche,* ed. Josef Hofer and K. Rahner, 2nd ed. (Freiburg: Herder, 1965), X, 305.

200 Cf. A. Poulain, *The Graces of Interior Prayer,* tr. L. Yorke Smith, 6th ed. (St. Louis, Mo.: Herder, 1950), pp. 169–170.

201 Cf. Joseph de Guibert, *The Jesuits their Spiritual Doctrine and Practice. A Historical Study,* tr. Wm. J. Young (Chicago: Loyola University, 1964), p. 62, footnote 83.

times a day, between February 2 and March 12, 1544.[202] This weeping took place principally whenever Ignatius celebrated mass and occurred with such frequency that Ignatius feared the loss of his eyesight.[203] Moreover, Ignatius explicitly directs the soul to beg for tears of compassion with regard to the meditations on the passion of Christ in the *Spiritual Exercises:*

> This will be to consider what Christ our Lord suffers in His human nature, or according to the passage contemplated, what he desires to suffer. Then I will begin with great effort to strive to grieve, be sad, and weep. In this way I will labor through all the points that follow.[204]

He also asks for compunction in the meditation on one's personal sins: "This is to ask for what I desire. Here it will be to ask for a growing and intense sorrow and tears for my sins."[205] Both of these themes recur in the *GTB* and the *TN*. The colloquy of tearful compassion with the beloved crucified is reflected in Christ's words to the soul in the *GTB* 164.10—16:

> Mein Kind, dein hertz ist betrübt, und meinem hertzen ist gar seltsam; spricht dein allerliebster Breutigam vom Creutz. Was wiltu machen? Gehe in dein kämmerlein, setze dich da nider zu meinen füssen, o mein hertziges ausserwehltes kind: Weine, und weine; seufftze, und seufftze; weine und seufftze; seufftze und weine, Lass fliessen dein hertz, und augen: lass winden und wehen deine seufftzer, lass gehen in lufften deine begierden. . . .

This is repeated in *GTB* 165.31—40. Correspondingly, the theme of compassion on the part of creation *(natura compatiens)* for Christ is found in the cycle of poems of the *TN*, the *Eklogen*, *TN* 37—41; the Passion Poems, *TN* 37—43; and Lamentations for the Crucified, *TN* 44—47; and in *GTB* 385.13,21; 387.25; 290.38; 391.11,15,20 and 523.18ff. Tears of compunction for sin occur in *GTB* 361.11—12, 388.30, and *TN* (15) and (16).

Other seventeenth-century poets, both secular and religious, employ the tear-motif.[206] But none of these poets employs the motif with the frequency and

---

202 *The Spiritual Journal of St. Ignatius Loyola,* tr. Wm. J. Young (Woodstock, Md.: Woodstock Press, 1958), pp. 1—34.

203 An authority on Catholic asceticism maintains that Ignatius' shedding of tears is unsurpassed in Catholic spiritual literature:

> Such is the fact in its material reality. I do not know of any equivalent example in Catholic spiritual literature. This Catholic tradition has indeed always had a very high esteem of tears, of compunction (the compunction of fear and that of love), and more still of the mystical gift of tears. But it seems to me that no other saint, man or woman, has in practice given to these tears a place equal to that of Ignatius.

Cf. de Guibert, *Jesuits,* pp. 62—63.

204 Cf. p. 195.

205 *Spiritual Exercises,* p. 55.

206 Cf. Jacobsen, *Metamorphosen,* pp. 122ff.; and Beckmann, "Motive," p. 42, for lengthy discussions of this motif. Nowak maintains that Johann Hermann Schein (1586—1630) influenced Spee in his use of this motif. Cf. "Versuch," pp. 321—322.

intensity of Spee. In addition, his similarity with Ignatius' own religious experience and expressions in this regard cannot be merely that of chance occurrence, but indicates the continued influence of Ignatius on his thought and poetry.

In comparing the GTB and the TN, the former has a far wider range of application with regard to the soul's tears. Consequently, all the tear-themes of the TN can be found expressed in the GTB. Functionally, tear-images in the TN can be summarized in the following basic, three-fold schema:

1) tears which result from the soul's painful longing for union with Christ;
2) tears of compunction over past sins and transgressions;
3) tears of compassion for Christ in His passion and suffering.

Divisions 2 and 3 compare with themes from the *Exercises* of Ignatius. The first two divisions (1 and 2) stem from poems originally in the GTB and, apart from TN (16) and (15), are all found in the GTB, Book II. The final division (3), embraces poems from the later section of poems in the TN poems on Christ's Passion which were the last to be composed by Spee.

With the basic, three-fold schema above (tears of yearning, tears of compunction, and tears of compassion) the following functional categories can be constructed to provide a complete analysis of tear-images in the TN. A corresponding list of occurrences in the GTB will be indicated where appropriate:

1) The soul weeps because of her painful love-experience with Christ (cf. Table 7.1, p. 144).
2) The soul weeps in longing for the heavenly Jerusalem and Christ.
3) The soul weeps because this world separates her from her beloved.
4) The soul weeps out of compunction and sorrow for her sins which have displeased and angered God. Correspondingly, in the GTB the soul weeps in joy over God's grace which has reconciled her to Him (46.31–33; 46.37–47.2), and in 47.5–12 where the soul's tears are compared to melting snow. A similar figure occurs in TN (11):2,1–3,8, where Mary Magdalen's tears of love are compared to melting, tearful snow:

> Zwar gleich / wan je zu weilen /
> Zur Frühlings morgen-stund /
> Mit ersten Sonnen-pfeilen /
> Mit erster hitz verwund /
> Herab von berg- und steinen /
> Von felssen hoch / und geh
> Zerfleusst in sanfftes weinen
> Der lind entlassen schnee:

> Fast eben gleicher massen
> Das weib von lieb verwund /
> In lauter zähr zerlassen /
> Zerfloss in thränen rund:
> Begierd mit heissen pfeilen
> Ihr beyde augen schmeltzt /
> Und abwerts beyder theilen
> Die runde tröpfflein weltzt.

5) Christ weeps in His search for the lost sheep.

6) Nature weeps at Christ's sufferings (*GTB* 523.24—31).

7) Halton weeps in sorrow at the thought of Christ's torment (*TN* 45:290,25—291,6), and in *GTB* 392.6ff. we find parallels to this.

8) Mary, Christ's mother, weeps at the death of her Son (*TN* 44:18,1—8).

Categories 1, 2, and 3 correspond to Book II of the *GTB*, "die liebe der begierlichkeit," which characterizes a love that is more introspective and self-satisfying. Categories 4 through 7 correspond to *GTB*, Book III, "die liebe der gutwilligkeit," which equals a selfless, altruistic love that is more concerned with the Thou than with the I.

Paraphrases for tears in the *TN* are (cf. Table 7.2, p. 145). An interesting metaphorical use occurs in *TN* (6):11,6 and *TN* 45:291,2,4, where the soul calls her tears "brod" and "speiss und trank."[207] In the first instance [*TN* (6):11,1—8], her tears help to nourish her in the face of her love-sickness:

> Drumb stätig nass von zähren /
> Die seufftzer steigen auff:
> Sie stündlich sich vermehren /
> Unzahlbar wird der hauff.
> Die thränen mich ernehren /
> Seind meine speiss / und tranck /
> Von zähren muss ich zehren /
> Weil bin von liebe kranck.

In *TN* 45:291,1—6 Halton is so overcome by grief at Christ's suffering that he falls exhausted to the ground, but his tears sustain him.

A variety of verbal metaphors occurs in connection with tears and weeping in the *TN* (cf. Table 7.3, p. 145). Similes occur in *TN* 2:3,1—4; (11):2,1—3,8; and 39:18,3—4. Oxymoron occurs only once, in *TN* (7):21,5—6. Where nature weeps in compassion for the suffering of Christ, paraphrase abounds. These have been

---

[207] This is a common Petrarchan motif discussed at length in Nowak, "Versuch," p. 149. A similar notion, tears as a means of strength, occurs in Ignatius' *Spiritual Journal* for February 18, 1544 (*Spiritual Journal*, p. 11.).

listed above under division 6. Simile and paraphrase are combined in *TN* 39:18,3–4, where the moon's tears are "wie der schwartze Mohr." Oxymoron is used to describe the paradoxical nature of the love-experience, its "freud und leid," in both the *TN* and the *GTB*. The images in this category with their emphasis on the soul's longing, compassion and compunction exhibit similarities with the baroque affective and mystical categories of style.

8. Taste and Smell

In this category, images based on the sense of taste and smell (principally taste), and the traditional "bitter-sweet" antithesis to describe the effects of love in the soul of the lover, are a pronounced feature in Spee. Sappho was the first to apply this antipodal notion to describe the joy and sorrow contrast of the love-experience.[208] The Petrarchan school appropriated the bitter-sweet love antithesis. Spee's use of this Petrarchan notion in the poems of the *TN* is another example of "geistlicher Kontrafaktur," the absorption of a secular theme or motif and its consequent "canonization" when put into the context of mystical or religious poetry. In Spee the bitter-sweet antithesis, a secular motif, is sacralized and applied exclusively to a description of the soul's love-relation to God or Christ.

Images based on the senses of taste and smell, while occurring with considerable frequency in the poems of the *TN*, appear only twice in the poems of the *GTB* which do not also appear in the *TN*. In *GTB* 51.35–37 the soul sings with King David that the wounds of her sin "stincken sehr; und faulen mehr;" in *GTB* 198.1–4 Cupid's arrows enflame the worldly heart "mit süsser hitz." However, neither of these two images recurs later in the *TN*. The majority of the taste and smell images are found in those *TN* poems that originated in the *GTB* and of these poems, aside from *TN* (28) and (43), all were composed in the context of the *GTB*, Book II, where the emphasis is on "die liebe der begierlichkeit."

In Book II, chapter 8, where Spee intends to lead the soul to a deeper trust in God when she finds herself in a mood of desolation, the cross is pictured as the source of sweetness: "Wers will mit *Jesu* tragen // Find endlich süssigkeit" [*TN* (17):6,7–8]. The cross as a source of joy and consolation, as previously noted, is a characteristic of Spee's spirituality.[209] This notion is repeated later in *GTB*

---

208 Cf. Hans Pyritz, *Flemings Liebeslyrik* (Leipzig: 1932), pp. 15ff.
209 For the relationship of this theme with Ignatian spirituality, cf. K. Rahner, "Ignatian Mysticism of Joy in the World," *Theological Investigations,* tr. Karl Kruger, III, 280ff.

403.7–8. In *TN* (18):5,5–8 and 6,1–8, Christ Himself is pictured in images reminiscent of the Song of Songs. In the application of these images to Christ, Spee desires to turn the soul's attention away from herself and from her self-pity by showing Christ as desirable and attractive. He can bring her joy and peace (*GTB* 166.38–167.2).

A preponderant number of bitter-sweet images occurs within the context of Book II, chapter 16. The aim of Spee's chapter is ". . . darauss du sehen kannst die natur der begierlichen liebe . . ." (*GTB* 220.5–6). Spee's poems in this chapter picture the soul yearning and sighing for her beloved. Here the taste of Jesus' love surpasses anything on earth: "Nichts schmäcket mir auff gatzer welt // Als JESU lieb alleine" [*TN* (8):8,1–2].[210] The painfulness and the bliss of the soul's interior state as a result of this longing are conveyed by means of the traditional Petrarchan bitter-sweet antithesis. Christ's love is a "süsses band" [*TN* (7):6,4]. The soul's heart could break "für süsser noth" [*TN* (7):13,4]. The pain of love is sweet and bitter:

> Süss ist der schmertz /
>   Gesund dass hertz /
>   Für freud ich muss ermatten?
> Ja kranck dass hertz /
>   Herb ist der schmertz /
>   Bey Sonnenschein ist schatten. [*TN* (7):14,1–6]

Spee continues to emphasize the antithetical nature of this love of the soul in several of the remaining sponsa poems. The arrows of *Christus-Cupido* are "süss/herb" [*TN* (11):8,3]. The torment and pain of love are sweet to the soul [*TN* 2:2,6 and (11):27,3].

These images describe the psychological and subjective reaction of the soul to her experience of Christ's love. They are used to describe the soul's paradoxical reaction when she loves Christ: her attraction to Christ is now shown to be a sweetness; her separation from Him, on the other hand, a bitterness or a sweet pain. Concern for the beloved, "die liebe der gutwilligkeit," is obliterated because of the soul's own self-involvement and absorption in her own experience and advantage ("die liebe der begierlichkeit"). The inner logic that connects Spee's aim in *GTB* Book II, the practice of the virtue of hope, and the poetic images contained in the poems of Bk. II is once again demonstrated. "Begierliche liebe" stresses the subject and not the object of love. Spee's images reflect this subjective aspect.

The bitter-sweet antithesis does not occur outside of the sponsa poems in the *TN*, of which the majority stem from *GTB*, Book II. Only in *TN* 34 are traces

---

210 Medieval mystics use similar expressions. Cf. Lüers, *Sprache*, pp. 256–259.

again found of the sweetness of love's fire (34:206,25; 207,1), or of the
sweetness of suffering from love; in *TN* 34:207,7—8: Damon and Halton reflect
upon the bitter-sweet effect of their love for the Christ-Child. The remaining
images from this category merely involve the use of "süss" adjectively, plus a
substantive:

1) to describe the beauty of nature as praising God [*TN* (28):9,5—8; 23:14,2;
   and (22):3,7];
2) to describe Christ's wounds (*TN* 48:308,17—20; *GTB* 385.27ff.; 406.21—23);
3) applied theologically to the Holy Spirit (*TN* 29:27,3,7—8; 30,1).

The basic image-structures occurring in this category are antithesis and
paraphrase. The seventeenth-century preference for antithesis and oxymoron has
already been noted. In the present category these figures occur when
image-function details the soul's psychological emotions of attraction and
distaste in her relationship with the beloved. The following paraphrases also
appear: Christ's love is described as a "süsses band" [*TN* (7):6,4—5]; Christ's
cheeks are called "Brunn und bach der süssigkeit" [*TN* (18):6,7—8]; the Holy
Spirit is a "süsse gab" (*TN* 29:27,3); bees are called "Völcklein honig süss" (*TN*
23:14,2).

The majority of these images of taste can be categorized from a stylistic point
of view as "geistlicher Petrarkismus" in the mystical mode. Where nature praises
God (category 1 above) the style is more decorative than mystical. Religious
poetry in the seventeenth century, as noted, abounds in these bitter-sweet
oxymoron borrowed from the Petrarchan school.[211]

9. The Human Anatomy

The analysis of images based on parts of the human body will center for the
most part on Christ since His figure predominates above all others in both the
TN and the *GTB*. Spee's picture of Christ, reconstructed on the basis of these
images, is typical of other contemporary seventeenth-century love poetry. The
beloved, Christ, seemingly differs little when compared with descriptions of the
coy mistresses and feminine beauties of seventeenth-century secular poets. As in
Gryphius, Harsdörffer, and Fleming, Christ, in Spee's descriptions, is rarely
portrayed as a total form or as a synthetic whole. He is analytically dissected and
described according to the various parts of His human profile, such as: the head,

---

211 For further examples among religious poets of this feature, cf. Marie-Luise
Wolfskehl, "Die Jesusminne in der Lyrik des deutschen Barock" (Diss. Giessen, 1934),
p. 148, footnote 135. (Sonderdruck aus den Giessener Beiträgen zur dt. Philol., hrsg. von
O. Behagel und A. Götze, 34. Bd.). Cf. also Nowak, "Versuch," p. 232. This rhetorical
feature is continued later in Pietistic circles. Langen, *Wortschatz*, pp. 374—375.

lips, teeth, eyes, and cheeks. His total human form is seen as a composite of isolated units. The tendency to consider the human form in its parts and not as a totality in the seventeenth century has been attributed to a general lack of subjectivity and to a more objective type of poetic vision and technique. The harmony which would result from an appreciation of the beloved's form as a totality is disrupted by the poet's description of the beloved's various physiognomic features.[212]

It is interesting to note that this tendency to emphasize analysis over synthesis, to consider an essence or object in its constituent elements rather than in its totality, is not only typical of Spee's poetic descriptions of Christ as a person, but also of the structural features of the chapters and exercises in the *GTB*. When Spee, for example, uses the cosmos as an illustration in an exercise whose aim is to offer praise to God, he does not view the cosmos as a total phenomenon, but reduces the cosmos to its various structural components: the ocean, land, heaven, earth, the classes of living creatures. This occurs, for example, in Book III, chapter 7, 303.34–304.18. Devotion to the various wounds of Christ is another instance of this tendency to emphasize the parts of the form over the synthetic whole. To increase the soul's devotional participation at Mass, the soul is advised "... die gantze Welt in die Funff Wunden Christi legen." Thereupon each of the five wounds of Christ is enumerated in succession: *GTB* 496.4–20, and 399.36–400.19. In Book III, chapter 20, 431.5–432.36 each hour of the day is assigned its special role in praising God.[213] Moreover this lack of synthetic approach and the emphasis on analysis is characteristic of the general philosophical outlook of the seventeenth century.[214]

The *locus classicus* for this analytical approach to reality with regard to the human anatomy image-field occurs in the *GTB* 522.14–526.20, "Liebreiches gebett zu Jesu den gekreuzigten, mitt dem mund und hertzen zu sprechen," which occurs in a context where Spee is preparing the soul for receiving Christ in communion during the celebration of Mass. Devotion to Christ under the aspect of His head, hair, face, eyes, cheeks, mouth, neck, hands, breast, and feet are presented in succession in *GTB* 522.14–526.20:

a) His hair is described as "gelber alss das golt aus Orienten" (523.3);
b) His face is compared to the "heller morgenstern, schöner Mon, heitere Son" (523.8–9);

---

212 Cf. Beckmann, "Motive," pp. 49ff.
213 This analytic process is further evident in the accumulation of endless metaphors for objects such as the cross. In Book III, chapter 8, devotion to the cross of Christ produces the following litany of poetic comparisons. The cross is a "Schifflein, Stab, Leiter, Thron, Schul and beth" (*GTB* 390.15–34). It is also called "Abendstern, brunnen, garten, Rosenbusch, blumen, Edelstein, feuer, Regenbogen, Apoteck." Cf. also *GTB* 402.25–403.26.
214 Cf. Van Oorschot, "GTB II," p. 156.

c) His eyes are like gleaming crystals and beaming diamonds (523.13–14);

d) His cheeks are "gleich wie die allerliebstichste lilgen und rosen" (523.38–524.1);

e) His neck is "schneeweiss," a "helffenbeinere thurn," a "marmere Seul" (524.15–16);

f) His feet are "weisse alabasterne" (525.19).

Many of these metaphors are literary conventions common to other seventeenth-century poets, some of which have already been indicated in the image-categories treated above, as: color, flowers, heart, and wounds. A comprehensive treatment of these images pertaining to Christ's physiognomy from the aspect of their rhetorical style and structure makes this evident. Their function is clearly apparent: to present Christ as a lovable poetic figure and humanly attractive to the Spouse.

The image of Jesus, as described in the poems in the *TN*, is not much different from the beautiful lovers portrayed elsewhere in seventeenth-century poetry. To the modern reader He appears effeminate, soft, and epicene but this results from Spee's frequent adoption of common secular motifs and current poetic conventions, in particular the Petrarchan tradition.[215]

The following analysis is confined to the ten poems of the *TN* where Christ is described at some length. These ten poems can be subdivided into three main groups. In the first group of poems Christ is the beautiful lover pursued and sought after by the soul. Here Christ appears not unlike the lover in the Song of Songs [*TN* 2, (8), and (18)]. In the second group He is the beautiful Christ-Child (*TN* 33 and 34). In the third group He is the suffering Christ [*TN* 9, 10, 42, and (43)]. Many common seventeenth-century conventional images are applied without discrimination to all three of these categories. Where these images occur in other baroque poets, reference will be made in the table to Windfuhr's catalogue of images and to Jacobsen's study in the examples which follow.[216] These images are stylistically all of the "dekorative Metaphorik" (cf. Table 9.1, p. 145).

Aside from these decorative and ornamental descriptions the following paraphrases occur (cf. Table 9.2, p. 146).

The following extended similes appear in *TN* 2:1 and 2, where "Jesu Wangen / stirn, und mundt" are compared to "die reine Stirn der Morgenröth" (*TN* 2:1,2); "Der Frühling nach dem Winter öd" (*TN* 2:1,3); "die weiche brust der

---

215 Cf. Jacobsen, *Metamorphosen*, pp. 83, 88, and 80; Beckmann, "Motive," pp. 26ff. It is quite likely that Spee himself read Petrarch; cf. Rosenfeld, *Fr. Spee*, pp. 238–239 and *Studien*, p. 153.

216 Cf. Jacobsen, *Metamorphosen*, and Windfuhr, *Bildlichkeit*. Nowak, "Versuch," pp. 174–178, discusses the frequent parallels between Spee and Silesius in this image-category.

Schwanen weiss" (*TN* 2:1,5); and "die gülden Pfeil der Sonnen heiss" (*TN* 2:1,7). In *TN* 34:205,7—10, Halton states:

> So frisch die saugend Lämmerlein
> Noch nie zun brüsten sprangen
> Als lieffen frisch die lefftzen mein
> Zur weid auff seinen wangen.

This image of grazing on Christ's physiognomy appears again in *TN* (8):12,8—10 where the soul begs Christ that:

> Mein augen beid
> Nur fuhr zur weid
> Auff dein so schöne wangen.

Spee's picture of the beloved, Christ, is composed almost entirely of literary conventions and images common to seventeenth-century decorative poets. A correspondence has been indicated for many of the descriptive images listed above describing Christ's anatomy such as: golden, yellow hair, ivory feet, purple lips, rosy cheeks and honey-sweet mouth. Spee shares the baroque tendency to view the beloved analytically in an extended description of the various features rather than the total form. This analytic tendency permeates the methodology and the structure of the *GTB* and is frequently apparent in the *TN* in several categories of images already subjected to analysis as: stars, trees, seasons, animals, wounds, and tears.

10. Death

The notion of death in Spee's *GTB* and *TN* can be analyzed from two basic points of view: physical death and eternal death. Physical death has been defined theologically as the separation of the soul, which continues to live on, from the corporeal body which is dissolved into its elements.[217] Eternal death, a religious concept, is the result of sin and brings about eternal separation from God. For Spee eternal death results from man's sinfulness: "Unsere sünd seind solche hoch verbottene waaren; bey deme sie gefunden werden, wird mit dem ewigen todt bezahlen müssen" (*GTB* 139.24—26 and 198.25—32). Eternal death results in hell and eternal damnation: ". . . gedencke du seyest in deinen sünden gestorben; gedencke du seyest nun in der höllischen verdamnuss . . ." (*GTB* 170.14—17). In the *GTB* it is eternal death or damnation which Spee emphasizes most. This emphasis on eternal death follows logically from the fact that Spee is developing

---

[217] Cf. Parente, *Dictionary*, p. 70.

a dogmatically structured religious ethos which is based on faith in an afterlife and on the concept of eternal salvation (cf. *GTB* 62.21–28; 64:9–15, and 64:27–34). Spee discusses physical death in the *GTB*, but his discussions on physical death are invariably a prelude or a presupposition for further discussion on the overriding possibility of eternal death because of mortal sin.

In the following analysis of Spee's death-imagery, only the more pertinent instances, rather than the almost innumerable allusions to eternal and physical death, have been selected from the *GTB* and the *TN*.

In the *GTB* Spee repeatedly attempts to imbue the spiritual daughter he addresses with a deep awareness of eternal death and eternal salvation, and her responses in the *GTB* indicate that she has learned her lesson well from Spee. She prefers physical death to eternal death rather than deny a single article of faith (*GTB* 93.39ff.); she is willing to accept physical death for her faith (95.20ff.); she does not fear physical death because she knows she will attain eternal life by reason of her trust and faith in God's mercy and goodness (130.1–3). She is constantly aware that sin causes eternal death (170.15ff.); she knows that a final judgment awaits her in the afterlife concerning her actions in this life (62.21–28). She would rather accept physical death than commit sin: ". . . Und da du sihen soltest, dass ich heut tödtlich darwider sündigen wurde, so straffe mich jetzo von stund an mit dem gehen Todt: dann ich lieber sterben will, dan dich verzürnen" (271.38–272.2). She knows that after death her soul will arise (96.25ff.) and that to die in Christ, is to live eternally: ". . . so begrabe mich in deine verwundte seyten, damitt mein todes hertz in deinem toden hertzen ewig lebe" (215.38–216.1).

Perhaps the soul's most striking experience with an aspect of death is her confrontation with physical death personified in *GTB* 343.11–345.5. Spee portrays physical death in all its horrifying aspects in order to induce the soul to commit herself to Christ in loving surrender: "Mein Kind, sage mir ohne schertz, wird es nit warhafftig und ohnfählbarlich einmal geschehen, dass der leidige grimme tod zu dir komme? " (343.11–13). In *GTB* 345.3–5 Spee says: "Da ist an einer seiten der grewlich Tod, die abschewlich bestia, dafür doch alle menschen erschrecken müssen: da ist an der ander seiten der Sohn Gottes. . . ." Spee continues in poetic form:

> Der grausam Tod kompt nur allein,
>   Dass er dich bring umbs leben,
> Doch all das dein: soll ihme sein
>   Ihm wilt es alles geben?
>
> Wolan fahr hinn: nach deinem sinn,
>   Hör niemands rath in trewen
> Gott sey schabab: Tod alles hab;
>   Sehr bald wirds dich gerewen.

> Die nass wird er dir schneiden ab,
>   Die läfftzen, und die ohren;
> Und wird dich schenden in dem grab;
>   Solch lohn gebürt den thoren. (*GTB* 346.22—33)

Spee personifies physical death in its horrifying and gruesome aspects to stress how necessary it is for the soul to surrender all to Christ and thus avoid the possibility of eternal death. Her basic choice lies between Death or Christ. Spee actually uses the term "marriage" as he spells out the soul's ultimate and decisive choice between Christ and Death: "Ob du dann dem Tod, oder dem Sohn Gottes heuraten, und zu theil werden wollest? Der Tod hat nichts umb dich verdienet; suchet nur dein verderben, kompt nur dass er dich schende, dich ermorde, dir nass und lefftzen abschneide" (345.32—36).

Spee constantly stresses the vanity of this world, warning the soul that too great a trust in this world's riches and honors can lead to self-deception (*GTB* 341.9—12; 21—24; 34—35) and to eternal sorrow (*GTB* 181.11—16; 17—30). In the *GTB* the world is termed a stench when compared to the glory of heaven: "O Gott, wie stincket mir die Erde, wan ich gen himmel schawe? " (210.5—6). The world is Satan's ally [*TN* (14):83,1—3]; it is a "zergengliches ellend" (*GTB* 70.21). He stresses that the soul must constantly evaluate the goods of this world in the face of the absolute certainty of physical death (*GTB* 343.20—23) and its consequences for possible eternal death of life (*GTB* 186.17—27). The vanity of this world, in addition to Satan's activity in tempting men to achieve worldly success and thereby suffer eternal death, and the corresponding necessity for indifference toward created things are all key Ignatian concepts.[218] Spee has incorporated these concepts into his own spiritual teaching.

The following analysis of the poems in the *TN* contains images of death that occur within the context of the *GTB*. In Book II, chapter 8, Spee imaginatively takes the desolate soul to the garden of Gethsemane in order that she may contemplate Christ in His struggle with death. Spee's purpose is to increase the soul's compassion and love for Christ because of what He has suffered for her. He translates this contemplation into the imagery found in *TN* 38. Deeply impressed by His suffering for her sins and by the fact that these very sins could cause her eternal death (*GTB* 170.19—20), she comes to realize, through the words of her confessor ". . . dan diser jetzigen deiner traurigkeit würdest nicht entgehen, sondern sie würde tausend, und tausendmahl grösser sein, und in alle ewigkeit nicht vergehen" (*GTB* 170.21—23). Christ's struggle with death in *TN* (38) serves as a model for the soul in her practice of the virtue of hope and in her willingness to accept mundane suffering and desolation, after the exemplary manner of Christ.

---

218 Cf. *Spiritual Exercises*, nos. 23 and 142.

In *TN* (13) the dying flower becomes an allegory to show the vanity and the fragility of man's existence in the face of certain, inexorable physical death. The concomitant need for reconciliation with God is also expressed [*TN* (13):12,1—8]. This poem occurs in the context of *GTB* Book II, chapter 9, "Andere Werck der Hoffnungh:" "Weil die hoffnung in sich begreifft ein verlangen und begierd, auch grossschetzung der himmlischen, hingegen aber verachtung der irrdischen sachen . . ." (*GTB* 179.3—5). Since the world is passing away, repentance and adherence to God are to the soul's benefit.

TN poems (7) and (8) occur in *GTB* Book II, chapter 16. Here the context is once again an exercise in "begierliche liebe," emphasizing the effect of the love of God in the soul. The love of the soul for Christ in these poems reaches such intensity that she: (a) dies and lives simultaneously in Christ's embrace [*TN* (7):15,1—8]; and (b) dies from the power of love [*TN* (7):7,4—6]. Physical death, in this instance, results from the intensity of love, and this motif recurs constantly in seventeenth-century poetry. It is frequently expressed by means of antithesis, as in Weckherlin and Silesius.[219]

TN poems (12) and (15) occur in *GTB* Book III, chapter 9, a chapter that is an exercise in ". . . Reu und leid uber die sünd, so man zerknirschung des hertzens nennet . . ." (322.7—8). Spee's death-images emphasize the suddenness and the inevitability of physical death [*TN* (12):4,1—4] and the consequences for the unprepared soul that is found not to be in "gnadenzeit" (4,5—8, eternal death). Since sin is a direct cause of this lack of grace, immediate repentance is necessary if reconciliation with God is to succeed and death is to be avoided.

The images of death in *TN* (43) (*GTB,* Book III, chapter 18) are intended ". . . zu erweckung aller-hand lieb-reichen affecten" (*GTB* 381.6—7) and ". . . zu allerhand wercken der hoffnung, liebe, zerknirschung dess hertzens, andacht, mittleyden, und dergleichen liebreichen anmütungen zubewegen . . ." (*GTB* 381.17—19). In *TN* (43):1,1—4; 2,5—6 and 47,7—8, Christ is pictured in His struggle with physical death. The images function to produce these "lieb-reichen affecten" in the soul as she contemplates Christ in His passion.

Death-images in the *TN* function according to the following four-fold schema:

1) Images of physical death are closely associated with the expression of the soul's intense longing and love for Christ. The death-image is frequently used in juxtaposition with life to indicate the paradoxical, perhaps mystical nature of this love [*TN* 2:7,5—8; (7):15,1—8; 13,5—6; (11):24,5—8]. The mystical love-experience reaches such a peak of ardor and intensity in these *TN* poems that poetic expression seems inadequate and the ineffable finds itself

---

[219] Cf. Beckmann, "Motive," pp. 74ff.; Van Ingen *Vanitas und Memento Mori,* pp. 255ff.; and for the "Liebes-Tod Antithetik," cf. Jacobsen, *Metamorphosen,* p. 138.

expressed through a *coincidentia oppositorum*,[220] in this instance "Ist todt im leben schweben" (*TN* 2:7,8) and also:

> Ohn leben ich noch lebe
> Bin todt ohn Todt zugleich
> Todt Lebend immer strebe
> Wo nur ich dich beschleich. [*TN* (11):24,5–8]

The image in *TN* (8):10,5–7 also occurs in the mystical terminology of Mechthild von Magdeburg.[221]

2) The soul is confronted directly by the incontrovertible fact that physical death is unavoidable, and, consequently, she must repent if she is to avoid eternal death. Physical death is personified as catching the soul unawares [*TN* (12):4,2–8; and (13):12,3–8; 14,3].

3) Christ is seen under two aspects: (a) in a struggle with physical death [*TN* (38):9,3–4]. His love is portrayed in the most concerete imagery to help produce a greater love-affect in the soul. (b) Christ overcomes physical death through His resurrection [*TN* (11):12,1–8].

4) The Eucharist is described in *TN* 51:17,1–8 as the key to eternal life and/or death.

Spee's imagery here reaches its theological and poetic zenith. Whoever receives the Eucharist unworthily, "... wird verleit // Zum Todt und schwartzen pforten" (17,3–4), that is, will experience both physical and spiritual death. On the other hand, whoever receives the Eucharist worthily will escape spiritual death and gain eternal life. Both of these concepts are clearly related to the Pauline notion of the Eucharist in I Corinthians 11,26–34. Interestingly, the treatment of the Eucharistic sacrifice and the reception of Holy Communion appear at the conclusion of both the *GTB* and the *TN*. The final chapters of the *GTB*, Book III, 31–34, are devoted to the worthy reception and preparation for communion: "Das 31 Capitel, Eine schöne Weiss andächtiglich zu Communiciren" (*GTB* 511.22–23); "Das 32 Capitel, Noch eine andere weiss zur H. Communion: und seind werck der dreyen Göttlichen Tugenden, des Glaubens, Hoffnung, und der liebe" (*GTB* 514.1–3); Das 33 Capitel, Noch andere Weiss zur H. Communion" (*GTB* 517.31–32); "Das 34 Capitel, Noch eine andere Weiss zur Heiligen Communion" (*GTB* 521.19–20). If, as has been suggested, the *TN* is composed of only fifty-one poems and *TN* 52 in the Arlt edition was dropped later by Spee,[222] then the attention Spee gives to the Eucharist cannot be merely that of coincidence. This sacrament is the

220 Cf. Lüers, *Sprache,* p. 107.
221 Lüers, *Sprache,* pp. 227, 265–266.
222 Cf. Rosenfeld, *Studien,* pp. 109–110.

theological and religious point of culmination in Spee's spirituality. Eternal death is now overcome. The Eucharist is the sign and the symbol of man's future resurrection (cf. John 6,53—59). In Spee's poetic terminology (*TN* 51:17,5—8) the efficacy of the Eucharist is proclaimed in clear terms:

> Hingegen wer sich prüffet vor
> Und dan der speiss geniesset
> Man ihm die schöne thür und thor
> Zum leben weit erschliesset.

Descriptions of death in Spee exhibit considerable similarity with Gryphius' epithets of death, and with other poets of the affective-pathetic mode of style[223] (cf. Table 10.1, p. 146). Antithesis predominates in the structure of the death-images listed above under functional category "1" (where the images of physical death are associated with the expression of the soul's longing for union with Christ), which is composed of poems from the first cycle of poems in the *TN*: [2:7,5—8; (7):15,1—8; (11):24,5—8; (8):10,5—8].

Throughout functional categories "2" (where the soul is confronted by unavoidable death) and "3" (where Christ confronts physical death), Spee employs personifications of death to convey the poignancy of Christ's struggle with death and the confrontation of the soul herself with physical death. Death is personified (cf. Table 10.2, p. 146). Verbal personifications of death in Spee portray death's agility, suddenness, certainty, and brutality (cf. Table 10.3, p. 146).

D. Realia

1. Arrows

The siginificance of the arrow, bow, and quiver in Spee's poetic imagery is clearly indicated by the frontispieces to various editions of the *TN*. The Strassburger manuscript, the Paris copy and the first edition of the *TN* (1649) portray Christ as *Christus Cupido cruciatus,* hanging from a tree and gazing down upon the soul who is pictured with an arrow piercing her breast.[224] These emblems express one of the major poetic themes permeating the *TN*: the mutual love of the soul and Christ. The Cupid-figure with bow and arrow was a favorite Ovidian device and one of its foremost imitators in the Renaissance was

---

223 Cf. Windfuhr, *Bildlichkeit*, pp. 188ff.
224 Cf. the emblems reproduced in Rosenfeld, *Fr. Spee*, p. 192; and Jacobsen, *Metamorphosen*, pp. 14, 16, and 18. The *Cupidus cruciatus* form is an ancient classical figure and first occurs in Ausonius. Cf. Jacobsen, pp. 48 and 60, Rosenfeld, *Spee*, p. 199, footnote 10, and Dimler, "Arrow-Motif," 280ff.

Petrarch.[225] Spee's fellow Jesuit, Hermann Hugo (1588—1629), employs the *Christus-Cupido* figure and the arrow-motif extensively in his *Pia Desideria*.[226] Most probably he borrowed the motifs from Otto Vaenius who was, in turn, strongly influenced by Ovid, Petrarch, and the medieval mystical tradition. Medieval mystics had employed the motif of Cupid with the bow and arrow wounding the soul,[227] but transformed Cupid into the divinity, as occurred in the works of Mechthild von Magdeburg.[228] The resultant "minne wunt" from the arrows of the divinity is a favorite formula to express the act of mystical union.

A study in the similarity that exists between the fourth emblem of Hugo's *Pia Desideria* and Spee's frontispieces reveals once again Hugo's considerable influence on Spee in this image-field.[229] Both Spee and Hugo portray "Cupido/Jesus am Baume gekreuzigt" with the spouse below gazing up from a seated position beneath the tree. In Spee's emblem, however, the arrow-motif is explicitly introduced,[230] i.e., the spouse is transfixed, an indication of its forthcoming importance in the *TN*.

The first appearance of the Cupid-arrow motif in Spee occurs in the poem in *GTB*, Book II, chapter 11, "O Venus Kind, du blinder Knab" (197.33). Here "Venus Kind" is asked to put down his bow and arrows and surrender them to "Marien Kind," who is Christ (197.39). "Venus Kind" and his love tools represent the world and sinful creation hindering the soul from union with God. The aim of the exercise in which the poem occurs is expressed in the title to this chapter: "Noch andere werck der Hoffnung oder der begierlichen liebe zu Gott: und ist für die jenige, so etwan eine Creatur zu sehr lieben" (*GTB* 192.2—3). To counteract the world of Cupid, Spee calls on "O Jesu mein, du schöner Knab" to disarm the "Venus Kind" and to aim his arrows at the soul:

> O Jesu mein, du schöner knab,
> Nim hin Cupidons waffen:
> Reiss ihm die pfeil und kocher ab,
> Und leg ihn ewig schlaffen. (*GTB* 198.9—12)

Although the *Christus-Cupido* figure is not explicitly formulated here, Jesus' appearance as *Cupido* in the *TN* is foreshadowed in *GTB* 198.13—16:

---

225 Cf. Jacobsen, *Metamorphosen*, p. 46.
226 For examples, cf. Emblems 4 and 19 in Jacobsen, pp. 13 and 35.
227 Cf. Nowak, "Versuch," pp. 197—198.
228 "Bei Mechthild wird die Gottheit als Minne mit der Armbrust schiessend dargestellt. . . ." Lüers, *Sprache*, pp. 77 and 78.
229 Cf. Jacobsen, *Metamorphosen*, p. 58; Rosenfeld, *Studien*, pp. 75—76; and Adolf Spamer, *Das Kleine Andachtsbild vom XIV. bis zum XX. Jahrhundert* (München: 1930), pp. 140ff., for a discussion of Jesuit emblem literature and the relationship between Hugo, the Dutch Jesuits of the seventeenth century and contemporary sevententh-century literature.
230 Cf. Rosenfeld, *Spee*, p. 192, and Jacobsen, pp. 14, 16, and 18.

Nur bitt du ich: du zihl auff mich;
Von dir will sein getroffen:
O reines gifft: wan Jesus trifft!
Alssdan ist heil zu hoffen.[231]

The conflict between the heavenly Cupid, Christ, and the earthly Cupid also occurs in emblem-literature, indicating the prevalence of this motif.[232] "Amor carnalis," moreover, "mit süssen pfeilen" appears later in TN (14):82,24—25.

The representation of Christ as a Cupid shooting His arrows of divine love, and kindling a fire of love in the soul, occurs again in the GTB 225.16—20. Spee expands this motif and employs it extensively throughout the TN [(3), (20), 1,2,10,40,34,46 and 41]. He does so particularly in those contexts where the soul describes her intense longing for Christ's love. This inward reflective glance of the soul on her love-experience is characteristic of "die liebe der begierlichkeit" (= hope).

Aside from the Christus-Cupido motif of GTB 198.9ff. and 225.16—20, where Christ pierces the soul with His tender arrows and his "reines gifft" as the effect of His love, arrows are also employed by Spee in connection with Satan and Death. Satan and Death also have their arrows of destruction and allurement among medieval mystics, and even in Gryphius.[233] In GTB 130.1ff. Satan's "pfeil und bogen" represent his wiles and snares used to divert the soul's attention from God. But in this instance, because of her trust in God, Satan's arrows have no effect on her. In GTB 144.9—16 the soul escapes the arrows of death because of God's mercy and kindness which increases her hope in Him. In GTB 181.21—22 the arrow, representing death's readiness to strike and cause untimely death, is employed by Spee to lead the soul from her attachment to the world and to the love of God.

Death's arrow makes its appearance again in TN (11):13,5—8. Here the image of Christ destroying the arrow and bow of death by fire is attributed to the power of His resurrection. In a penitential poem TN (12):4,2—4 the possibility of being struck by death's swift arrows is an image similar to GTB 181.21—22, used again by Spee to lead the soul to a spirit of true repentance, which is the aim of the exercise in Book III, chapter 9 (322.4—6).

Thus the relationship existing between arrow-imagery and motifs in the GTB and those which reappear in the TN is frequently determined by their specific context and function in the GTB exercises. An overall categorization of arrow-imagery, by function, for the complete TN follows:

---

231 Cf. Jacobsen, Metamorphosen, p. 29, for an emblem from O. Vaenius picturing Cupid shooting his arrow at a lover and p. 30 for "Cupido/Jesus" shooting his arrow at the spouse.

232 For examples, cf. Jacobsen, pp. 35 and 39.

233 Cf. Lüers, Sprache, p. 220, and Fricke, Bildlichkeit, p. 89.

1) Nature
   a) The sun is pictured at dawn, filling her quiver with arrows as she prepares
      for the light of day [TN (8):3,5—7]. The sun's rays are called arrows [TN
      (13):8,6—8; and 2:1,7—8]. The sun bears down on the flower [TN (13)]
      with great intensity, and is pictured pulling back on the bow and shooting
      "den besten schein" (9,1—3). Aside from this last instance of per-
      sonification, the images are purely decorative and non-functional or what
      has been termed "composition of place." The personification in TN
      (13):9,1—3, where the arrows of the sun function as agents of destruction,
      indicates the fragility of human existence symbolized by the wilting
      flower.
   b) Fountains are pictured as shooting from the mountain-side like arrows [TN
      (8):2,5—7]. Here the image in the form of a simile serves a contrastive
      function. The languid mood of the soul contrasts with joyful springtime,
      streaming fountains, and bright sunshine, a typical Petrarchan character-
      istic.
2) Death's arrows appear in TN (12) and (11):
   a) to stress the need for repentance in the light of the suddenness of death
      represented by his arrows (personification) [TN (12):4,1—4];
   b) to demonstrate the power of Christ's resurrection and its destructive hold
      over Death's arrow [TN (11):13,3—6].
3) In the context of the Our Father the soul asks the divinity to set her free
   from the allurements of the world. Here the attractiveness of this world is
   symbolized by its sweet arrows [TN (14):82,24—27].
4) In this category the emblematic context of the frontispieces picturing
   Christus-Cupido unleashing His arrow of love at the soul and piercing her
   heart predominates:
   a) The soul in TN (3):5,1—4, complains of the pain of the love-arrow. In TN
      2:2,3—8 the arrow wounds the soul with sweet pain; in TN 10:3,5—6
      arrows strike her heart with a bitter-sweet fire; in TN (20),3—4 the arrows
      are sharp and hot — symbolizing the soul's distress and languor from love.
      from love.
   b) Damon is wounded with a sweet arrow from the Christ-Child (TN
      34:205,15—19). This increases his desire to love Christ.
   c) The "Trutznachtigall" herself is wounded with the sweetness of Christ's
      love (TN 1:6,1—2); her heart burns with a fiery love for Christ, and she
      despises worldly pomp.
   d) In TN 40:11,1—2 Christ's love for the lost sheep is symbolized by the
      "Blinde pfeil / und bogen blind." The arrow-image shows the effect of
      divine love on Christ:

Blinde lieb / nun mag ich sagen /
Blinde pfeil / und bogen blind!
Dich ich freilich muss beklagen
Daphnis hoch verliebtes kind:
Ach! wie mochtest je doch lieben
Nur das einig Schäfflein arm?
Wo der ander hauff ist blieben?
Ach / und ach / das Gott erbarm?   (*TN* 40:11,1–8)

This is the sole instance in the *TN* where the positions are reversed. Christ Himself becomes the victim of Cupid's arrow – *Cupidus divinus*. Divine love drives him to seek the lost sheep. Only in one other instance is Christ portrayed as the victim of love's arrows; in the *GTB* Book II, chapter 12, 199.24–28 the soul's sighs and aspirations are intended to wound Christ's heart as "nur lautere schöne pfeil der liebe,"

... so bilde dir für, als wan die folgende liebspruch nur lautere schöne pfeil der liebe waren: deren dein hertz, als ein pfeilkocher, voll stecke; und die du gleich als von einem bogen durch einen anmütigen seufftzer in das hertz des gecreuzigten Jesu könnest abgehen lassen, einen nach dem anderen.

This is a poeticization of an emblem occurring in Hugo's *Pia Desideria*.[234]

e) Mary Magdalen is wounded "Mit süsslich-herben pfeilen" [*TN* (11):8,1–4]. The arrows represent the effects of Christ's love on her soul.

The effect of these arrows: sweet-pain, bitter-sweet fire, and searing wounds have been analyzed extensively in the image-categories above under pain, wounds, and fire. The source of these arrows is *Christus-Cupido* in general, except in two instances (*TN* 2:2,3–4 and 10:3,4–4,4), where the arrows shoot from Jesus' eyes: "äuglein rundt," "äuglein theur," "gläser-bogen," and "auss beiden fensterlein." The metaphor of arrows shooting from the beloved's eye and wounding the lover is an ancient one, occurring in Aeschylos as ὀμμάτων βέλος.[235] It appears in contemporary emblem literature and among orthodox Petrarchans.[236] A related notion also occurs in the *GTB* 523.13–14, where Jesus' eyes are called "pfeilkocher der Liebe."

Epithets modifying arrows in the *TN* and the *GTB* are (cf. Table 1.1, p. 147). Verbal forms in this category describing the destructive nature of the love-arrows are (cf. Table 1.2, p. 147).

Spee's incorporation of arrow and Cupid imagery, which was initially the sole preserve of secular or worldly poetry, and his application of these motifs to a

---

234 This emblem is reproduced in Jacobsen, *Metamorphosen*, p. 32.
235 *Agamemmon*, 742.
236 Cf. Jacobsen, *Metamorphosen*, pp. 41–42.

religious context is another instance of a general tendency operative during the Counter-Reformation and among seventeenth-century Jesuits in particular. In canonizing these secular motifs and metaphors, expressed in a mystical mode of style, Spee is carrying out his announced intention in the introduction to the TN as set forth in the "Vorred dess Authoris:"

> Derohalben hab ich solchen zu helffen understanden / und befliessen mich zu einer recht lieblichen Teutschen Poetica die baan zu zeigen / und zur grösseren ehren Gottes einen newen geistlichen Parnassum / oder kunstberg algemach anzutreten.[237]

2. Precious Objects

Images of precious jewels and metals have been treated indirectly in some categories already analyzed as: flowers, cosmology, the human anatomy, wounds, and stars. A more complete analysis of this precious-object image-field follows.

Images of precious objects occur with great frequency among German baroque poets of the decorative mode. Religious poets also employ the decorative style and incorporate it into their imagery, among them Kuhlmann and Silesius. Spee's application of the Petrarchan's flowery, stilted descriptions of feminine beauty to the figures of "Jesus-Cupido," "Daphnis," and the Christ-Child is aesthetically striking. Many of these Petrarchan characteristics have already been alluded to in Spee's descriptions of Christ, which were analyzed above under "human anatomy" as an image field. The frequent occurrence of this type of imagery in the TN and the GTB attests to Spee's affinity with the general seventeenth-century tendency to seek striking and colorful effects. This emphasis on picture-images, found especially among decorative poets, is manifested in their predilection for the ornate style over the stylistic categories of clarity and purity.[238]

In the TN Spee's images in the category of precious objects is applied in various ways:

1) "Geld / Pomp / und Pracht auff Erden" (TN 1:6,5) are used to represent the spirit of the world, its vanity, and transitory character as opposed to God.

The "Trutznachtigall," the symbol of the poet himself, despises these worldly treasures in its desire to love Christ above all else:

---

237 Cf. Arlt Edition, p. 5*, ll. 18—23.
238 Cf. Dych, Ticht-Kunst, p. 68.

>   Geld / Pomp / und Pracht auff Erden
>   Lust / Freuden ess verspott /
>   Und achtets für beschwerden
>   Sucht nur den schönen Gott. (*TN* 1:6,5—8)

"Die Gesponss Jesus" in *TN* 10 bids adieu to worldly trappings: "Ade golt / gelt in Kasten // Ade nun alle welt" (*TN* 10:19,7—8). She desires only to rest in her spouse Christ. In the *GTB* Spee frequently uses precious objects as symbols of the world and its vanity. The images in *TN* 1:6,5 and 10:19,7—8 are a continuation of this representative aspect behind precious objects in the *GTB*. The "Frau von Babylon" and her spirit of worldly vanity appear in the *GTB* and are represented by a chalice full of precious objects:

>   Ey was hat mich betrogen,
>   O Frau von Babylon?
>   Dass je nach dir thet frogen,
>   Weil nur trag leid darvon?
>
>   Dein kelch ist zwar gezogen
>   Von lauter golt so rein,
>   Stehn drin schön aussgebogen
>   Vill perl, und edel stein:
>   Doch wers mit dir darff wogen,
>   Und drincket ein süssen sauss,
>   Find lauter höllisch plogen,
>   Die man thut sauffen drauss. (*GTB* 143.27—38)

In *GTB* Book II, chapter 3, 274.15ff., Christ asks the spouse to destroy her "ring, perlen . . . Ketten . . . Kleinodien . . ." to show her love for Him above all. In her choice between the Eucharist and the precious goods of this world (gold, silver, jewels and treasure) in a later chapter in the *GTB*, the soul chooses the Sacred Host (*GTB* 515.19ff.). Christ Himself is proposed as the model of detachment from the world: "Ade, o welt, ade o schöne welt; schöne kleyder trag ich nit mehr, gross lob und preiss such ich nit mehr, sag ab dem pomp und pracht der erden; . . ." (*GTB* 394.18—20). Conversely, the cross of Christ and the Holy Eucharist are true objects of substance and value described in connection with precious objects (*GTB* 389.30; 403.15—16).

2) God's omnipotence is represented by the scepter and crown in *TN* (24):10,7—8: "Sein ist der Scepter / sein die Cron; // Vor ihm erde / himmel bebet."

3) The beauty of creation is pictured in all its glory in order to give greater praise to the Creator.

This glory of creation is studded with images of precious objects (cf. Table 2.1, p. 147).

4) Nature herself takes on an active role.

In *TN* 44:2,1—4 the stars are called golden apples, pearls, and jewels by Mary as she asks them to be sympathetic onlookers at her sorrow and grief for her Son. The soul, bursting with repentance, calls on the stars (which are termed shining pearls) to listen to her sorrowful tale [*TN* (15):2,1—2]. The sun, in envy, steals the glow on Christ's forehead that is characterized as "Den gold-und perlen schein" (*TN* 10:10,8).

5) The beloved, Christ, is transformed by Spee into a Petrarchan beauty (cf. Table 2.2, p. 148).
6) In *TN* 52:1,5—6 the beaks of the nightingales are carved of ivory, and their song is fashioned in marble as they sing praise to the Creator (52:5,1—2).

Images from this category can be reduced to four main structural components: metonym, personification, simile, and metaphor-paraphrase. Metonym occurs in *TN* 1, 10, and (24). In *TN* 1:6,5 and 10:19,7—8 precious objects represent wordly vanity. In *TN* 24:10,7—8 the scepter and crown stand for God's majesty and power.

Personification, in this image-category, occurs only once (*TN* 26:1,1—2), where the poet calls on the stringed-instruments to speak with silver-tongues in giving praise to God. Simile occurs more frequently. In *TN* 2:3,1—2 the spouse's tears of love are compared to pearls from the Orient. In *TN* (18):4,5—6 the brooks murmur like pure "Silberschein." In *TN* (21):7,1—4 fountains shoot forth like silver beams and in *TN* 26:5,3—4 the waters gleam like silver and glass. Other similes, already mentioned above, occur in *TN* (28):12,2-4; (43):2,1—4 and 46:5,1—8.

By far the outstanding structural features in this image-field are metaphor and paraphrase. Many of these have already been indirectly noted above in the functional categories and in other image-areas. The following list is a summary of all the occurrences in this category. Similarity with Gryphius and the decorative poets in Windfuhr's list is noteworthy (cf. Table 2.3, p. 148).

In correlating image-structure with the six functional categories in the image-category of precious objects, the following correspondences between function and structure may be drawn. Metonym predominates in divisions 1 and 2 where precious objects represent the spirit of the world. Simile and paraphrase show creation in its praise-function in division 3. Compassionate nature in division 4 functions through metaphor and paraphrase. Petrarchan descriptions of Christ in division 5 abound in metaphor and, less frequently, in simile. In division 6, the images of the nightingales are comprised of purely decorative metaphor.

CHAPTER IV
CONCLUSION

As was indicated in the opening chapter of our investigation, Spee the poet and Spee the reformer seem to represent two divergent almost irreconcilable aspects of his personality. On the one hand, he did not hesitate to venture onto controversial even highly dangerous ground in his forthright condemnation of the witchcraft trials which were prevalent in the cities where he spent his Jesuit life: Cologne, Speyer, Wurzburg and Paderborn. He condemned the injustice of these trial-procedures in the *Cautio,* and, above all, the trial-judges, many of whom operated under the principle that the end justifies the means. In many cases, any means was considered licit and valid which could produce an admission of practicing witchcraft from the suspect. Many of these suspects were in fact innocent women. An outstanding example was the celebrated case in Cologne in the late 1620's of the patrician lady, Katharina von Henot, an innocent victim who was tortured to such an extent that she finally confessed to witchcraft.

In boldly speaking out on these matters, Spee brought himself into open conflict with his superiors in the Society and became a highly controversial figure with his fellow Jesuits. Moreover, it took great courage to speak out against the trials which in many instances were openly supported by the leading secular and religious figures of his time and place. Several of these prominent people were favorable to the Society and were wealthy benefactors as, for example, Ferdinand and Maximilian of Bavaria.

On the other hand, one is astonished at the mystical, tranquil nature of the love poetry of the TN which seems so far removed from the polemics of the *Cautio.* The TN and the GTB are, for the most part, love-songs to God express-ed in a mood of basic peace and confidence, even if at times interspersed with themes of impatient longing and languor. Many of the poems were composed at a time when Spee was recovering from serious wounds resulting from the assassination attempt in Peine which nearly cost Spee his life. Yet, he wrote his poetry under great duress, but with such artistry and skill that he has become a leading literary figure in the baroque age. However, it has been our contention that a literary investigation of the images and their motifs could shed light on this seeming discrepancy.

At this point, after our analytical inquiry into his imagery, we can now return to some of the basic questions raised at the beginning of our investigation. Is Spee's poetry a type of escapism, a flight from man's inhumanity to man, a retreat to an inner oasis or to a platonic beauty removed from reality? Or is his poetry rather a return to a more meditative preoccupation with the basic problematic behind his own commitment as a Jesuit priest, a man preoccupied and vitally involved with the issues of his own age? Has our analysis of the motifs and themes behind his poetic imagery led us any nearer to the well-springs and dynamics of his personality? Do his poetic writings document his social commitment and enable us to contact the inner man? Are Spee the poet and Spee the reformer irreconcilable aspects of his life?

From the analysis of Spee's poetry and his imagery, it is our conviction that contact has been made with the inner dynamic of his heroic personality which so impressed the great Leibniz. The motifs from the *Spiritual Exercises,* scholastic theology, from the Bible, the mystics and the Pietists point to the ultimate motivating force behind his courage and tenacity: his love for God and for man. His poetry constantly revolves around these two polarities. It is particularly in the discussion above on Spee's love-images and the chapters on the heart, arrow, and death where these themes were revealed as dominant characteristics in Spee's poetic consciousness. It was also at that point in our inquiry where it was considered necessary to look beyond the *TN* to the *GTB* where many of Spee's love-images are discussed from a philosophical and theological point of view. Thus, rather than seeking a mere retreat, an oasis, or an escape into beauty from the problems brought on by the publication of the *Cautio,* or the day-to-day tension brought on by conflict with his fellow Jesuits, Spee's poetry presents us with the ultimate dynamic, the basic spring-board for his social involvement and awareness. The love-images and the poetic motifs are the linguistic documentation of his social commitment which in turn leads to the conclusion that Spee the poet compliments Spee the reformer.

With regard to the second major-problem-area, one which is more literary than psychological: how and why does Spee so often fuse secular and spiritual motifs in his imagery and how does Spee use the conventional themes of the seventeenth-century, the solution to this problematic was touched upon in the discussion of arrow and love-images above and bears repetition at this point. Here again Spee's poetry is closely intertwined with his religious and Jesuit *Weltanschauung.* Spee's incorporation of countless secular motifs which were originally the sole preserve of secular poetry and his continual application of these motifs to a religious context is another instance of a general propensity operative during the Counter-Reformation and among seventeenth-century Jesuits in particular. Spee is clearly within this tradition and in canonizing these motifs and metaphors from Petrarchan, from seventeenth-century sources and the classics, expressed frequently in a mystical style, he is carrying out his announced intention in the introduction to the *TN* as set forth in the Vorred dess Authoris (cf. above, p. 116).

Spee has applied traditional motifs of the heart, precious materials, arrows, fire, and heat, etc., in line with his own purposes, the building of a new spiritual Parnassus *(Kunstberg)* for God's greater glory. Previous Spee-scholarship has not given sufficient attention to this typical Jesuit quality in his poetic handicraft: the adoption of predominantly secular motifs for what is basically a spiritual message. Spee, however, refused to confine his spiritual message to his poetry. The full record of his message is contained in one of the most courageous documents of the seventeenth-century, the *Cautio Criminalis,* in the heroic activity of his own life whether as father-confessor to those suspected of witchcraft, or as a force for greater ecumenism during his activity among Protestants near Paderborn, and finally in the sacrifice of his own life for plague-stricken soldiers in Trier.

CHAPTER V
TABLE OF IMAGE-CATEGORIES

The compilation, in tabular form, that concludes this study is a synthesis of the twenty-four image-categories in the *TN*. Each image-category in the table is divided according to its various functions, structures, and styles in accordance with the methodology pursued in the preceding analysis of Spee's poetry. The table is not exhaustive; it attempts to provide a tabular summary of the results of the analysis. It cannot be adapted to coordinate every function, all the structures, or each stylistic variation in the *TN*. Only the more prominent characteristics of Spee's rhetorical style, function, and structure are listed. Nor does it relate these factors to the all-important role of the influence of the *GTB* upon the *TN*, or to Spee's historical relationships and literary motifs.

The poems of the *TN* that are related to the various functional categories are listed under the heading "Function." The table indicates the multiplicity of image-functions and the variations of structure and style according to each function. From the variations of style indicated in the last column, it is evident how incorrect it is to term Spee simply a poet of the decorative mode or a poet of the mystical or of the affective-pathetic mode. Spee employed a combination of styles, and his style varies with the function of each image. Combination of styles and variants also applies to his structures. Spee employs many personifications, antitheses, and paraphrases, but he employs them in conjunction with function and theme, and in subordination to function and theme. Each type of figure can and frequently does vary with the image-function, as is shown in the table.

General statements with regard to Spee's imagery must be eschewed. Frequently general statements regarding Spee's imagery and poetic style have been made by Spee scholars without sufficient investigation. Through the foregoing analysis and study of the intricacies of Spee's images and stylistic traits (indicated in the table) previous broad and general conclusions are shown to be inaccurate. Analysis of the imagery in Spee, when extended to all the poems of the *TN* and based on the twenty-four image-fields of major import, and in terms of the inner mechanism of the image itself (function, structure, and style) shows clearly the depth, detail, and substance of Spee's creative fabric that has clearly emerged within the context of German baroque poetry.

The image-fields in the following table are listed in the order in which they were analyzed in Part II, ie., progressing from images involving inorganic nature to organic nature, and from images of human existence to *realia*.

Key to abbreviations:

aff. = affective	descr. = descriptive
alleg. = allegory	meta. = metaphor
amor *ben.* = *benevolentiae*	myst. = mystical
amor *conc.* = *concupiscentiae*	*n.c.* = *natura compatiens*
anti. = antithesis	oxy. = oxymoron
com.pl. = composition of place	para. = paraphrase
conc. = conceit	pers. = personification
dec. = decorative	sim. = simile
	theol. = theological
	Xt. = Christ

Image-Field	Function	Structure	Style
Light	a) com.pl.: (3), (8), 9, (13), (21), (22), (26)	para. pers	dec.
	b) contrast-heighten: (7), (11), (21), (17–18), (24)	anti, oxy.	conc.
	c) theol.: (11), 26, 51, 29, (42)	anti. oxy.	myst.-conc.
Night	a) com.pl.: (7), 44, (38), 47	pers. para.	aff.
	b) contrast: (18), 49	pers. para.	aff.
	c) praise: (25), 26, 30	pers. para.	dec.
	d) theol.: (15)	ant. oxy.	myst.
Color	a) descr. Xt., Nature: 9, 10, (11), (18), (22–23), 27	anti. pers. para.	dec.
	b) theol.: (7), (16)	pers. meta.	myst.
Water	a) com.pl.: (8), (18), (21), 26, (28)	sim. meta. pers.	dec.
	b) *n.c.*, praise, sorrow: (11) (6), (24–25), (15), 40	pers. sim.	dec.
	c) theol.: (6), (16), 47	ship-sym, sim.	myst.
Fire	a) love-experience: (3–4), (6–7), (11)	anti. para. meta.	myst.-aff.
	b) theol.: 29	para. anti. oxy.	myst.
Stars	a) praise: (21), (28)	pers. para.	dec.
	b) com.pl.: (6), (8), 9–10, (11)	para. pers.	dec.
	c) *n.c.*: (14–15), 39, 41	para. pers.	dec.
	d) theol.: 29, 49	meta. alleg.	myst.
Firmament	a) praise: (24), 27, (28)	para. meta.	dec.

Image-Field	Function	Structure	Style
Air-Wind	a) praise: (24–25), (17–28)	pers. para. sim.	dec.
	b) heighten: (6), (8), (18), 35	pers. para. sim.	dec.-aff.
	c) *n.c.:* 1, (4), 23, 44–45	pers.	dec.
	d) theol.: 29	meta.	myst.
Flowers	a) com.pl.: (5), 9, (51)	pers.	dec.
	b) penitence, vanity: (8), (13), (17)	sim. pers. alleg.	myst.-dec.
	c) theol.: (21–22), 23, 26–27	pers. meta.	myst.
Trees	a) praise: (21), (24), 26, (28), 50	sim. pers.	dec.
	b) com.pl.: 1, 49	pers. meta.	dec.
	c) *n.c.:* (4), (18), 45	pers.	dec.
	d) contrast: 5, (8)	pers.	dec.
	e) theol.: (17), (38), 48	sym.	myst.
Seasons	a) com.pl.: (4), (11), (13), (20), 48, 51	pers.	dec.
	b) penance: (5–6), (16–18), (8), 49	meta.	myst.
	c) praise: (22), (25), 27, 30, 32	pers.	dec.
Animals	a) *n.c.:* 2, 45, (38)	pers. para.	dec.
	b) cpm.pl.: 1, (6), (8), 9, 49	para, pers.	dec.
	c) praise: (20–22), 23, 27, (28), 30, (52)	pers.	dec.
	d) contrition: 8, (18)	meta.	myst.
	e) theol.: 9, (24), 33, 47–48	alleg. sim.	myst.
Love	a) *amor ben.:* (8–9), 10, 40, (42), 46, 49	para. sim.	aff.-myst.
	b) *amor conc.:* 2, (3), (6–7), (11)	anti. oxy. sim.	aff.-myst.
	c) theol.: 29	meta.	myst.
Heart	a) *n.c.:* 9, (38), 39, (43)	pers.	myst.-aff.
	b) *amor conc.:* 2, (6–7), (15), 38	para. meta.	myst.-aff.
	c) *amor ben.:* (5), (7), (11), 46	para. meta.	myst.-aff.
	d) theol.: 29	meta. para.	myst.

Image-Field	Function	Structure	Style
Pain	a) *n.c.*: (38), 39, (44–45), 49	pers.	aff.
	b) contrast: (6), (8), (17–18), 32	descr. pers.	aff.
	c) penance: (12), (15–16)	pers. para.	myst.
	d) love: 2, (6–8), (11), 10	oxy. para. anti.	aff.-myst.
Wounds	a) Xt.: (7), (42–43), 46–49	pers. para. anti.	dec.-myst.
	b) soul: 2, (3), (7), (11)	anti, oxy.	myst.
Joy	a) praise: (20–22)	pers.	dec.
	b) love: (3), (7), (11), (18)	oxy. anti.	aff.
	c) penance: (15–17)	meta.	myst.
	d) Xt.: 2, (7), (17)	oxy.	aff.
	e) theol.: 29	meta.	myst.
Sighs	a) theol.: 29	meta.	myst.
	b) *amor conc.*: (4–8)	anti.	myst.-aff.
	c) penance: 9, (14–16)	pers.	myst.-aff.
	d) Xt.: 37, 39, 43	meta.	myst.
Tears	a) longing: (3), (5–8), (11)	oxy. meta.	aff.-myst.
	b) sorrow: (6), (11), (15)	sim. para.	aff.-myst.
	c) compassion: 44, 49	pers. para.	aff.-myst.
	d) *n.c.*: (38), 39–41, 45, 49	pers. para. sim.	aff.-myst.
Taste	a) *amor conc.*: (7–8), (11), 2, (34)	oxy. para.	myst.-conc.
	b) praise: (22), 23, (28)	para. meta.	dec.
	c) theol.: 29	para.	myst.
Anatomy	a) Xt.: (8), 9–10, (18), 33–34, (42–43)	sim. meta. para.	dec.
Death	a) longing: 2, (7–8), (11)	anti.	myst.
	b) physical: (12–13)	pers.	aff.
	c) Xt.: (11), (38), (43), 49–50	pers. para.	aff.
	d) theol.: 51	meta.	myst.
Arrows	a) nature: (8), (13)	para. pers. sim.	dec.-aff.
	b) death: (11–12)	pers.	aff.
	c) world: (14)	para.	aff.
	d) *Cupido-Xtus*: 1–2, (3), 10, 20, 34, 40	anti, pers.	aff.-myst.
Precious	a) world: 1, 10	metonym.	dec.

Image-Field	Function	Structure	Style
Objects	b) praise: (21—22), (25—26), (28)	para. sim. pers.	dec.
	c) Xt.: 9—10, (18), 34, 39, (43), 44, 46	para. sim. meta.	dec.
	d) God's power: (24)	metonym.	dec.

A. Elemental Images (Inorganic)

1. Light

Table 1.1

"Sonnenschein" [*TN* (3):3,4; (8):9,2; (20):1,2; (21):2,1–2; 32:189,23–24]; stars: [*TN* 9:1,6–7; (24):1,2–3]; moon: [(21):2,1–2]. These later images, which are more specifically cosmic, will be treated as a group below. Verbal expressions of light occur as: "glitzend blümelein:" (*TN* 23:13,6); "erglitzet" (32:189,24); "entzünd" [(17):20,6]; "leuchten" [(16):3,8]; "scheinen" [(16):13,1,5–6]; "glitzen" (26:3,4). Substantives occur such as: "stralen" [(21):7,3]; "augen-licht" [(17):20,5]; "flämlein" [(11):56,3–4]; "augenstrahl" [(16):3,8]; "hertzen-licht" [(11):21,2]; "fackeln" (27:2,6); "glantz" (29:7,5). Adjectives are: "klar und hell" (9:1,6); "lauter" [(18):4,6]; "wohlgezündet" [(24):1,2]; "liechtes" [(6):13,2]; and "gülden" (29:31,3).

---

2. Night-Darkness

Table 2.1

"Schwarze stunden" (*TN* 45:291,24); "gar braunem kleid" (*TN* 44:1,6); "Braune stunden" (*TN* 49:324,4); simple adjectival use: "In lauter schwartzen dunst" (*TN* 23:20,4); "guter nacht" [*TN* (38):10,1]; "Finstren nacht" [*TN* (18):2,2]; "schwere finsternüsse" (*GTB*, 205.22).

Table 2.2

"Wan morgenröth // Die nacht ertödt" [*TN* (7):1,1–2]; "Erd und himmel schwartz benachtet // Stunden in gar braunem Kleid" (*TN* 44:1,5–6), or as in *TN* (16):1,5–6 where the brown night carries the day to rest. In *GTB* 294.21 night chases away the day.

---

3. Color

Table 3.1

The nightingales are called: "wilde färbelein" [*TN* (52):4,3—4]; their songs are described as: "Die Färblein" [*TN* (5):4,4] and also as: "starcken ferben" [*TN* (21):14,7] and [*TN* (20):5,3—4]. The flower in *TN* (21):5,7 is replete with color: "ohne zahl hast farb;" bird's feathers are: "zart feder-farben" [*TN* (21):15,6]. Jesus' lips are "die schöne rosenfarb" (*TN* 10:11,4). When Mary Magdalen feels Christ's love in "ihr marck in beinen," it "colors" her heart and spirit: "Und farbet hertz und muth" [*TN* (11):57,1—4]. When Christ's wounds bleed, then He is described as "viel zu starck gefärbet" [*TN* (42):2,3]. In a verbal image referring to the beauty of God's creation, Spee writes: "Grün färbet Er den erdenklotz / Mit blümlein untermahlet" (*TN* 26:6,1—2). See also *TN* 30:179,20 and 31:184,20—24.

Table 3.2

The blood of Christ [*TN* 9:9,3—4; 10:11,5—6; (18):9,5—7 and 39:8,6];[1] to Christ the hero [*TN* (10):12,8; 13,2]; to flowers (*TN* 39:8,8); to Christ's teeth (*TN* 47:301,8—9); to His tears (*TN* 39:7,4).

[1]Red-colored blood is Spee's adaptation of Conrad Vetter's translation of the famous medieval hymn *Jubilus de nomine Jesu*. For Vetter's influence on Spee cf. Rosenfeld, *Neue Studien*, pp. 78ff.

Table 3.3

His hands and feet are "marmer-weiss" (*TN* 9:9,1—4); "weisser als das helffenbein" (*TN* 44:6,2); His hair is "gülden" [*TN* 9:14,2; (11):10,2; 34:204,7—8]; "gelb" (*TN* 44:8,2). Golden hair is also a Petrarchan trait and Spee shows a special preference for this image. Christ's sides are "corall und purpur" (*TN* 10:11,1 and 18,4); His skin is "weisses helffenbein" (*TN* 10:12,4; 13,8); His feet are "purpur" (*TN* 33:3,3); "purpur-schwesterlein" [*TN* (43):2,2]; His tears are "silber-weiss" [*TN* (18):9,6]. Christ Himself is compared to the moon: "weiss und bleicher dan der Mon" [*TN* (38):3,3]; His wounds are "rothe bächlein" (*TN* 42:1,7); "roth" (*TN* 42:12,4); "rothe rosen" (*TN* 48:307,24);

His blood is "warme purpur" [*TN* (43):14,5]; "purpur farbe" (*TN* 48:312,3); "purpur uber marmer bleich" (*TN* 46:4,8); "purpur-schaum" (*TN* 47:2,4). Compared to Christ's red cheeks the dawn is: "gleich dem koth" (*TN* 10:10,2).

Table 3.4

The heavens are a "blaues feld" (*TN* 27:3,2; 30:180,23); "blaue strassen" [*TN* (9):2,3]; "blaue-gefarbten weiden" (*TN* 30:179,20). The stars are "gülden Woll" (*TN* 39:14,4); "gülden fräulein" [*TN* (9):6,2]; "Schäfflein gülden-gelb" (*TN* 39:1,2); "gelb" [*TN* (24):2,1]; "gülden Lämerlein" (*TN* 30:180,13); "gülden Herd" (*TN* 30:181,15). Sheep are "silber-weiss" [*TN* (9):14,6]; "schwanen-weiss" [*TN* (9):17,2]; the sun has a "purpur schoss" (*TN* 10:1,4); the day is "Schwanen-weiss" [*TN* (11):21,7]; the moon is "bleich" (*TN* 39:17,2); and "gülden perll" (*TN* 44:2,4); the dawn is "purpur" (*TN* 48:311,16); the beams of the sun are golden [*TN* (7):1,3]; and also [*TN* (8):11,7]; swans are "In schnee gefärbte" [*TN* (22):18,6]; bees are "gelbe kriegerlein" (*TN* 23:5,4); and "gülden-gelbe schaar" (*TN* 23:33,6).

---

4. Water

Table 4.1

"Der hagel wie die perlen voll" [*TN* (28):12,3]; "Die wässer all mit lindem schein // Wie glas / und silber leuchten" (*TN* 26:5,3—4);

> Die brünlein sich ergiessen
> Und ihre wässer klar
> Wie silber stralen schiessen
> Von felsen offenbahr. [*TN* (21):7,1—4; cf. also (18):4,5—6]

Brooks are like crooked snakes:

> Die blümlein sich nun melden.
> Wie Schlänglein krumb
> Gehn lächlend umb
> Die bächlein kühl in Wälden. [*TN* (8):1,8—10]

And the brooks flow from the hills "Wie pfeil von Felsen ziehlen" [*TN* (8):2,7].

Table 4.2

The spring is a "feuchte brust der erden" [*TN* (28):26,6]; brooks are "reines wasser-glas" (*TN* 27:12,5); "Crystallen klar" [*TN* (22):18,1]; "geschmoltzen glass" [*TN* (21):9,8]; the paths of streams are "feuchter strass" (*TN* 9:5,8); fountains are "silber-weisse töchterlein" [*TN* (8):2,3]; rain is described as: "Der lieblichst Göttertranck" (*TN* 33:15,6).

Table 4.3

"Die feuchte reich zerschneidet // So stumm / ohn stimmen / ohn discurs" (*TN* 26:5,7−8); the dew crowns the fields as: "die felder lieblich crönet" [*TN* (22):6,7−8]; and the fountains "frölich springen" [*TN* (22):7,2; (7):2,3−4]. Brooks "zancken mit den steinlein" [*TN* (21):8,2−3]; "frölich klingen zu" [*TN* (20):8,5−6]; "sausen" [*TN* 1:3,8; (18):4,5; (21):8,5]; "schwitzen" [*TN* (4):1,10]; "spatziren" (*TN* 33:14,5−8). The brook Cedron sings verses and pipes a shepherd-song (*TN* 1:9,5−8).

5. Fire, Heat, Flame, Bruning

Table 5.1

In the prose text of *GTB* Bk. II, chapter 13, Christ is called "du flamm meiner begirden," "du süsser brand" (211.16−17) which is repeated in *TN* 32:196,22 and *TN* 34:207,1. *GTB* 200.25: "du feuer meines hertzens" is Christ and *TN* (6):2,6. *GTB* 408.24: "die Liebe ist ein starkes Feuer" and *TN* (7):17,1. *GTB* 224.34−36: "O Jesus, Jesu Wunden Nahm, / Wie brinnest mir im Hertzen! / Bist warlich nur ein lauter flamm" and *TN* (3):4,1−2. *GTB* 224.17: "O Flämmlein süss" and *TN* 34:206,22−207,1. *GTB* 219.15−16: "Das brint gleich einer kertze // Von Jesu lieb gerührt" and *TN* (3):1,5 −8.

Table 5.2

Jesus' name is a "Flämmlein" [*TN* (3):4,1], a metaphor expressing the spouse's reaction to the intensity of Christ's love [*TN* (3):3,5—6; (3):1,5—6; (3):6,5—6]; for the stars (*TN* 26:3,1—2; 44:2,1—2); for the love emanating from Christ's eyes (*TN* 10:4,3).

Table 5.3

"hertzen-brandt" [*TN* (6):2,6; 32:196,22]; "brand" [*TN* (4):2,4]; "augen--brandt" (*TN* 42:10,6); "feuer" [*TN* (7):17,1]; "hitz" [*TN* (11):15,8]; "hertzen-feuer" (*TN* 34:205,25); "glut" (*TN* 47:303,24; 29:28,7); "fieber" (*TN* 48:309,24). Verbal forms are "entzünden" [*TN* (7):20,4—6]; "kühlen" [*TN* (3):6,7—8]; "einfressen" [*TN* (3):4,3—4]; "zehren" [*TN* (3):4,3]; "brennen" [*TN* (4):20,2; (4):4,2]; "überwinden" [*TN* (43):47,7]; "anzünden" [*TN* (42):4,6]; "toben" [*TN* (11):15,8]; "erbrinnen" [*TN* (13):9,7; 29:29,4; 29:25,6].

Stars

Table 6.1

The stars are: "fackel-pracht" [*TN* (28):4,5]; "feuer und flamm" [*TN* (15):2,4; 40:14,1]; "sternen kram" [*TN* (14):80,24]; "Himel-kertzen" (*TN* 9:2,7); "geld-gewaffnet Heer" (*TN* 33:9,(6)); "gülden perll und Edelstein" (*TN* 44:2,3). The sun is a "himmlisch augenball" (*TN* 23:21,2); "klares goldt" (*TN* 31:184,16); "runden-schein" (*TN* 49:324,3); "schöne bildtnuss" (*TN* 49:319,7). Personifications occur frequently, taken from the animal world: "Schäfflein gülden-geld" (*TN* 39:1,2); "gelbe schaar" [*TN* (24):2,1]; "gülden Ross und Wagen [*TN* (22):2,2]. These animal personifications, of cosmic nature, are also typical of the decorative mode.[1]

[1]Windfuhr, p. 260, lists many such personifications from Lohenstein, Weckherlin, and Hofmannswaldau.

Table 6.2

The "Sonnenwagen" occurs [*TN* (6):3,1–4; (11):20,506; (22):2,1–6; 41:13,1–2; 47:297,17–20; 31:185,13–14; 32:191,4–7; 49:322,16–17]; "Rossen" [*TN* (11):1,1–4; 31:185,11–14; 49:319,4–9; 51:8,1–4]. "Pfeil" and "Köcher" referring to the sun's rays [*TN* (8):3,5–10; 31:185,2–5; 49:322,14–17].

===

Table 6.3

"weinen" referring to the stars [*TN* (38):14,3–4]; to the moon (*TN* 45:292,4–5; 39:18,3); to the sun (*TN* 45:287,26–288,1). "leiden" refers to the moon (*TN* 38:14,1–2); and to the moon and the stars together (*TN* 45:292,2–3). "Lachen" referring to the sun [*TN* (21):2,6]; "laufen" referring to the sun (*TN* 50:326,3). The moon and the stars put the sun to bed (*TN* 49:321,22–23). The moon's heart breaks (*TN* 39:6,2); the moon drives the stars (personified as sheep) to pasture (*TN* 39:1,1–4). The sun sits (*TN* 49:322,17); curls her hair (*TN* 50:325,22); climbs the heavens (*TN* 32:191,16) and pretties herself (*TN* 32:191,6–7).

===

7. *Firmament*

Table 7.1

"blaue strassen" (*TN* 9:2,3); "marmor glatten-meilen" [*TN* (8):3,10]; "blaues feld und wasen" (*TN* 27:3,2); "weit und breites feldt" [*TN* (28):4,1]; "blau gefarbten weiden" (*TN* 30:179,20); "runde Wiesen" (*TN* 34:207,26); "geründter blauen Heiden" (*TN* 39:1,3). The concept of the rounded firmament as "in die rund gebogen" cited above from *GTB* 301.8 and also *TN* (11):20,3: "himmel rund-gebogen;" and the phrase "blau gewölb" (*TN* 32:191,16) is found also in Gryphius.[1]

[1]Cf. Windfuhr, *Bildlichkeit,* p. 195.

===

8. Air, Wind and Clouds

Table 8.1

(a) through His action in the universe [TN (25):3,5−6; 26:4,1−2; 7,3−4; 10,1−2; 11,1−4; 12,5−6]; (b) through the beauty of their very existence [TN (13):3,5−6; (8):4,1−4; (21):11,7−8; (22):4,8]; (c) by reason of the fact that as creatures they owe fitting praise to their Creator [TN (24):6,7−8; (28):7,8,9,10; (14):1−2; (11):21,5−8; 27:6,1−2].

Table 8.2

The following uses of paraphrase occur in the TN: "Du web gar zart gesponnen" [TN (28):7,2] as the air; hyperbole occurs: "Ihr wind zween uber fünffmal sechss" [TN (28):11,3]. This is a rhetorical paraphrase for the thirty-two directional readings on the compass.[1] The clouds are called "lufftgewächss" [TN (28):11,1]; "schnauffend lufft-gesind" (TN 26:11,3). Thunder appears under the following image: "stoltzer wolcken-stimm" (TN 26:12,5). The winter-wind is called: "Der fliegend winter-bott" (TN 35:1,6).

Personifications are: (a) nominal: "All Jüngling still von sitten" as the cool summer wind [TN (8):4,1−4]; animal personifications: God puts wings on the wind [TN (28):14,1]; the wind shakes its wings (TN 1:4,1−4 and 35:1,1−2) and contracts its wings (TN 41:11,1−2). (b) verbal: greifen (TN 25:1,7); lachen [TN (18):2,4]; rühren [TN (13):3,6]; verschnauffen [TN (6):6,4]; stossen [TN (21):11,8]; bestraffen (TN 26:10,1−2); umhalsen [TN (28):21,7−8]; musicieren (TN 27:6,2); dienen (TN 40:22,2); schlafen (TN 44:1,4); feiern (TN 45:286,18); trauren (TN 45:287,22); weinen (TN 45:287,25); and schwimmen [TN (21):11,7].

[1]Cf. Van Oorschot's notes on this passage, p. 608.

B. Organic Nature

1. Flowers

Table 1.1

---

stoltzieren (TN 50:4,3); *lächeln* (TN 27:9,5); *loben* (TN 27:10,3); *gaffen, gienen* (TN 23:4,3–5); zieren (TN 1:1,1–4); hälslein nidersencken [TN (13)10,6]; *bravieren* [TN (13):14,1]; "Da nehret sich dass leben // Und seel in grünem blut" [TN (21):12,7–8]; and *wänglein* [TN (13):6,4].

Table 1.2

Christ's wounds are called: "rothe röselein" (TN 10:15,2); "rothen Blümelein" (TN 10:16,6); "beyden Rosen roth" (TN 10:17,2); "Daphnis wunden rosenroth" (TN 48:305,22); "rothe rosen" (TN 48:307,24). Close parallels exist also in the *GTB*. The wounds in Christ's head are "purpurfarbe rosen" (GTB 522.35) and Christ's cheeks are compared to "die allerliebste lilgen und rosen" (TN 523.38). Jesus' lips are "blumen" [TN (18):8,6]; "Rosen" (TN 34:205.6). The wounds in Christ's side are called "rothes Rosenkleid" (TN 48:311,22).

Table 1.3

"gülden öpffel / gülden kernen" (TN 44:2,3). Flowers themselves are paraphrased as "du garten Sternelein" [TN (13):7,2]; "frisch und zartes blut" [TN (21):5,6]; "wol gemahlter hauff" (TN 50:4,4). The activity of bees in collecting honey is described as "süsser blumen Krieg" (TN 23:9,6).

---

3. Seasons of the Year, Hours of the Day

Table 3.1

"guter nacht" [TN (38):10,1]; "trüben winter-tag" [TN (17):1,6; (8):1,1]; "schöne Frühlingszeit" [TN (17):4,2]; "schöne Frühling" [TN (4):2,1]; "edle sommer zeit" [TN (13):1,2]; "werthen Sommerzeit" [TN (21):4,4]; "edler Mey" [TN (8):9,8]; "zarter morgenschein" [TN (16):1,1]; "schöne morgenröth" (TN 30:179,8); "klare morgenstunden" (TN 32:191,8); "purpur morgen stunden" (TN 51:1,1).

Table 3.2

"gehen zu grab" [Winter in TN (17):1,4]; "gebrochen" (winter in TN 18:2,5); "ertöden" [dawn in TN (7):1,2]; "entfliehen" [day in TN (3):3,1]; "verkün-den" [summer in TN (3):1,3]; "leiten" [spring in TN (22):3,4]; "verkleiden" [evening in TN (15):1,2]; "sich zieren" (dawn in TN 1:1,1); "erbleichen" (dawn in TN 10:10,1); "wachen" (dawn in TN 30:183,17); "sich crönen" (dawn in TN 30:179,9); "Haar entbinden" (dawn in TN 32:191,8—10); "in lüfften spreiten" (dawn in TN 32:191,11); "sich schmucken" (spring in TN 33:14,1); "an die thür klopfen" (spring in TN 48:307,22); "aus dem beth erstehen" (morning in TN 48:311,16—18); "todt ligen" (winter in TN 49:316,6).

---

4. Animals

Table 4.1

She is a more beautiful singer than other birds (TN 1:5,1—2); she is wounded with the arrow of love (TN 1:6,1—2); she seeks only God and dies in the attempt and despises worldly pomp (TN 1:6,3—8); and she is engaged in the singing of God's praises [TN (22):4,1—10]. In TN (5) her heart breaks from singing out the name "Jesum." In TN 20 she sings God's praise and surpasses all other in her ability to do so (TN 20:5,1—8). The nightingale appears again briefly in TN 45:282,7—8 as "schönes fräulein," called so by Daphnis (Christ).

Table 4.2

---

a) in a *natura compatiens* role "die wilden thier" grieve along with the soul contemplating Christ's agony in the garden [TN (38):15,3]; birds collectively mourn over Christ (TN 45:282,25—283,6).

b) as poetic preludes and "compositions of place" birds appear collectively [*TN*
   1:2,1–2; (8):1,3–4; and (17):2,1]; dawn's horse is clad with roses [*TN*
   (6):3,3–4]; the moon rides on a "braune Rappen" (*TN* 9:1–2); the
   nightingale (*TN* 49:315,21–316,2).
c) in praising God's creation: birds [*TN* (21):13,1–8; (20):2,1–8; 27:6,5–8;
   50:2,1–8; (28):8,1–4]; the nightingale [*TN* (21):14,1–8 and (22):4,1–6];
   nightingales collectively [*TN* (52):1,1–6; 3,1–3]; the bees (*TN* 23:5,3–4;
   8,5–6; 29,7–8); sheep (*TN* 30:180,11–21).

Table 4.3

The tiny flower [*TN* (13)] sways like a bird on a string (3,7–8). In *TN* (8)
flowers look like crooked snakes (1,6–7). In *TN* 26:3,1–3 the stars gleam like
the proud peacock. In *TN* 40:21,1–2 Daphnis sheep are as white as swans.

Table 4.4

Birds are called "feder-vieh" [*TN* (24):7,5]; "schönes feder volck" (*TN*
45:282,2); "gefedert Schwesterlein" [*TN* (52):2,1]; "süsse Schwesterlein" [*TN*
(52):3,1]; "lufft- und wolcken-Sängerlein" [*TN* (52):3,3]; "marmer-weisse
schaar" (*TN* 49:317,20); "flügend psälterlein" [*TN* (20):7,4]; "pfeifflein" (*TN*
1:1,7). Bees are called "stolze Bürgerschaft" (*TN* 23:23,2); "gülden-gelbe
schaar" (*TN* 23:33,6). Sheep are "weisse wüllen ballen" (*TN* 32:193,19);
"Schwanen-weisse zucht" (*TN* 9:17,2), and "wüllen völcklein" (*TN* 45:282,7);
"Schwester zart" [*TN* (5):3,1]; "mütigs hertz" [*TN* (5):10,5]: "gülden kertz"
[*TN* (5):10,3]; "die Meisterin in Walden" [*TN* (5):4,2]; and "Fräulein reich von
stimmen" [*TN* (5):7,7]. Nests are paraphrases as "Kindbettlein" [*TN* (18):3,8];
wings are "rüderlein" (*TN* 1:2,8). Occasionally religious figures are referred to
under the guise of animals. Mary Magdalen is called "Täublein" [*TN* (17):5,2].
Christ is a "halbes hirschlein" (*TN* 47:301,24); "Lämlein zart" (*TN* 48:313,5),
and "frisches Hirschen-kindt" (*TN* 10:5,8). The daughters of Jerusalem are
referred to as "tauben-reine Tochter" (*TN* 51:1,5).

C. Human Existence

1. Love

Table 1.1

In the soul's concentration on love's painfulness [*TN* 2:2,3–6; *GTB* 408,8–10; (7);3,6; (6):10,1; (11):27,7–8]; its restless character [*TN* 2:2,7; (6):1,3–4]; its searing quality [*TN* (3):1,5–6; 5,1–4; (11):49,8]; the sharpness of its heat (*TN* 2:4,1); its debilitating effect [*TN* (6):2,1–2; *GTB* 202.15–16; 214.17; 181.37; *TN* (11):58,7]; the soul's sorrow [*TN* (6):10,1]; her sickness [*TN* (6):11,8; *GTB* 208.33; 211.5 and 181.37]; love's force [*GTB* 134.1–15 and *TN* (7):22,1]; love's poison [*TN* (11):9,5–6]; the soul's confusion [*TN* (11):15,5–6]; the soul's losing sight of her beloved and centering on her own subjective state.

Table 1.2

Supreme [*TN* (8):8,1–2 and *GTB* 151.32ff.]; as affective [*TN* (9):11,1–2; 33:3,3–5; 34:204,20–205,1]; their mutual embrace (*TN* 10:17,5–7; 19,3); its contrition [*TN* (11):5,5–8]; the exclusivity of her love (*TN* 46:5,1–8 and *GTB* 197.23–25); her willingness to suffer for the beloved (*TN* 49:317,26–318,4; 318,22–25); and her eagerness to die for him (*GTB* 215.37ff., 525.32ff. and *TN* 2:7,5–8; 10:6,3–4).

Table 1.3

"erbrinnen" (*TN* 29:25,6); "durchrissen" [*TN* (11):59,7]; "brennen" [*GTB* 219.21; *TN* (11):49,8]; "verfolgen" [*TN* (7):11,5]; "ubernehmen" [*TN* (7):12,6]; "durchstecken" [*TN* (7):22,6]; "zehren" [*TN* (3):5,5]; "einnehmen" [*TN* (6):1,2]; "Kräncken" [*TN* (6):2,2]; "plagen" [*TN* (6):9,1]; "schmecken" [*TN* (8):8,1]; "erfrieren" [*TN* (16):14,6]; "Zerschmeltzen" [*TN* (16):13,8; *GTB* 406.31ff.]; "verblenden" [*TN* (43):45,5]; "küssen" (*TN* 9:11,2): "entäugen" [*TN* (11):11,2]; "bethören" (*TN* 40:4,4); "tödten" (*TN* 40:13,3); "Verwunden" (*TN* 34:208,1; *GTB* 227,30): "Zünden" [*TN* (43):42,5; *GTB* 203.35].

Table 1.4

"blind" (*TN* 40:11,1–2); "Scharpff" (*TN* 2:4,1); "starck" [*TN* (7):22,1];
"keusch" (*TN* 2:3,5); "unvermessen" (*TN* 29:25,2); "kühl" [*TN* (7):16,2];
"süss" (*GTB* 408.25). Love appears under a variety of metaphors, paraphrases,
and personifications: "abentheuer" [*TN* (7):17,2]; "flammen" (*TN* 29:21,7);
"feuer" [*TN* (7):17,1]; "hertzen Dieb" [*TN* (7):22,2]; "Kühle Brunst" [*TN*
(7):16,2]; "brenn/und kühl" [*TN* (7):16,4]; "Cupido rein" (*TN* 2:3,5);
"hertzen-brandt" (*TN* 10:6,4); "wasser" [*TN* (7):17,3]; "Flügel" (*TN* 2:4,2);
"Mündelein" (*TN* 34:204,20–23).

Table 1.5

Love is both fire and water [*TN* (7):17,1–3]; it is joy and sorrow [*TN*
(7):17,4–5]; it is sweet and bitter [*TN* (3):6,1–2]; it is a "kühle Brunst" [*TN*
(7):16,2]; "brennt und kühlt" [*TN* (7):16,4]; "zehrt und nehrt" [*TN* (3):5,5–8];
it is both love and sorrow [*TN* (11):27,7]. In *TN* 2:3,5ff. the spouse cries out "O
keusche Kieb / Cupido rein // Alda dein hitz erkühle" and in *TN* 2:2,6: "O wee
der süssen peine!" (also *GTB* 408.9); and "süsse marter."

---

2. Heart

Table 2.1

---

zerfliessen[1] (Langen, 292); *brennen* (Langen, 72); *zerbrechen* (Langen, 78);
zerschmelzen (Langen, 292 and 421); *zerschlagen* (Langen, 421).

[1]References in parentheses are to the page in Langen, *Wortschatz,* where a
similar expression occurs in pietistic circles.

Table 2.2

---

zerbrechen [*GTB* 120.9–10; 227.3; 369.8; and *TN* (7):13,6; 9:13,6; (15):8,8;
39:10,7 and (43):28,4]; *zerschmeltzen* [*GTB* 145.39–40; 393.6; and *TN*
(16):13,8]; *zerspalten* [*GTB* 213.1; 226.16; 368.13; and *TN* (5):8,2]; *zersprin-*

gen [*GTB* 216.13; 168.21–22; 218.7; and *TN* (38):9,2]. Other *TN* verbal expressions for love are: *spalten* (*TN* 39:6,2); *reissen* [*TN* (38):8,4]; *krachen* [*TN* (5):10,1; and (20):4,7]; *weichen* [*TN* (7):5,2]; *befangen* [*TN* (11):23,3]; *kräncken* [*TN* (15):7,6 and (20):4,7]; *zerschlagen* (*TN* 41:8,3); *abstehlen* (*TN* 44:12,7); and *brechen* (*TN* 41:8,8).

Table 2.3

"gülden Kertz" [*TN* (5):10,1] standing for the heart of the *Trutznachtigall;* Christ is called "hertzen-dieb" [*TN* (7):22,2] and "Hertz des Hertzen" [*TN* (43):27,6]. "hertzen winde" are the sighs of Mary Magdalen [*TN* (11):32,3] and the sighs of the soul (*TN* 46:10,3–6). "Hertz-concept" is the name given the Son in the Trinity (*TN* 29:15,5); and "hertz von seinem hertzen" (*TN* 29:17,6). The wound in the side of Christ (*TN* 46:13,2) is called "hertzen-kast." "Hertzen-grund" [*TN* (3):7,5–6; *GTB* 56.31, and 57.2] is a standard mystical term used among the German mystics and probably originated with Augustine.[1] It is defined in Sandaeus, *Clavis*, p. 219, as: ". . . designare in Mysticorum arcanis, intentionem, finem, propositum, appetitum, desiderium, cor."[2]

[1]Cf. Lüers, *Sprache*, p. 189.
[2]For the use of the term "Herzensgrund" among the Pietists, cf. Langen, *Wortschatz*, p. 167.

Table 2.4

Here the heart reflects the soul's pain (*TN* 2:2,5); sorrow [*TN* (6):9,5–6]; dissolution [*TN* (7):8,5–6]; metaphorical state of dying [*TN* (7):13,5–6]. In *TN* (38):9,1–4 Christ tells His mother that His heart will burst for pain.

---

3. Pain and Sorrow

Table 3.1

---

a) In *TN* (38):15,3 the wild animals mourn with Christ in His passion;
b) In *TN* (38):14,1–2 and 39:18,5–8 the moon can no longer shine because of her sorrow for Christ;

c) In *TN* 44:1,7—8 the sun, moon, and stars sorrow at Christ's death;

d) In *TN* 45:284,18—25 Halton commands the brooks, streams, fountains and mountains to lament Christ's death;

e) In *TN* 45:283,17—24 and 47:302,20—24 the birds lament Daphnis;

f) In *TN* 49:321,19—20 the waters lament Christ's death.

Table 3.2

---

a) Mary, Christ's mother, in *TN* 44:9,1—3 and 18,1—4;

b) The soul laments Christ crucified in *TN* 40:19,1 and 46:10,7—8 as do Phidaemon in *TN* 47:301,1—4 and Halton in *TN* 49:320,7—10.

3. Christ Himself sorrows in His passion and death:

a) In *TN* 37:7,7—8 Christ's head is torn in pieces by heat and fire;

b) In *TN* 37:5,1—8 Christ suffers seeking the lost sheep;

c) In *TN* (38):11,1—2 the cross hovers before Christ's eyes and He suffers profound inner pain and sorrow;

d) In *TN* 39:10,5—6 Daphnis experiences such mental anguish that he cannot speak;

e) In *TN* 43:24,5—8 Christ communicates, in sorrow, with His mother, Mary;

f) In *TN* 51:7,1—4 the soul contemplates Christ's pain and death in the bread of the Eucharist.

Table 3.3

---

a) contrast:

   i) the soul is in deep torment while the world is in joy [*TN* (8):6,5—10];

   ii) during the beauty of spring [*TN* (8):11,1—10];

   iii) during the brightness of nature [*TN* (17):3,1—8];

b) in agreement with the soul's sorrow:

   i) in pain late at night [*TN* (6):3,7—8];

   ii) the soul tells pain to flee into the darkness of the night [*TN* (18):2,1—2].

Table 3.4

a) The painful effects of Christ's love in the soul cause: restlessness [TN 2:2,7; (6):5,5–8; (7):9,4–6]; sweet pain [TN 2:2,3–6; (3):4,5–6; (7):14,1]; torment [TN (3):3,5–6; (6):5,1–6]; pain [TN (6):2,5; (7):3,6]; love-plaint [TN (6):9,5–6]; constant torment [TN (6):10,1–4]; general malaise [TN (6):11,8]; exhaustion [TN (7):4,1–2]; distress [TN (7):7,6]; sweet distress [TN (7):13,4]; speechlessness [TN (7):13,3; 24,3]; and both pain and joy [TN (7):21,5–6];

b) The soul's love-yearning is expressed in her pain and her absence from Jesus [TN (3):2,5–8; 32:197,25–198,2]; in her loneliness [TN (8):7,1–10; 10,3–4]; in her fevered searching for Him [TN (11):26,1–8];

c) There is also the pain which results from actual union with the beloved:
   i) The soul expresses her indifference to pain and even death itself (TN 2:6,7–7,8);
   ii) The soul professes her continual torment since her marriage with Christ [TN (8):6,5–10];
   iii) The soul experiences sweetness in pain and pain in sweetness (TN 10:19,1–2).

Table 3.5

queelen [TN (3):3,5]; verkräncken (GTB 208.33); ermatten [TN (7):14,3]; achtzen [TN (11):19,1]; schmeltzen [TN (11):27,8]; zerfliessen [TN (15):7,8]; verderben [TN (16):6,6]; erstochen [TN (18):2,7]; zerplagen (TN 44:9,3); zerspleissen (TN 44:9,1); zerschlagen [TN (18):7,1]; verletzen (TN 34:205,26 tödten (TN 40:13,3).

Table 3.6

"süsse peine" referring to the effect of God's love on the soul (TN 34:206.25), and to the effect of the arrows of love (TN 2:2,3–6). The searing flame of Jesus' love is described as: "O süssigkeit in schmertzen // O schmertz in süssigkeit" [TN (3):4,5–6]. Both "leidt" and "ergetzlichkeit" are a further result of this flame of love [TN (3):6,5–8]. The soul's love for Christ causes the following reactions:

"süsser noth" [*TN* (7):14,1]; "freud und leyd" [*TN* (7):21,5]; "lieb und leyd" [*TN* (11):27,7].

---

4. Wounds

Table 4.1

---

a) a place of refreshment for the soul (*GTB* 392.14ff.; 399.21−22 and 522.34ff.);
b) a means of purification (*GTB* 201.16);
c) a place of joy (*GTB* 385.27ff.; 385.5ff.);
d) a place of refuge and rest (*GTB* 389.1ff.);
e) a source of virtue and a bulwark against the deceits and wiles of the worldly way of life (*GTB* 399.23−32; 400.1−19);
f) a means for deep union with Christ the beloved (*GTB* 399.38ff.);
g) a place where the soul can die for love (*GTB* 413.6ff., and 525.32ff.);
h) a supremely desirable treasure above every created good (*GTB* 405.38−406.25).

Table 4.2

Christ's wounds are:
a) a joy [*TN* (17);7,5−8; 46:12,1−4; 49:318,22−25; *GTB* 385.27, and 388.5ff.];
b) a source of peace (*TN* 46:13,4);
c) a source of rest (*TN* 46:14,8; 49:317,8−15; *GTB* 389.1ff.);
d) a place of refreshment (*TN* 49:320,24−321,2; *GTB* 399.21−22; 392.12ff.; and 522.34ff.);
e) an object of contemplation [*TN* (42):1,5−8; 2,1−8; 46:1,1−8; 47:301,20−22; 48:305,22];
f) a means of purification (*TN* 46:6,1−8; 49:316,14−19; *GTB* 201.16);
g) a help against the spirit of the world (*TN* 48:308,4−11; *GTB* 399.23−32; 400.1−19);
h) a place for mystical dying in Christ (*TN* 46:13,3−4; *GTB* 413.6ff.; 525.32ff.).

Table 4.3

"bronnen" (*TN* 46:8,1); "safft" [*TN* (42):1,6]; "bächlein" (*TN* 49:320,23);
"rothe bächlein" [*TN* (42):1,7]; "heisse brünlein" [*TN* (42):2,8]; "strämen" [*TN*
(43):47,6]; "Bächlein von Corall und glass" (*TN* 46:5,6); "rothe rosen" (*TN*
48:305,22; 307,24 and *GTB* 404.22–23); "blumen-strauss" (*TN* 48:308,9);
"rubin und perlen gass" (*TN* 46:5,8); "pforten" (*TN* 46:12,5 and *GTB* 399.39);
"seiten-thür" (*TN* 46:12,6); "hertzen-kast" (*TN* 46:13,2); "matratz" (*TN*
46:13,8); "bettlein" (*TN* 46:13,8).

---

5. *Joy*

Table 5.1

Christ is the source of joy [*TN* (3):7,4–8; 6,7–8 and (7):19,1–6]; the love of
Christ is opposed to the love of the world [*TN* (3):7,1–8]; the subjective
love-experience brings tears of joy [*TN* (7):21,4–6]; the awaited love-embrace
between the soul and Christ will be a joyous experience [*TN* (6):12,7–8].

Table 5.2

---

a) Joy as an effect of the love between the spouse and Christ [*TN* (3):5,5–8;
   6,7–8; 7,7–8; (7):17,5; 21,4–6; (11):56,8 and (18):7,3–4].
b) The joy which accompanies the soul's reconciliation with God after she has
   done penance and shown sorrow for sin [*TN* (15):18,1–8; (16):16,7–8;
   17,3–4: and (17):11,1–4].
c) The soul experiences joy in nature's praise to the Creator [*TN* (20):1,5–8;
   8,5–6; (21):13,5–8; (22):5,1–8; 7,1–8; 12,1–2].
d) Christ's passion and suffering are a source of joy to the soul [*TN* (17):7,5–8;
   49:318,22–25; (17):6,5–8; 9,1–4].
e) Christ himself is a joy to the soul [*TN* 2:6,1–8; (7):19,3].
f) In the theological poem on the Trinity, *TN* (29), the epitome of joy and
   pleasure is expressed to indicate: (i) the trinitarian community existing
   between the Father and the Son (26,8); (ii) the Holy Spirit as the supreme
   joy: "O freud / ob allen freuden!" (27,4).

---

6. Sighs

Table 6.1

"aufsteigen" [*TN* (6):11,2]; "blasen in winde" [*TN* (8):10,8—10]; "sich heben" [*TN* (11):23,5]; and the phrases: "durch Wolcken" [*TN* (14):80,19]; "Zun Sternen" (*TN* 32:192,9); "in lufft und Wolcken" (*TN* 37:2,2). In *TN* 32:192,6—9, the sighs are acts of praise to God (cf. also *GTB* 486.25ff.). In *TN* 37:2,1—8 Christ sighs in longing for the lost sheep. In *TN* 39:10,5—6; 40:16,1—2 and (43):1,8 Christ emits sighs of agony in His passion. In *TN* 46:9,1—4 the nightingales are pictured as emitting sighs of sorrowful compassion over Christ's passion.

---

7. Tears

Table 7.1

---

1) The soul weeps because of her painful love-experience with Christ [*TN* (3):2,5—8; (5):3,4, and *GTB* 225.12; 226.5—6 and 229.17—20].
2) The soul weeps in longing for the heavenly Jerusalem and Christ [*TN* (6):12,1—3; (8):10,8—10; (7):3,1—2; (11):3,3—8; 19,1—2; 38,3—8; 39,1—4 and *GTB* 181.37—38; 210.32; 211.20—24].
3) The soul weeps because this world separates her from her beloved [*TN* (6):13,7—8 and *GTB* 190.27—30; 217.24—30].
4) The soul weeps out of compunction and sorrow for her sins which have displeased and angered God [*TN* (15):1,5—8; 4,1—2; 7,1—2; 17,1—8; (16):3,4—6; 4,5—8; 6,3 and *GTB* 361.11—12; 388.30].
5) Christ weeps in His search for the lost sheep (*TN* 37:2,1—8 and *GTB* 134.40ff.).
6) Nature weeps at Christ's sufferings (*GTB* 523.24—31):
   a) the moon (*TN* 39:18,3—4);
   b) the stars [*TN* (38):14,3—4];
   c) the rivers (*TN* 40:23,3);
   d) the brook Cedron (*TN* 41:1,5—6);
   e) the swans (*TN* 45:283,26—284,4);
   f) the cattle (*TN* 45:288,9—12);
   g) the trees (*TN* 45:290,16—23);
   h) the cliffs (*TN* 49:320,12—15).

Table 7.2

"bächlein" [*TN* (15):17,3–4; 44:14,7–8, and *GTB* 47.22; 229.19–20]; "augen-schweiss" [*TN* (15):17,7]; "weisse perl" and "corallen roth" (*TN* 39:7,3–8); "thränen bad" [*TN* (15):4,1]; "augen tropfen" (*TN* 39:18,3).

Table 7.3

"in zähren baden" [*TN* (5):3,4; (7):21,5–6; (16):4,5–6 and *GTB* 211.22]; "ernehren" [*TN* (6):11,5]; "zerfleussen" [*TN* (11):2,7; 3,4]; "rinnen" [*TN* (15):1,6]; "wangen träncken" (*TN* 40:18,7); "in zähren schwimmen" [*TN* (42):17,5; 45:284,4, and *GTB* 190.27–30]; "in thränen ersauffen" (*TN* 45:291,5); "wangen zerschleissen" (*TN* 37:2,5–8).

---

9. *The Human Anatomy*

Table 9.1

Christ's hair is "gülden" [*TN* 9:14,1–2, a Petrarchan convention (Jacobsen, p. 83), and *GTB* 523.1ff.]; "güldengelb" [*TN* 34:204,7–8 (Windfuhr, p. 242)]; "gelben" (*TN* 44:8,2); His cheeks are "süsse" [*TN* 44:14,5–8; (18):9,1 (Windfuhr, p. 246)]; "schöne" [*TN* 42:11,5–6; (8):12,10]; "purpur" (*TN* 34:204,21); His eyes are "theur" (*TN* 10:3,6); His lips are "schöne rosenfarb" [*TN* 10:11,4 (Windfuhr, p. 259)]; on his lips "nirgend besser blumen sein" [*TN* (18):8,3–5 (Windfuhr, pp. 240 and 259)]; "corallen stein" [*TN* (43):2,1–4 (Windfuhr, p. 259; Jacobsen, p. 90)]; "purpur" [*TN* (33):3,3–6 (Windfuhr, p. 240)]; His forehead is "mit rothen Blümelein besteckt" [*TN* 10:16,5–6 (Windfuhr, pp. 240,258)]. His mouth is "süssem honig-mund" [*TN* 34:205,16 (Windfuhr, p. 259)]. Jacobsen links this motif with a classical motif stemming from Ovid and Plautus.[1] His head ". . . raucht und windet" // Nach Zimmet und Zebeth" (*TN* 10:9,5–6). His hands and feet are compared to "weisses Helffenbein" [*TN* 9:9,1–2 (Windfuhr, p. 242)]. Another Petrarchan motif, where the lover's lips are a source of not only honey but life and refreshment, occurs in *TN* (18):7,7–8: "Nunmehr hab ichs leben sogen // Nur auss JESU lefftzen roth." Interestingly, Spee uses this motif in the *GTB*, Book II, chapter 8, where he seeks to lift the soul's spirits when she is in a mood of desolation.

[1]Cf. *Metamorphosen*, pp. 90–91.

Table 9.2

Christ's arms and hands are called: "Schwesterlein der Schwanen" (*TN* 2:5,1–2); Christ's eyes are "gläser-bogen" (*TN* 10:4,1); "fensterlein" (*TN* 10:4,4); "brünlein reich an feuchte" (*TN* 16:3,5–6); His cheeks are compared to "Winter-Blümelein" (*TN* 33:3,3–6); "Rosen" (*TN* 34:205,3–6); His lips are called "purpurschwesterlein" [*TN* (43):2,2]; and "corrallenstein" [*TN* (43):2,4].

10. Death

Table 10.1

"falb" [*TN* (5):12,2; (43):2,5; 47:302,1]; "süss" [*TN* (7):13,5]; "tief" [*TN* (38):13,2]; "kalt" [*TN* (43):47,8]; "bleiche" (*GTB* 368.22; *TN* 44:12,1; 50:10,3); "blindt" (*TN* 44:12,2); "schnöd" (*TN* 49:323,21); "grausam" (*GTB* 346.22); "bitter" (*GTB* 497.1).

Table 10.2

"haut- und beinen-Knecht" [*TN* (11):12,6]; "menschen-prasser" [*TN* (11):25,1]; "ungeheures Tier" [*TN* (11):25,2]. In the *GTB* the term "abscheuliche bestia" is used (345.3).

Table 10.3

"citieren" [*TN* (13):14,3]; "holen" [*TN* (13):12,3]; "entleiben" [*TN* (11):12,1]; "bestreichen" [*TN* (43):2,5]; "beschleichen" (*TN* 44:12,3); "beissen, weissen"

(*TN* 47:301,26); "bauen" (*TN* 50:10,3). In the *GTB* "bestricken" (121.3); "bringt ums leben" (346.22–23); "kompt heimlichen bucken" (198.6).

D. Realia

1. Arrows

Table 1.1

"süss" (*TN* 1:6,2) [*TN* (14):82,24; 34:205,18–19]; "gülden" (*TN* 2:1,7); "schnell" [*TN* (4):3,9]; "süsslich-herben" [*TN* (11):8,3]; "heiss" [*TN* (11):3,5]; "bleich" [*TN* (12):4,4]; "scharf und hitzig" [*TN* (20):1,4]; "stark" (*TN* 23:21,5); "blind" (*TN* 40:11,1); "zart" (*GTB* 225.18); "vergiffte" (*GTB* 198.1).

Table 1.2

"verschiessen" (*TN* 2:2,4); "durchstreichen" [*TN* (3):5,4]; "verwunden" [*TN* (12):4,3; 34:205,18; *GTB* 198.4]; "durchschiessen" (*TN* 34:205,19; *GTB* 225.16); "entzünden" (*GTB* 198.3); "brennen" (*GTB* 225.17).

2. Precious Objects

Table 2.1

Brooks shoot forth like silver beams [*TN* (21):7,1–4]; the dew is brilliant with white pearls [*TN* (22):6,7]; flowers are called gems [*TN* (22):8,1–4]; the sun and moon are clothed in gold and silver [*TN* (25):2,1–2]; stringed-instruments praise God with their silver-tongues (*TN* 26:1,1–2); the heavens are vaulted in crystal [*TN* (28):3,1–2]; the bowels of the earth are composed of gold and silver [*TN* (28):24,3–4]; hailstones fall from the heavens like pearls [*TN* (28):12,2–4]; precious objects are called upon to laud their Creator [*TN* (28):25,2–3]; and the sun is called pure gold (*TN* 31:184,16–17).

Table 2.2

His hands and feet are ivory (*TN* 44:6,1–2; 9:9,1–4). He is called "Schatz" (*TN* 10:1,6). His ivory skin is reddened with His blood in His passion (*TN* 10:11,3–4). The bees graze on His silver tears and red-coral face [*TN* (18):9,6–7]. The Christ-Child has pearly-white eyes (*TN* 34:204,8); golden hair (*TN* 34:204,7). In the Garden of Gethsemane Christ's tears are white pearls and the blood drops are compared to coral (*TN* 39:7,3–8). His lips are coral-stones [*TN* (43):2,1–4 and *GTB* 523–525]. In *TN* 46:5,1–8, when Christ's side is opened with a spear, the blood pours out red as coral and the water from His side is like crystal. The spear-wound itself is called "rubin und perlen gass."

Table 2.3

Christ is called "Schatz" (*TN* 10:1,6); Christ's skin is "So weisses helffenbein" (*TN* 10:12,3–4); stars are "perlen klar" [*TN* (15):2,1]; flowers are "kleinod stoltz in garten" [*TN* (22):8,4]; heaven is a "zelt von glas geblasen" (*TN* 27:3,4); and "crystallen baan" (*TN* 47:297,20); brooks are "manche fliessend silbergas?" (*TN* 27:12,7); the sun is "du klares goldt" (*TN* 31:184,16); the dew is "Die morgen perlen rund / und weiss" (*TN* 32:189,21); Christ's tears are "Weisse perl / corallen roth" (*TN* 39:7,7); Jesus' lips are "Corallen-stein" [*TN* (43):2,4]; the heavenly constellations are "Gülden öpffel gülden kernen // Gulden perll und Edelstein" (*TN* 44:2,2–3); the blood from Christ's side is "Rothe stralen wie Corall" and the water is "Weisse wässer wie Crystall" (*TN* 46:5,1–4); the voices of the nightingales are ". . . klarer brünnelein // Gefasst in marmersteine" (*TN* 52:5,1–2).

A FEW REMARKS ON SPEE AND DIMLER
By Heinrich Meyer

Dr. G. Richard Dimler, a native of Baltimore, Maryland (b. 21 October 1931), is a member of the Jesuit order. He took his courses largely at Roman Catholic schools, but his Master of Arts at Middlebury College and his Ph D. (in 1970) at the University of California at Los Angeles. He is at present Associate Professor of German at his own alma mater, Fordham University. His list of publications includes translations from Karl Rahner, S.J., and a number of articles both of an educational and a religious content. The subject of his first major work in the area of German studies is a member of the same order, Friedrich von Spee.

Public opinion concerning the Jesuits is hardly *vox Dei,* since so much of it is ill-informed and deliberately derogatory. I am not aware of any study reflecting the changes of attitudes toward the Jesuits from the time of their foundation and success through the suspension of the order in the late eighteenth century, the presence of "Crypto-Jesuits" for some decades, the liberal assault, the effect of Count Hoensbroech's conversion to Protestantism (1895) and his subsequent attacks on his former associates, nor could I even name a specialized study dealing with the literary treatment of Jesuit undertakings, like the Jesuit state in Paraguay. Spindler's novel comes to mind, but no doubt there must be many other treatments. Then there is, inevitably entwined with these literary processes, the political history of Freemasonry against the Catholic Church and, for that matter, other churches, a history which is especially emphasized in the Latin lands, but which emerges then again in troubled times and minds to feed propaganda about "International" powers, as in the Ludendorff group. All of this, hardly studied objectively by those within or without the S.J., affects somewhat all those who mention any Jesuit, present or past. For there is clearly no image of Jesuitism that has historical substance and general approval. Today, we often find the Jesuits in the forefront of progressive thinking and thus in partial conflict with the bureaucracy of the Vatican, yet only a hundred years ago the same order was supposed to be a chief instrument in the management of the first Vatican Council and the promulgation of the Infallibility Dogma.

Obviously, this is not the place to find a suitable formula for an order of such long standing, such successes as the Counter-Reformation in German speaking countries, such superior wisdom as the management of the Chinese and Indian missions, and many other highly creditable achievements. But it may be worth saying that the Jesuits were usually the least hide-bound, the most advanced, and the most courageous of all the orders that were established to serve their church. The very fact that one held it against them that they did not literally interpret what the verbalists insisted on expecting and demanding proves that they were the most modern and liberal group most of the time. Friedrich II of Prussia knew why he offered them a refuge in his practical concept of "Enlightenment."

When I emphasize courage, I think of the Chinese missionaries and of men like Spee.

No doubt, the cautious contemporaries preferred to keep silent and believe in witches when everybody else did or said he did. Whatever the various motivations, not the least of which was greed for the belongings of these single women, the populace at large and its judges and confessors were not given to psychological scrutiny and self-analysis. The only order in which psychology had been conceived of as essential and in which self-analysis was made a daily exercise and more than a routine of verbal repetitions thus has the glory of Spee's attack on the dull, cruel and stupid belief in witchcraft. He belongs for this reason among the truly great heroes of the spirit. It was risky, but he risked everything to fight what he considered wrong.

What a complex and subtle man he was, how he created a poetic language of his own and fled from the meanness of daily life into the beauty of religious poetry at its finest has always been felt. Much in this area remains to be investigated. One of the most promising studies of Spee's artistic methods and innate gifts is here before us. It will not only stimulate further research, it will also redound to the credit of the great liberal mind which Spee was and which the Jesuits nurtured, harbored and regard as a model.

A SELECTED BIBLIOGRAPHY

Aquinas, Thomas. *Summa Theologiae.* I—II. Ottowa, 1941.

Bachem, Rolf. *Dichtung als verborgene Theologie. Ein dichtungstheoretisches Topos vom Barock bis zur Goethezeit und seine Vorbilder.* Bonn: Bouvier, 1956.

Balthasar, Hans Urs von. *Herrlichkeit. Eine theologische Aesthetik.* Vol. 3. Einsiedeln: Johannes Verlag, 1965.

Bankl, Susanne. "Friedrich von Spee von Langenfeld und die europäische Mystik." Diss. Masch. Wien, 1959.

Becker, Adolf. *Die Sprache Friedrichs von Spee. Ein Beitrag zur Geschichte der nhd. Schriftsprache.* Halle, 1912.

Beckmann, Adelheid. *Motive und Formen der deutschen Lyrik des 17. Jahrhunderts und ihre Entsprechungen in der französischen Lyrik seit Ronsard. Ein Beitrag zur vergleichenden Literaturgeschichte.* Hermaea. Germanistische Forschungen Neue Folge. Vol. 5. Tübingen: Max Niemeyer, 1960.

Berger, Kurt. *Barock und Aufklärung im geistlichen Lied.* Marburg, 1951.

Böckmann, Paul. *Formgeschichte der deutschen Dichtung.* Vol. 1. *Von der Sinnbildsprache zur Ausdruckssprache.* 3rd ed. Darmstadt: Wissenschaftliche Buchgesellschaft, 1967.

Bruni, J. T. "Devotion to the Wounds of Our Lord." *New Catholic Encyclopedia.* Vol. 14. New York: McGraw-Hill, 1968. P. 1036.

Cirlot, J. E. *A Dictionary of Symbols.* Tr. Jack Sage. London: Rutledge & Keagan, 1962.

Conrady, K. O. *Lateinische Dichtungstradition und deutsche Lyrik des 17. Jahrhunderts.* Bonner Arbeiten zur deutschen Literatur, Vol. 4. Bonn, 1962.

Curtius, Ernst Robert. *European Literature and the Latin Middle Ages.* Tr. Willard R. Trask. New York: Harper, 1963.

Denziger, H., and Umberg, J. B. *Enchiridion Symbolorum. Definitionum et Declarationum.* 26th ed. Freiburg i. Breis.: Herder, 1946.

Deutsche Barockforschung. Dokumentation einer Epoche. Neue Wissenschaftliche Bibliothek 7 Literaturwissenschaft. Ed. Richard Alewyn. 2nd ed. Berlin: Kiepenheuer & Witsch, 1966.

Donnely, M. J. "The Holy Spirit." *New Catholic Encyclopedia.* Vol. 7. New York, 1928. Pp. 96—98.

Duhr, Bernard. *Geschichte der Jesuiten in den Ländern deutscher Zunge.* Vol. 2. Freiburg i. Breis: Herder, 1907.

Durrwell, F. X. "Lamb of God." *New Catholic Encyclopedia.* Vol. 8. New York, 1968. Pp. 338—340.

Dych, Joachim. *Ticht-Kunst. Deutsche Barockpoetik und rhetorische Tradition.* Ars Poetica 1. Bad Homburg: Verlag Gehlen, 1966.

Eikel, Elfriede. "Die Entstehung der religiösen Schäferlyrik. Von Petrarca bis Spee." Diss. Masch. Heidelberg, 1957.

Flemming, Willi. "Die Auffassung des Menschen im XVII. Jhdt." *DVJ,* 6 (1928), 403—446.

— *Der Wandel der deutschen Naturgefühle vom XV. bis XVIII. Jhdt.* Halle, 1934.

Frenzel, Elisabeth. *Stoff-, Motiv- und Symbolforschung.* 2nd ed. Stuttgart: Metzler, 1966.

Fricke, Gerhard. *Die Bildlichkeit in der Dichtung des Andreas Gryphius. Materialen und Studien zum Form-problem des deutschen Literaturbarock.* Neue Forschung, 17. Darmstadt: Wissenschaftliche Buchgesellschaft, 1967.

Fülop-Miller, Rene. *The Power and Secret of the Jesuits.* Tr. F. S. Flint and D. F. Tait. New York: Viking Press, 1930.

Gentner, Margarete. "Das Verhältnis von Theologie und Aesthetik in Spees 'Trutznachtigall.'" Diss. Tübingen, 1965.

Graef, H. C. "Dionysius Areopagites." *Lexikon für Theologie und Kirche.* Vol. 3. Freiburg: Herder, 1957. 402—403.

Greenewald, G. M. "Spiration." *New Catholic Encylcopedia.* Vol. 13. New York McGraw-Hill, 1968. Pp. 567—568.

de Guibert, Joseph. *The Jesuits, Their Spiritual Doctrine and Practice. A Historical Study.* Tr. William J. Young. Ed. George E. Ganss. Chicago: Loyola University Press, 1964.

Hankamer, Paul. *Die Sprache, ihr Begriff und ihre Bedeutung im XVI. und XVII. Jhdt.* Bonn, 1927.

Jacobsen, Eric. *Die Metamorphosen der Liebe und Friedrich Spees "Trutznachtigall."* Studien zum Fortleben der Antike, 1. Copenhagen, 1954. (Det Kongelige Danske Videnskabernes Selskab, Historisk-filologiske Meddelelster, bind 34, nr. 3.)

The Jerome Biblical Commentary. Ed. Raymond E. Brown, S. S., Joseph Fitzmeyer, S. J., and Roland E. Murphy, O. Carm. Englewood Cliffs, N.J.: Prentice-Hall, 1968.

The Jerusalem Bible. Ed. Alexander Jones. London: Darton, 1966.

Jöns, Dieter. *Das Sinnen-Bild. Studien zur allegorischen Bildlichkeit bei A. Gryphius.* Germanistische Abhandlungen, 13. Stuttgart: Metzler, 1966.

Jungbluth, Alphons. "Beiträge zu einer Beschreibung der Dichtersprache Friedrichs von Spee." Diss. Bonn, 1906.

Jungmann, Josef. *Pastoral Liturgy.* New York: Herder & Herder, 1962.

Karrer, Otto. "Deutsche Mystik." *Lexikon für Theologie und Kirche.* Vol. 3. Freiburg i. Breis., 1959, Pp. 266—270.

Koch, Ludwig. *Jesuitenlexikon.* Paderborn: Verlag Bonifacius, 1934.

Langen, August. "Deutsche Sprachgeschichte vom Barock bis zur Gegenwart." *Deutsche Philologie im Aufriss.* Vol. 1. Munich, 1957. 931ff.

— *Der Wortschatz des deutschen Pietismus.* 2nd ed Tübingen: Max Niemeyer, 1968.

Lanham, Richard A. *A Handlist of Rhetorical Terms. A Guide for Students of English Literature.* Berkeley: California University Press, 1969.

Lausberg, Heinrich. *Elemente der literarischen Rhetorik.* 2nd ed. Munich: Max Hueber, 1963.

Lieder, Frederick W. C. "Friedrich Spe and the Theodicee of Leibniz." *Journal of English and Germanic Philology,* 11 (1912), 149—172, 329—354.

Loyola, Ignatius. *The Spiritual Exercises of St. Ignatius.* A new translation by Louis J. Puhl, S. J. Westminster, Md.: Newman, 1951.

— *The Spiritual Journal of St. Ignatius Loyola.* Tr. William J. Young, S. J. Woodstock, Md.: Woodstock Press, 1958.

Lüders, Eva. "Die Auffassung des Menschen im 17. Jahr. Dargestellt an Hand der poetischen Handbücher." Diss. Köln, 1935.

Lüers, Grete. *Die Sprache der deutschen Mystik des Mittelalters im Werke der Mechthild von Magdeburg.* Darmstadt: Wissenschaftliche Buchgesellschaft, 1966.

Lüthi, Max. "Eine Ringerzählung (Clock-Tale) bei Friedrich von Spee." *Fabula,* 4 (1961), 209—230.

Märtens, Ilse. "Die Darstellung der Natur in den Dichtungen Friedrichs von Spee." *Euphorion,* 26 (1925), 564—592.

Martz, Louis L. *The Poetry of Meditation. A Study in English Literature of the Sevententh Century.* Rev. ed. New Haven: Yale University Press, 1962.

Maurer, Warren R. "Spee, Southwell and the Poetry of Meditation." *Comparative Literature,* 15 (1963), 15—22.

McGovern, L. J. "Processions, Trinitarian." *New Catholic Encyclopedia.* Vol. 11. New York, 1968. Pp. 821—823.

McKenzie, John L. *A Dictionary of the Bible.* Milwauke: Bruce, 1965.

Murphy, F. X. "The Creed." *New Catholic Encyclopedia.* Vol. 4. New York, 1968. Pp. 432—438.

Neveux, Jean-B. "Friedrich von Spee SJ (1591—1635) et la société de son temps. La grâce et le droit." *Études germaniques,* 19 (1964), 399—428.

Nix, Udo. "Sprache und Mystik." *Muttersprache* (1962), 129—135.

Nowak, Wolfgang. "Versuch einer motivischen Analyse des Schäferhabits bei Friedrich von Spee." Diss. Masch. Berlin, 1954.

Ohly, Friedrich. *Vom Geistigen Sinn des Wortes im Mittelalter. Sonderausgabe aus Zeit. f. deutsches Altertum und deutsche Literatur,* 89 (1958/1959), 1—23. Darmstadt: Wissenschaftliche Buchgesellschaft, 1966.

Ott, Ludwig. *Fundamentals of Catholic Dogma.* Ed. James C. Bastible, tr. Patrick Lynch. 5th ed. St. Louis: Herder, 1962.

Oxford Dictionary of the Christian Church. Ed. F. L. Cross. London: Oxford University Press, 1957.

Parente, Pietro; Piolanti, Antonio; and Garafalo, Salvatore. *Dictionary of Dogmatic Theology.* Tr. Emmanuel Doronzo. Milwaukee: Herder, 1957.

Peter, J. "Generation of the Word." *New Catholic Encyclopedia.* Vol. 6. New York, 1968. P. 323.

Poulain, A. *The Graces of Interior Prayer. A Treatise on Mystical Theology.* Tr. Leonora Smith. 6th ed. St. Louis, 1950.

Praz, Mario. *Studies in Seventeenth Century Imagery.* Sussidi Eruditi, 16. 2nd ed. Rome, 1964.

Pyritz, Hans. *Paul Flemings deutsche Liebeslyrik.* Göttingen: Vandenhoeck & Rupprecht, 1963.

Quint, Josef. "Mystik und Sprache. Ihr Verhältnis zueinander, insbesondere in der spekulativen Mystik Meister Eckeharts." *Altdeutsche und Altniederländische Mystik.* Wege der Forschung, Vol. 23, hrsg. Kurt Ruh. Darmstadt: Wissenschaftliche Buchgesellschaft, 1964. Pp. 113—151.

Raby, F. J. E. *A History of Christian-Latin Poetry. From the Beginnings to the Close of the Middle Ages.* 2nd ed. Oxford: Clarendon Press, 1953.

Rahner, Karl. *Theological Investigations.* Vol. 3. *Theology of the Spiritual Life.* Tr. Karl-H. and Boniface Kruger. Baltimore: Helicon, 1967.

— and Vorgrimler, Herbert. *Kleines Theologisches Wörterbuch,* 4th ed. Freiburg: Herder, 1964.

Reichert, Ernst. "Einflüsse und Anregungen auf die Dichtung Friedrichs von Spe. Ein Beitrag zur Kennzeichnung eines jesuitischen Dichters." *Programm Neuruppin,* 1913.

Rosenfeld, Emmy. *Friedrich Spee von Langenfeld. Eine Stimme in der Wüste.* Quellen und Forschungen zur Sprach- und Kulturgeschichte der germ. Völker, N. F. Hrsg. Hermann Kunisch. Vol. 2. Berlin: de Gruyter, 1958.

— *Neue Studien zur Lyrik von Friedrich von Spee.* Mailand: Univ. Bouani, 1963.

— *Weltliche und Geistliche Lyrik im Zeitalter des Barock.* Editrice Viscontea, Mailand, 1960.

Rüttenauer, Isabella. *Friedrich von Spee, 1591—1635. Ein lebender Märtyrer.* Freiburg, 1951.

Sandaeus, Maximilian. *Pro Theologia Mystica Clavis Elucidarium. Onomasticon Vocabulorum et loquutionum obscurarum, quibus Doctores Mystici, tum veteres, tum recentiores utuntur ad proprium suae disciplinae sensum paucis manifestum.* Köln, 1640. Louvain, Editions de la bibliothèque S.J., 1963. rept.

Schachner, Heinrich. "Naturbilder und Naturbetrachtung in den Dichtungen Friedrichs von Spe." *Programm des Obergymnasiums Kremsmunster.* Linz: Kremsmunster, 1906.

Schoene, Albrecht. *Emblematik und Drama im Zeitalter des Barock.* Munich: Verlag Beck, 1964

Schulte, R. "Tränengabe." *Lexikon für Theologie und Kirche.* Ed. J. Hofer and K. Rahner. Vol. 10. 2nd ed. Freiburg: Herder, 1965. P. 305.

Sloyan, Gerard S. *The Three Persons in One God.* Foundations in Catholic Theology Series. Englewood Cliffs, N.J.: Prentice-Hall, 1964.

Spamer, Adolph. *Das Kleine Andachtsbild von 14. bis 20. Jhdt.* Munich, 1930.

Spee, Friedrich von. *Güldenes Tugend-Buch, das ist/Werck unnd übung der dreyen Göttlichen Tugenden. dess Glaubens, Hoffnung, und Liebe. Allen Gottliebenden/ andächtigen/frommen Seelen: und sonderlich den Kloster und anderen Geistlichen personen sehr nützlich zu gebrauchen.* Köln: Friessen, 1649.

— *Goldenes Tugendbuch das ist: Werke und Übungen der drei göttlichen Tugenden, das Glaubens, der Hoffnung, der Liebe. Allen Gott liebenden, andächtigen, frommen Seelen nützlich zu gebrauchen.* Hrsg. Clemens Brentano. Koblenz, 1829.

— *Güldenes Tugend-Buch.* Hrsg. Theo G. M. van Oorschot. Friedrich Spee Sämtliche Schriften. Historisch-kritische Ausgabe in drei Bänden. Hrsg. Emmy Rosenfeld. Vol. 2. Munich: Kösel, 1968.

– *Trutz Nachtigal/oder Geistlichs-Poëtisch Lustwäldlein/dessgleichen noch nie zuvor in Teutscher Sprach gesehen.* 5th ed. Köln, 1683.
– *Trutz Nachtigal ein geistlich poetisches Lustwäldlein, dessgleichen noch nie zuvor in deutscher Sprache gesehen worden.* Berlin, 1817.
– *Trutznachtigall von Friedrich von Spee.* Hrsg. Gustav Balke. Deutsche Dichter des Siebzehnten Jahrhunderts, hrsg. Karl Goedecke and Julius Tittmann. Vol. 13. Leipzig, 1879.
– *Trutznachtigall.* Mit Einleitung und kritischem Apparat. Hrsg. Gustave Otto Arlt. Neudrucke deutscher Literaturwerke des XVI. und XVII. Jhdts. Nr. 292–301. Halle: Max Niemeyer, 1936.
Stierli, Josef. *Heart of the Saviour. A Symposium on Devotion to the Sacred Heart.* Tr. Paul Andrews, S.J., ed. Joseph Stierli. Freiburg: Herder, 1957.
Strich, Fritz. "Der lyrische Stil des 17. Jahrhunderts." In *Deutsche Barockforschung*, hrsg. R. Alewyn. Köln: Kiepenheuer, 1966.
Szöverffy, Josef. "Hymnology." *New Catholic Encyclopedia.* Vol. 8. New York, 1968. p. 294.
Thesaurus Spiritualis Societatis Jesu. Rome, 1948.
Van Ingen, Ferdinand. *Vanitas, und Memento Mori in der deutschen Barocklyrik.* Groningen: Wolters, 1966.
Van Oorschot, Theo G. M. "Friedrich Spees Güldenes Tugend-Buch II. Literarhistorische Abhandlung." Diss. Nijmegen: Dekker, 1968.
Viëtor, Karl. "Vom Stil und Geist der deutschen Barockdichtung." *Deutsche Barockforschung*, hrsg. R. Alewyn. Köln: Niemeyer, 1966. Pp. 39–71.
Wellek, Rene. *Concepts of Criticism.* Ed. Stephen G. Nichols, Jr. New Haven: Yale University Press, 1963.
Wentzlaff-Eggebert, Friedrich W. *Deutsche Mystik zwischen Mittelalter und Neuzeit.* 2nd ed. Berlin: de Gruyter, 1947.
– *Das Problem des Todes in der deutschen Lyrik des XVII Jhdts.* Palaestra, Nr. 171. Leipzig, 1931.
Windfuhr, Manfred. *Die Barocke Bildlichkeit und Ihre Kritiker. Stilhaltungen in der deutschen Literatur des 17. und 18. Jahrhunderts.* Germanistische Abhandlungen, 15. Stuttgart: Metzler, 1966.
Wolfskehl, Marie-Luise. "Die Jesusminne in der Lyrik des deutschen Barock." *Giessener Beiträge zur dt. Philologie,* 34 (1934). Giessen, 1934.
Das Zeitalter des Barock. Texte und Zeugnisse. Hrsg. Albrecht Schöne. *Die deutsche Literatur,* Vol. 3. Munich: Beck, 1962.
Zeller, Paul. "Friedrich von Spee und seine Weltschau." Diss. Fribourg, 1956.
Ziemendorff, Ingeborg. *Die Metapher bei den weltlichen Lyrikern des deutschen Barock.* Germanische Studien, 135. Berlin, 1933.
Zoepfl, Friedrich. "Die Frömmigkeit Friedrichs von Spe." *Geist und Leben. Zs. f. Aszese und Mystik,* 20 (1947), 36–53.

INDEX

(The numbers refer to pages)

A

Aeschylos (525—456 B.C.), 115
Agnus Dei Motif, 66, 67
Alewyn, Richard, 29n, 151
Anchor-Motif, 32, 33, 33n
Anselm (1033—1109), 46
Aquinas, Thomas (1225—1274), 70, 151
Aristotle (384—322/1), 70
Arlt, Gustave Otto, 21, 21n, 22, 45, 110, 116n, 154
Arnobius (died, 451 A.D.), 46
Arnold, Gottfried (1666—1714), 85n
Augustine (353—430), 80, 139
Ausonius (310—395), 111n

B

Balde, Jakob (1604—1668), 65n, 77, 86
Balke, Gustav, 154
Bankl, Susanne, 16, 16n, 151
Bavingh, Hermann, 12
Beckmann, Adelheid, 32n, 34n, 43n, 47n, 52n, 62n, 63n, 75n, 76n, 77n, 98n, 104n, 105n, 109n, 151
Bernard of Clairveaux (1091—1153), 86
Böckmann, Paul, 19n, 151
Bonaventure (1221—1274), 54, 65, 65n, 66, 77
Brentano, Clemens (1778—1842), 66n, 153
Brown, Raymond E., 25n, 152
Browning, Robert M., 17n
Bruni, J.P., 86n, 151

C

Canisius, Peter (1521—1597), 10, 77
Canticle of Canticles, 25n, 30, 30n, 35, 62, 78, 102
Cautio Criminalis, 10, 11, 12, 14, 119, 120, 121
Chrysostom, John (347—407), 46
Cirlot, J.E., 25n, 31n, 51n, 56n, 62n, 76n, 151
Cologne, 10, 11, 12, 119
Counter-Reformation, 9, 116, 120, 149
Cross, Frank L., 92n
Cupido, 58, 58n, 59, 64n, 72, 72n, 102, 111, 111n, 112—113, 113n, 114—116, 125, 138
Czepko, Daniel (1605—1660), 34n, 75n

D

Damon, 41, 41n, 42—43, 49, 54, 59—60, 84, 88, 103, 114

Daphnis, 37, 49, 49n, 54, 62—63, 67, 74, 74n, 116, 135—136, 140
Denziger, Henricus, 50n, 74n, 151
Dietrich von Fürstenberg (1585—1618), 11
Dimler, G. Richard, 72n, 111n, 149
Donne, John (1571—1631), 28n
Donnelly, M.J., 74n, 81n, 151
Duhr, Bernard, 151
Durrwell, F.X., 151
Dych, Joachim, 29n, 116n, 151

E

Eckhart, Meister (1260—1327), 28, 35, 153
Eikel, Elfriede, 16, 151
Emblems, 19, 58, 58n, 59, 59n, 61n, 72n, 77n, 78n, 111—112, 112n, 113, 113n, 114, 153

F

Father, God the, 33, 33n, 34—35, 40, 43, 50—51, 74—75, 77, 80—81, 95—96, 143
Ferdinand of Bavaria (1578—1637), 11—12, 119
Fitzmeyer, Joseph, 152
Fleming, Paul (1609—1640), 29, 30n, 43, 75n, 77n, 101n, 103, 153
Flemming, Willi, 151
Francis of Assis (1181—1226), 38
Frederick of the Palatinate, 9
Frenzel, Elisabeth, 19n
Fricke, Gerhard, 15—16, 19, 19n, 27n, 28n, 32n, 34n, 41n, 52n, 62n, 68n, 113n, 151
Friedrich II of Prussia (1740—1786), 149
Fulda, 11

G

Gentner, Margarete, 16—19, 151
Goethe, Joh. Wolfgang von (1749—1832), 15, 19
Greenwald, G.M., 80n, 151
Gregory of Nyssa (330—395), 46
Grimmelshausen, Hans Jakob von (1621—1676), 10
Gryphius, Andreas (1616—1664), 10, 15, 15n, 19—20, 26—27, 28n, 29, 29n, 32, 34, 41, 52, 52n, 56, 58, 62—63, 68, 76, 103, 111, 113, 118, 132, 151—152
Guibert, Joseph de, 97n, 98n, 151

H

Halton, 41—43, 49, 54—55, 59—60, 76, 100, 103, 140

Harsdörffer, Georg Philipp von (1607–1658), 29, 58, 103
Henot, Katharina von, 11
Hofer, Josef, 97n
Hölderlin, Friedrich (1770–1843), 19
Hofmannswaldau, Christian Hofmann von (1617–1679), 30n, 62n, 75n, 131n
Holy Eucharist, 20, 26, 33, 34, 53, 55–56, 110–111, 117
Holy, Spirit, 20, 26, 30, 31n, 34, 49–51, 74, 74n, 80–81, 81n, 96, 143, 151
Horace (65–8 B.C.), 29
Hugo, Hermann (1588–1629), 59n, 72, 112, 112n, 115

I
Ingen, Ferdinand Van, 19n, 109n
Isaiah, 54, 66

J
Jacobsen, Eric, 16, 18, 18n, 30n, 34n, 35n, 37n, 40n, 54n, 55n, 57n, 58n, 59n, 61n, 62n, 64n, 64, 65n, 66n, 72n, 75n, 77n, 78n, 86n, 98n, 105, 105n, 109n, 111n, 112n, 113n, 115n, 145, 152
Jesuits, 9–14, 17, 21, 24, 33n, 37, 57, 65, 71–72, 76–77, 77n, 97n, 98n, 112n, 116, 119–120, 149, 151, 152
John's Gospel, 25, 25n, 28, 52n, 66–67, 80
Jones, Alexander, 28n, 152
Jöns, Dieter, 15, 15n, 16, 26n, 32n, 52n, 152
Jungbluth, Alphons, 16, 152
Jungmann, Josef, 86n, 152

K
Kiesel, Philip, 77
Kleist, Heinrich von (1777–1811), 19
Koch, Ludwig, 77
Köln, 44n
Kontrafaktur, 11, 70, 73, 101
Kuhlmann, Quirinus (1651–1689), 33, 43n, 56, 116

L
Langen, August, 19n, 28n, 33n, 43n, 44n, 55n, 62n, 75, 75n, 76n, 84n, 85n, 97n, 103n, 138, 139n, 152
Langton, Stephen (d. 1228), 31n
Lanham, Richard A., 152
Leibniz, Gottfried Wilhelm (1646–1716), 12–13, 18, 120, 152
Lieder, Frederick W.C., 18, 152

Lohenstein, Daniel Casper von (1635–1683), 29, 30n, 131n
Loyola, Ignatius of (1491–1556), 9–10, 13–14, 24, 24n, 47, 53, 53n, 56–57, 60, 69, 69n, 70–71, 82n, 87n, 89, 89n, 94, 94n, 97–98, 98n, 99, 100n, 101n, 152
Lüders, Eva, 26n, 29n, 32n, 52n, 152
Lüers, Grete, 26n, 28n, 30n, 33n, 34n, 35n, 44n, 50n, 61n, 63n, 65n, 75, 75n, 76n, 77n, 78n, 85n, 102n, 110n, 112n, 113n, 139n, 152
Lüthi, Max, 58n, 152

M
McGovern, L.J., 96n, 152
McGuire, M.R.P., 69n
McKenzie, John L., 50n, 54n, 152
Männling, Johann Christoph (1658–1723), 52n, 56
Mainz, 11, 12
Märtens, Ilse, 16, 29n, 152
Martz, Louis, 24n, 28n, 152
Mary Magdalen, 25, 31, 44, 50, 79, 99, 115, 136, 139
Maurer, Warren R., 24n, 152
Maximilian of Bavaria, 12, 119
Mechthild of Magdeburg (1207–1277), 26n, 28, 30, 33n, 35, 50n, 61n, 65, 75, 75n, 77, 85, 110, 112, 112n, 152
Medieval Mystics, 17, 26, 33, 35, 44, 65, 75–76, 78, 85, 102n, 112, 139
Münzius, Georg, 86
Murphy, F.X., 26n, 151
Murphy, Roland E., 152

N
Nakatenus, Wilhelm (1617–1682), 77
Neukirch, Benjamin (1665–1729), 19
Neveux, Jean-B., 18, 152
Nowak, Wolfgang, 16, 41n, 49n, 74n, 91n, 98n, 100n, 103n, 105n, 112n, 152
Nürnberg, 43
Nugent, Dominicus (1641–1717), 65n

O
Ohly, Friedrich, 41n, 152
Oorschot, Theo Van, 17n, 18, 22, 24n, 33n, 44n, 46n, 69n, 71n, 76n, 86n, 92n, 104n, 133n, 153–154
Opitz, Martin (1597–1639), 19, 34n, 43, 75n, 76
Ott, Ludwig, 71n, 74n, 152
Ovid (43 B.C.–18 A.D.), 30, 32, 40, 111–112, 145

P

Paderborn, 12, 44n, 119, 121
Parente, Pietro, 27n, 34n, 55n, 80n, 106n, 153
Pastor-Bonus, 67
Pecham, John (1225–1292), 65
Peter, J., 80n, 153
Petrarch, Francesco (1304–1374), 11, 16, 17, 19, 21, 30, 35, 62n, 63–64, 66, 70, 73, 75–77, 84, 91n, 100n, 101, 103, 105, 105n, 112, 114–116, 118, 120, 145, 151
Philip of Schönborn (1607–1668), 12
Pietists, 33, 43n, 44, 55, 62, 75n, 76, 78, 84–85, 97, 97n, 103n, 120, 138, 139n, 152
Plautus, Titus Maccius (244–184 B.C.), 145
Poulain, A., 97n, 153
Prague, 11
Procopius (475–538), 46
Psalm 48:44, 46n
Psalm 50:30
Psalm 65:46n
Psalm 102:52n
Psalm 103:46, 52n
Psalm 104:46n
Psalm 129:34
Psalm 148:46, 51
Pseudo-Dionysius (C. 500), 33n, 35, 151
Puhl, Louis J., 24n, 69n
Pyritz, Hans, 101n, 153

Q

Quint, Josef, 76n, 153

R

Raby, F.J.E., 65n, 153
Rahner, Karl, 25n, 36n, 50n, 55n, 97n, 101n, 149, 153
Reichert, Ernst, 65n, 76n, 153
Reinhardt, Kurt F., 9n
Ritter, Joachim-Friedrich, 10n
Ronsard, Pierre de (1521–1585), 32n, 151
Rosenfeld, Emmy, 11n, 16, 17n, 18, 25n, 30n, 32n, 34n, 36, 36n, 39, 42n, 44n, 49n, 54n, 59n, 64, 64n, 65n, 66n, 72n, 74n, 85n, 87n, 88n, 105n, 110n, 111n, 112n, 128, 153
Rosenroth, Knorr von (1636–1689), 43n
Rothe, Johann Andreas (1688–1758), 33n
Rüttenauer, Isabella, 153
Ruysbroek, Jan Van (1293–1381), 33n, 35, 75n

S

Sacred Heart, 76n, 77, 77n
Saint Agnes, 66
Saint Margaret Mary, 76n
Sandaeus, Maximilian (1578–1656), 33n, 75, 75n, 76, 139, 153
Sappho, 101
Satan, 35, 108, 113
Schachner, Heinrich, 16, 153
Schein, Johann Hermann (1586–1630), 98n
Schoene, Albrecht, 65n, 153, 154
Schulte, R., 97n, 153
Schwieger, Jakob (1624–1667), 62n
Seuse, Heinrich (1295–1366), 26n, 28, 50n, 75, 77, 78n, 85
Silesius, Angelus (1624–1677), 33, 43n, 56–57, 66n, 77n, 86–87, 105n, 109, 116
Sinaita, Anastasius, 46
Sloyan, Gerard S., 50n, 153
Son, God the, 33n, 33, 34–35, 43, 50–51, 74–75, 77, 80–81, 95–96, 143
Song of Songs, 35, 102
Southwell, Robert (1561–1595), 24, 24n, 37, 152
Spamer, Adolf, 112n, 153
Spener, Philipp Jakob (1635–1705), 62n
Speyer, 119
Spiritual Exercises, 9, 13, 24, 24n, 47, 47n, 53, 53n, 56–57, 57n, 60, 60n, 69, 69n, 70–71, 72n, 82n, 87n, 89n, 94, 94n, 98, 98n, 99, 108n, 120, 152
Spiritual Journal, 97, 98n, 100n, 152
Stieler, Caspar (1632–1707), 30n
Stierli, Josef, 76n, 77n, 86n, 154
Strich, Fritz, 29n, 154
Szöverffy, Josef, 31n, 154
Szyrocki, Marian, 19n

T

Tauler, Johann (1300–1361), 26n, 28, 33–35, 50n, 75n, 77
Teresa of Avila, 97
Tersteegen (1697–1769), 62n
Theocritus (300 B.C.), 49n, 74n
Theodoretus, 46
Trent, Council of, 80
Treuer, Wilhelm (1632–1711), 52n, 56
Trier, 9–10, 12–13, 121
Trinity, 33, 35, 43, 49, 50–51, 74–75, 77, 80–81, 95–96, 96n, 139, 143, 152
Tscherning, Andreas (1611–1659), 52n

U

Ulenberg, Caspar (1544–1617), 44, 44n

V

Vaenius, Otto (1556—1629), 112, 113n
Vetter, Conrad (1548—1622), 36n, 65, 128
Virgin Mary, 10, 38, 43, 49, 62, 79, 139—140

W

Weckherlin, Goerg Rodolph (1584—1653),
    34n, 43, 47n, 62n, 77, 109, 131n
Weise, Christian (1641—1708), 19
Westfalia, Treaty, 9
Windfuhr, Manfred, 15, 15n, 19n, 20n, 27n,
    28n, 30n, 33n, 34n, 36n, 43n, 52n, 62n,
    63n, 76n, 88n, 105, 105n, 111, 118, 131n,
    132n, 145, 154

Wolfskehl, Marie-Louise, 103n, 154
Worms, 11
Wurzburg, 11, 119

X

Xavier, Francis (1506—1552), 11, 31

Z

Zeller, Paul, 16, 16n, 18, 154
Zesen, Philipp von (1619—1689), 29, 77n
Zeus-Semele, 35
Ziemendorff, Ingeborg, 154
Zoepfl, Friedrich, 16, 16n, 154